latest edn 02/12

D1142805

DRIVING STANDARDS AGENCY
SAFE DRIVING FOR LIFE ™

The **OFFICIAL DSA GUIDE** to
DRIVING
GOODS VEHICLES

23

Approved by
Plain

Written and compiled by Driving Standards Agency Learning Materials.

First edition Crown copyright 1994
Second edition Crown copyright 1997
Third edition Crown copyright 1999
Fourth edition Crown copyright 2001
Fifth edition Crown copyright 2002
Sixth edition Crown copyright 2003
Seventh edition Crown copyright 2005
Eighth edition Crown copyright 2007
Ninth edition Crown copyright 2009
Second impression 2009

ISBN 978 0 11 5530814

A CIP catalogue record for this book is available from the British Library

Other titles in the Driving Skills series

The Official DSA Guide to Driving - the essential skills
The Official DSA Theory Test for Car Drivers
The Official DSA Theory Test for Car Drivers (CD-Rom)
Theory Test Extra - the official DSA guide
The Official DSA Guide to Learning to Drive
Prepare for your Practical Driving Test DVD
DSA Driving Theory DVD Quiz
The Official Highway Code Interactive CD-Rom

The Official DSA Guide to Riding - the essential skills
The Official DSA Theory Test for Motorcyclists
The Official DSA Theory Test for Motorcyclists (CD-Rom)
The Official DSA Guide to Learning to Ride
Better Biking - the Official DSA Training Aid (DVD)

The Official DSA Guide to Driving Buses and Coaches
The Official DSA Theory Test for Drivers of Large Vehicles
The Official DSA Theory Test for Drivers of Large Vehicles (CD-Rom)
Driver CPC - the official DSA Guide for Professional Bus and Coach Drivers
Driver CPC - the official DSA Guide for Professional Goods Vehicle Drivers

The Official DSA Guide to Tractor and Specialist Vehicle Driving Tests

The Official DSA Guide to Hazard Perception (DVD)

Every effort has been made to ensure that the information contained in this publication is accurate at the time of going to press. The Stationery Office cannot be held responsible for any inaccuracies. Information in this book is for guidance only. All metric and imperial conversions in this book are approximate.

Acknowledgements

The Driving Standards Agency (DSA) would like to thank the staff of the following organisations for their contribution to the production of this publication:

Volvo Trucks   Skills for Logistics
Bennetts of Malvern

Business Link

Business Link is the place to find all government motoring information for professional drivers. Go to:

www.businesslink.gov.uk/transport

Theory and practical tests

www.direct.gov.uk/drivingtest

Practical & Theory Tests
Enquiries & Bookings **0300 200 1122**
Welsh speakers **0300 200 1133**

Practical Tests
Minicom **0300 200 1144**
Fax **0300 200 1155**

Theory Tests
Minicom **0300 200 1166**
Fax **0300 200 1177**
Customer Enquiry Unit **0300 200 1188**

DVA (Northern Ireland)
Theory test **0845 600 6700**
Practical test **0845 247 2471**

Driving Standards Agency

www.dsa.gov.uk

The Axis Building,
112 Upper Parliament Street,
Nottingham
NG1 6LP

Tel **0115 936 6666**
Fax **0115 936 6570**

Driver & Vehicle Agency (Testing) in Northern Ireland

www.dvani.gov.uk

Balmoral Road, Belfast BT12 6QL

Tel **02890 681 831**
Fax **02890 665 520**

Driver & Vehicle Licensing Agency
(GB licence enquiries)

www.dvla.gov.uk

Longview Road, Swansea SA6 7JL

Tel **0300 790 6801**
Fax **0300 123 1278**
Minicom **0300 123 0798**

Driver & Vehicle Agency (Licensing) in Northern Ireland

www.dvani.gov.uk

County Hall, Castlerock Road,
Coleraine BT51 3TB

Tel **02870 341 469**
24 hour tel **0345 111 222**
Minicom **02870 341 380**

Office of the Parliamentary Commissioner for Administration

(The Parliamentary Ombudsman)

Millbank Tower, Millbank, London
SW1P 4QP

Tel **020 7217 4163**
Fax **020 7217 4160**

The Driving Standards Agency (DSA) is an executive agency of the Department for Transport. You'll see its logo at theory and practical test centres.

DSA aims to promote road safety through the advancement of driving standards, by

- establishing and developing high standards and best practice in driving and riding on the road; before people start to drive, as they learn, and after they pass their test
- ensuring high standards of instruction for different types of driver and rider
- conducting the statutory theory and practical tests efficiently, fairly and consistently across the country
- providing a centre of excellence for driver training and driving standards
- developing a range of publications and other publicity material designed to promote safe driving for life.

The Driving Standards Agency recognises and values its customers. We will treat all our customers with respect, and deliver our services in an objective, polite and fair way.

www.dsa.gov.uk

The Driver and Vehicle Agency (DVA) is an executive agency within the Department of the Environment for Northern Ireland.

Its primary aim is to promote and improve road safety through the advancement of driving standards and implementation of the Government's policies for improving the mechanical standards of vehicles.

www.dvani.gov.uk

Contents

01 Getting started

02 Understanding large goods vehicles

03 Limits and regulations

04 Driver skills

05 Preparing for the driving test

06 The LGV driving test

07 Additional information

About this book

This book will help you to

- understand what is expected of a Goods Vehicle driver
- prepare for your practical large vehicle driving test
- prepare for and maintain your Certificate of Professional Competence qualification.

The information in this book should be read in conjunction with the general driving advice given in *The Highway Code* and *The Official DSA Guide to Driving - the essential skills,* which provide valuable information on driver skills in general.

You will need this information in addition to the specific skills detailed regarding driving goods vehicles, shown in Section Four of this book.

All publications are available by mail order by calling **0870 241 4523**. They are also available from good bookshops or online at **www.tsoshop.co.uk/dsa**

The important factors

Reading this book should help you to appreciate the principles of driving goods vehicles and so lead you to become a safer driver. However, this book is a guide, and should not be taken as a training manual. It is only one of the important factors in your training. The others are

- a good instructor
- plenty of practice
- your attitude

Once you have obtained your goods vehicle licence you should take pride in your driving. Your professionalism will be seen and appreciated by other road users.

Driving is a life skill.

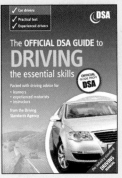

section **one**
GETTING STARTED

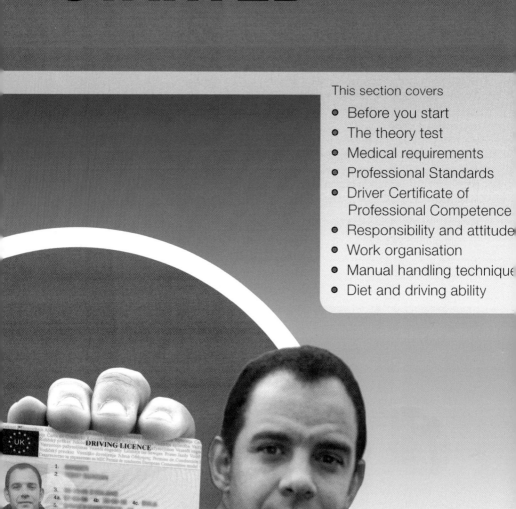

This section covers

- Before you start
- The theory test
- Medical requirements
- Professional Standards
- Driver Certificate of Professional Competence
- Responsibility and attitude
- Work organisation
- Manual handling technique
- Diet and driving ability

A message from the Chief Driving Examiner

As the driver of a goods vehicle you have a special responsibility - not just to yourself, but to all other road users. A professional driver should set an example to other drivers by ensuring that the vehicle is driven, at all times, with the utmost safety and with courtesy and consideration for everyone else on today's busy roads.

To become a goods vehicle driver you must possess the right attitude and approach to your driving, together with a sound knowledge of safe, modern driving techniques and the ability to apply those techniques. A high degree of skill in the handling of your vehicle and also being prepared to make allowances for the mistakes and errors of others are essential attributes.

By successfully passing your car driving test, you've already shown that you've reached the standard set for driving a motor vehicle unsupervised on today's roads. This book sets out the knowledge and skills that you must now demonstrate in order to pass a vocational driving test.

Included in this revised edition is lots of additional information to help prepare for the extended theory and practical tests that link to the introduction of The Driver Certificate of Professional Competence (CPC) in September 2009. Put the information this book contains into practice and you should be able to reach the higher standards demanded. Having passed your test, you will have demonstrated the skills necessary to become a goods vehicle driver and, above all, to continue to follow DSA's slogan of 'safe driving for life'.

Trevor Wedge

Trevor Wedge

Chief Driving Examiner and
Director for Safer Driving

Before you start

Selecting an instructor

It is important that you have the correct training and instruction before taking your large goods vehicle (LGV) test. DSA has developed a voluntary register of instructors. If you would like to take instruction from a registered instructor, contact

The LGV Register Section
Driving Standards Agency
The Axis Building,
112, Upper Parliament Street
Nottingham, NG1 6LP
Tel: 0115 936 6502

Applying for your licence

You should apply to the Driver and Vehicle Licensing Agency (DVLA) in Swansea (DVA in Northern Ireland) for the provisional entitlement to drive large goods vehicles. An application form is available online from DVLA or DVA.
www.dvla.gov.uk / www.dvani.gov.uk

Licence restrictions

To drive a small goods vehicle (category C1) you must be 18. To drive a small goods vehicle with a trailer (category C1+E) you must be 18, as long as the maximum authorised mass of the combination does not exceed 7.5 tonnes. If the maximum authorised mass **does** exceed 7.5 tonnes, you may still drive a C1+E at 18 if you hold a CPC. Otherwise you must be 21.

In order to drive a large goods vehicle (category C or, if driving with a trailer, C+E) you must be 21, unless you are 18 and

- you hold an initial CPC qualification authorising you to drive a motor vehicle of that class, *or*
- the vehicle is being used in the course of a driving lesson or driving test for the purpose of enabling you to obtain a driving licence or the driver CPC. You will also need a full driving licence for a category B vehicle and to hold a

provisional LGV driving licence for the category of vehicle that you wish to drive, *or*

- you have been issued with a document authorising you to drive the relevant vehicle for a specified period of up to 12 months, while undertaking a vocational training course leading to a professional qualification relevant to the carriage of goods by road. You will also need a full driving licence for a category B vehicle and to hold a provisional LGV driving licence for the category of vehicle that you wish to drive, *or*

- you hold one of the following documents on 10 September 2009

  (a) a current driving licence in the appropriate category

  (b) a current driving licence in the appropriate category, issued by a Member State other than the United Kingdom

  (c) a current driving licence in the appropriate category, recognised as equivalent to a document described at (a) above

  (d) a current test pass certificate entitling its holder to a driving licence authorising the driving of any relevant vehicle.

See page 13 for eyesight and medical requirements for Category C vehicles.

Automatic transmission

If your vehicle doesn't have a clutch pedal, it's classed as an automatic. If you take the LGV driving test in an automatic vehicle, your full LGV licence will restrict you to driving only LGVs fitted with automatic transmission.

Some modern vehicles have transmission systems where sensors select the next gear without the driver using the clutch pedal. Although the vehicle is predominantly driven in an automatic style, it still has a clutch pedal and is therefore classed as a manual transmission vehicle. The clutch is used for moving off and stopping, or for manoeuvring in a slow-speed situation, eg while controlling the vehicle in a yard.

Articulated vehicles

You must already hold a full licence to drive a rigid large goods vehicle (C1 or C) before you can apply for a provisional licence to drive an articulated vehicle (C1 + E or C + E). You don't have to pass a test in category C1 before taking a test in category C.

You'll already have experience of driving large vehicles. The information in this book about driving articulated vehicles will help you to prepare for your test and learn how to deal with the various characteristics of this type of vehicle. If you're taking your test with a trailer you'll be expected to demonstrate uncoupling and recoupling during your test.

The theory & practical tests

All new drivers wishing to drive large goods vehicles (LGVs) will have to pass a theory test before taking a practical driving test. You can start your lessons before passing the theory test but you must pass before a booking for a practical test can be accepted. The theory test pass certificate has a two-year life. If the practical test isn't passed within that time, the theory test will have to be re-taken.

When driving as a learner you must

• be accompanied by a qualified driver over the age of 21 who has held a full licence for the category of vehicle being driven for at least three years

• display L plates (or D plates, if you wish, when driving in Wales) to the front and rear of the vehicle.

You'll have to

• pass a category C test before taking a category C + E test

• pass a category C or C1 test before taking a category C1 + E test.

You won't have to gain a C1 before taking a test in category C.

A DVD entitled *The Official DSA Guide to Hazard Perception* for all drivers and riders will help candidates prepare for the hazard perception part of the theory test. This DVD can be obtained by mail order by calling 0870 241 4523. Alternatively, it can be purchased from good bookshops or online at **www.tsoshop.co.uk/dsa.**

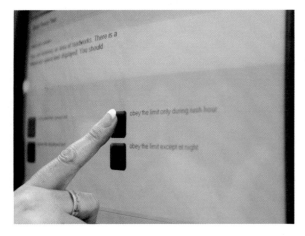

Medical requirements

Eyesight

All drivers, for whatever category of vehicle, must be able to read a number plate in good daylight at 20.5 metres (67 feet), or 20 metres (about 66 feet) if the new narrow font letters have been used on the number plate. If glasses or contact lenses are needed to do this then they must be worn while driving.

In addition, any applicant for an LGV licence must have a visual acuity of at least

- 6/9 in the better eye
- 6/12 in the other eye

when wearing glasses or contact lenses, if needed. There must also be normal vision in both eyes (defined as a 120° field) and no evidence of double vision (diplopia). Satisfactory uncorrected visual acuity is also required for applicants.

All applicants must have an uncorrected visual acuity of at least 3/60 in each eye. This visual field requirement is the normal binocular field of vision.

Your doctor will use the standard Snellen test card to test your eyesight. If you only have eyesight in one eye you must declare this on the relevant medical form.

A licence-holder who held an LGV licence before 1 January 1997 and whose eyesight doesn't meet the required new standard should contact

Drivers Medical Group
DVLA
Swansea
SA99 1TU

Tel: 0870 600 0301.

If you require any further general information you should contact DVLA on 0870 240 0009 or DVA on 0845 402 4000.

> **Remember,** if you normally wear glasses or contact lenses, always wear them whenever you drive.

Medical examination and form D4

Driving a goods vehicle carries a heavy responsibility towards all other road users so it's vital that you meet exacting medical standards.

Consult your doctor first if you have any doubts about your fitness. In any case, if this is your first application for LGV entitlement, a medical report must be completed by a doctor. You'll also need to send in a medical report with your application if you're renewing your LGV licence and you're aged 45 or over, unless you've already sent one during the last 12 months.

You'll need to have a medical examination in order to complete form D4.

Only complete the applicant details and declaration (Section 8 on the form) when you're with your doctor at the time of the examination. Your doctor will complete the other sections. The medical report will cover

- vision
- nervous system
- diabetes mellitus
- psychiatric illness
- general health
- cardiac health
- medical practitioner details.

Study the notes on pages 1 and 2 of form D4 then remove these two pages before sending in your application and keep them for future reference.

This medical report isn't available free under National Health rules. Your doctor is entitled to charge the current fee for this report. You're responsible for paying this fee: it can't be recovered from DVLA. In addition, the fee isn't refundable if your application is refused.

The completed form must be received by DVLA within four months of the date of your doctor's signature.

Change in health

It's your responsibility to immediately notify the Drivers Medical Group at DVLA, Swansea, (DVA in Northern Ireland) if you have, or develop, any serious illness or disability that's likely to last more than three months and which could affect your driving.

Medical standards

You may be refused an LGV driving licence if you suffer from any of the following

- liability to epilepsy*/seizure
- diabetes requiring insulin (unless you held a licence on 1 April 1991 and the Traffic Commissioner who issued that licence had knowledge of your condition)
- eyesight defects (see the eyesight requirements on page 13)
- heart disorders
- persistent high blood pressure (see the notes on form D4 for details)
- a stroke within the past year
- unconscious lapses within the last five years
- any disorder causing vertigo within the last year
- severe head injury, with serious continuing after-effects, or major brain surgery
- Parkinson's disease, multiple sclerosis or other chronic nervous disorders likely to affect the use of the limbs
- mental disorders
- alcohol/drug problems
- serious difficulty in communicating by telephone in an emergency.

> ***Remember,** a driver who remains seizure-free for at least 10 years (without anticonvulsant treatment within that time) may be eligible for a licence but with restricted entitlement. Contact DVLA (DVA in Northern Ireland) for further information.

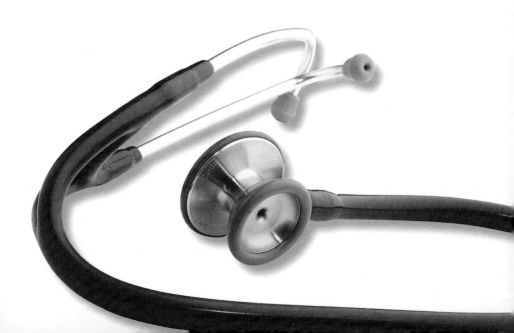

Professional standards

Driving an LGV requires skill combined with knowledge and the right attitude and driving techniques.

To become a professional driver you'll need

- demanding driving skills
- the knowledge to deal with all the regulations that apply to your work
- a comprehensive knowledge of *The Highway Code* including the meaning of traffic signs and road markings, especially those which indicate a restriction for LGVs.

From the start, you'll need to appreciate the differences between driving small and large goods vehicles. It's also essential to understand the forces at work on your vehicle and its load.

Remember, no risk is ever justified.

As a professional driver you have a responsibility to use your vehicle in a manner which is sympathetic to the environment. For more information, go to Section Four and refer to the sub-section entitled *Green issues - helping the environment*.

Initially, the most important thing to learn is that the way you drive is of great importance.

- Drive properly and safely and the goods entrusted into your care will arrive safely at their destination.
- Drive dangerously or even carelessly, and the potential for disaster is enormous.

Whether you're driving an unladen lorry of 7.5 tonnes or a fully laden articulated vehicle of 38 tonnes or more, acting hastily can have serious consequences.

Driver Certificate of Professional Competence

Driver Certificate of Professional Competence (CPC) is a new qualification that all professional lorry drivers in the EU must have in addition to their vocational licence. In the UK, it starts on **10 September 2009.**

Benefits are expected to include improvements to road safety and enhanced professionalism. Additional advantages include a reduction in fuel consumption and emissions resulting from a better knowledge of environmentally-friendly driving techniques.

You can get full and up-to-date information on Driver CPC on the web or from DSA (GB) or DVA (Northern Ireland). Contact details are given on page 19.

How you get your Driver CPC will depend on whether you are already a professional driver or a newly qualified driver. New drivers will need to pass additional theory and practical tests and then maintain their knowledge with 35 hours of periodic training in each five-year period after that. A new CPC will automatically be issued, provided that the periodic training has been delivered and recorded in accordance with regulations. The syllabus for these training courses covers safe and fuel-efficient driving, legal requirements, health, safety, service and logistics.

Existing drivers will have 'acquired' rights. This means that a driver who already holds a vocational driving licence on the start date will be deemed to hold the Driver CPC. They will not need to take any new tests, but they will need to undertake 35 hours of periodic training every five years to maintain their Driver CPC.

This training can be taken at any time within the five years, as one block or split into periods of at least 7 hours, which can be further split into two parts as long as the second part starts within 24 hours of the first part finishing. Their first five-year period starts on 10 September 2009.

driver cpc®
GETQUALIFIEDSTAYQUALIFIED

The tests

Theory Test (module 1) - the test is very similar to the current driving theory test. It is split into two parts that can be taken consecutively or at different times. The multiple choice part has 100 questions and the hazard perception part has 19 clips (with 20 scoreable hazards). In total the two parts take about two hours and 30 minutes.

Driver CPC Case Studies (module 2) - in addition to passing the Theory Test (module 1), drivers wishing to obtain their Driver CPC, and drive professionally, will also need to pass the Case Studies test (module 2). Each case study will be based on a real life scenario which you may encounter in your working life, and aims to test your knowledge and basic understanding, as well as how you put this knowledge into practice.

Questions will be based around this scenario and you will be asked to answer in a number of different ways, such as selecting from multiple choice answers, clicking on an area of a photograph or image, listening to audio information, or giving a short text answer.

There will be seven case studies, each with between five and ten associated questions. The test will take about one hour and 30 minutes.

Practical Driving Test (module 3) - this is the practical driving test which all new lorry drivers will need to pass. It will be slightly longer than before to allow you to show the examiner how you drive in various situations and types of road. Those taking the test will be assessed on their ecosafe driving, but they will not be failed on these factors. If the examiner finds that a driver could improve certain areas of their vehicle control and the way they plan their drive, the driver will be given further information to help them improve things like fuel economy.

Driver CPC Practical Demonstration Test (module 4) - this is also a practical test but it is for new professional drivers only, who require Driver CPC. It assesses your knowledge and abilities on matters of safety and security. For example, safe use of the vehicle, the security of the vehicle and yourself, preventing criminal acts and trafficking, assessing emergencies and preventing risks.

Periodic training

On completion of 35 hours training, drivers who hold a GB photocard licence will be automatically issued with a Driver Qualification Card (DQC) at no additional cost. The DQC will be sent to the address that is on the driving licence, so it is very important that drivers always keep DVLA (DVA in Northern Ireland) informed of their current address. Your DQC must be carried with you at all times when driving professionally.

Legal issues

It is an offence for an operator to cause or permit a driver who needs a Driver CPC or DQC to drive without one and there are penalties for drivers and operators who do this. You are guilty of an offence if you

- are a driver and you knowingly drive a large vehicle without a CPC DQC
- are an operator and you cause a driver to drive a large vehicle without a CPC DQC.

Both driver and operator can be fined up to £1000, if convicted of an offence.

Paper Licence and other EU Licences

At the time of publication, procedures for holders of EU and GB paper licence holders were not yet finalised. Note, however, that any qualifying GB paper licence holders opting to upgrade to a photocard licence will automatically receive their DQC without any need for a further DQC application process or fee.

A newly-qualified driver with a GB photo-card licence will get their DQC automatically when they have passed all four parts of the driving test.

Further information

DSA leaflet: *Driver CPC - Get Qualified, Stay qualified*

Great Britain
PO Box 280
Newcastle upon Tyne
NE99 1FP
Tel **0191 201 8161**
www.transportoffice.gov.uk/cpc
Email: **drivercpc@dsa.gsi.gov.uk**

Northern Ireland
66 Balmoral Road
Belfast
BT12 6QL
Tel: **028 9054 1832**
Email via **www.dvani.gov.uk**

Responsibility and attitude

A loaded LGV travelling at speed and colliding with another vehicle will cause serious damage. You're the one with the responsibility of driving your vehicle safely at all times.

Your vehicle will probably have the owner's name on display, and so your driving will be similarly on display. Make sure that your vehicle is clean and well maintained, and that your driving reaches the same high standards. Show a good example of skill, courtesy and tolerance to other road users. Be a credit to yourself, your company and your profession.

Your LGV licence is a privilege which requires effort to gain and even more effort to keep.

You could also take further training under the *Safe And Fuel Efficient Driving (SAFED)* Standard which helps you develop skills that promote your safety and that of your vehicle, load and other road users. It helps you build confidence in vehicle control and driving techniques as well as reducing stress levels and enhancing your satisfaction from driving. Some of the benefits of SAFED and other similar courses include

- improved road safety
- improved fuel consumption
- longer service intervals
- more relaxed drivers.

Many of these benefits should also result in less overall costs for operators.

Through fuel-efficient driving, drivers raise their levels of professionalism and become more of an asset to their employers.

Appropriate behaviour

As a professional driver you should set a good example of driving to others. You should always have an idea of how other road users see you. Be aware that they might not understand why you take up certain positions to make turns or take longer to manoeuvre.

You'll spend a great deal of time at the wheel of your vehicle. Losing your temper or having a bad attitude towards other road users won't make your working life pleasant. A good attitude will help you to enjoy your work and is safer for others around you.

Many operators participate in an initiative called the 'Driven Well' scheme. Each vehicle displays a freephone number on the rear so that other road users can praise or complain about the driver's actions.

Intimidation

Don't use the size, weight and power of your vehicle to intimidate other road users. Even the repeated hiss from air brakes being applied while stationary gives the impression of 'breathing down the neck' of the driver in front.

The sheer size, noise and appearance of a typical LGV often appears somewhat intimidating to a cyclist, motorcyclist or even the average car driver. Travelling dangerously close behind a smaller vehicle (tailgating) at speed can be very intimidating for the vehicle in front. When an LGV appears to be being driven in an aggressive way other road users can often feel threatened.

Tailgating

If you drive too close to the vehicle in front, your view of the road ahead may be severely restricted. You may not be able to see or plan for any hazards that might occur. The room in which you have to stop is also reduced, probably to less than the stopping distance for the speed at which you're travelling. This is a dangerous practice.

Police forces are concerned at the number of incidents that are caused as a direct result of vehicles driving much too close to each other. A number have mounted campaigns to video and prosecute offenders.

In an effort to improve the image of the transport industry, some large retail organisations are reviewing the placing of contracts with any distributor whose vehicles have been seen repeatedly tailgating on motorways.

Speed

The introduction of 'just in time' flow-line policies reduces the need for manufacturers to hold large stocks of materials. These policies are also intended to ensure the delivery of fresh foods at the supermarket, for example.

Don't allow your employer to set delivery targets which are unrealistic. You should never be under extreme pressure to meet deadlines.

You can never justify driving too fast simply because you need to reach a given location by a specific time, whether it be a ferry, loading bay or depot. If an incident results and you injure someone, there's no possible defence for your actions.

Retaliation

You should resist, at all times, impatience or the temptation to retaliate. Always drive

- courteously
- with anticipation
- calmly, allowing for other road users' mistakes
- with full control of your vehicle.

You can't act hastily without the possibility of serious loss of control when driving an LGV.

The horn

Because LGVs are often equipped with powerful multi-tone air horns, their use should be strictly confined to the guidance set out in *The Highway Code* – to warn other road users of your presence.

See page 176 for more information about using the horn.

The headlights

To avoid dazzle, don't switch the headlights onto full beam when following another vehicle.

Don't

- switch on additional auxiliary lights that may be fitted to your vehicle unless the weather conditions require their use (they must be switched off when the weather improves)
- repeatedly flash the headlights while driving directly behind another vehicle.

Flashing the headlights lets other road users know that you're there. It doesn't mean that you wish to give or take priority. You may be misunderstood by others when using an unauthorised code of headlight flashing, which could lead to road traffic incidents.

Neither the headlights nor the horn(s) must be used to rebuke or to intimidate another road user. Courtesy and consideration are the hallmarks of a professional driver.

Mobile phones

It is illegal to use a hand-held mobile phone whilst driving. Using hands-free equipment can also distract your attention from the road. Do not accept calls whilst driving. You are strongly advised to make sure your mobile phone is switched off before starting to drive. Use a messaging service and only pick up or return calls after you've stopped in a safe, convenient and legal place.

Driving a large goods vehicle requires all of your attention, all of the time.

Effects of your vehicle

As a competent LGV driver you must always be aware of the effect your vehicle and your driving have on other road users.

You need to recognise the effects of turbulence or buffeting caused by your vehicle, especially when passing

- pedestrians
- horse riders (on the road or grass verge)
- cyclists
- motorcyclists
- cars towing caravans
- other lorries and buses.

On congested roads in built-up areas, particularly in shopping areas, take extra care when you need to drive closer to the kerb. Be aware of

- the possibility of a pedestrian stepping off the kerb (and under the wheels)

- the nearside mirror striking the head of a pedestrian standing at the edge of the kerb
- cyclists moving up the nearside of your vehicle in slow-moving traffic.

Cyclists

Over a quarter of cyclist deaths are as a result of collisions with LGVs. You need to be aware of the limited vision you have around your vehicle due to its size and shape. Use your mirrors so that you have a constant picture of what's happening all around. Always check any blind spots before you move away.

Also remember that cyclists could become unbalanced by the buffeting effect of a large vehicle passing closely.

Work organisation

Your route or delivery sequence may be set by your operator or it could be one of your duties to plan the optimum route yourself, whether single or multi-drops are involved. Scheduling and organisation are important in terms of fuel costs and in respect of Drivers' hours of work/rest periods.

Equally though, in most if not all cases, you will be the face-to-face contact with the customer on behalf of your operator. If you find you are going to be delayed in any way whilst en route, it is important to be able to let the customer know so do take any available contact details with you. The customer will appreciate being advised of any delay, as it will allow them to be proactive in adjusting their activities, if required, to suit your amended estimated time of arrival (ETA).

This is especially important if specific load/unload timeslots are necessary, due to space constraints at the customer's premises. Any delays can also affect your working hours, rest periods, tachograph records etc, so stay aware of where you are in your work/rest cycle too. Remember that an apology, eg for a late delivery, can help to reduce a customer's anger or frustration. If goods are damaged, you should encourage the customer to sign the delivery note describing the damage.

Delivery notes

Any delivery should have supporting paperwork which tallies with the load you are carrying. This will list the goods to be delivered, along with the customer's details. Before departure from base, always check the paperwork. There may be special instructions which may need to be followed when you reach the customer's site.

On arrival at the delivery point, make sure that you have the paperwork to hand. The customer should check the goods against the delivery note during unloading. You also need to obtain the customer's signature on your paperwork. This is your confirmation that the goods have arrived safely to the customer's satisfaction.

Commercial and financial aspects of a dispute

Keeping the customer updated is also important from another point of view - it shows efficiency and customer care. This reflects well on both your operator and yourself, as you are seen to be taking an active role in helping the customer as much as possible.

Drivers become trusted company ambassadors and form a vital part of the liaison process. This can be especially important if there is a dispute of some sort, eg faulty goods or order discrepancies. When encountering 'just the driver who only delivers the goods and who knows nothing', the customer can become frustrated and angry. This could, in turn, affect supplier-customer relationships and lose business.

When dealing with 'the driver who is always helpful, courteous and who knows the name and number of who to call back at base if there is a problem', the customer sees efficiency, receives assistance and feels well looked after. This helps maintain good customer-supplier relationships, and could gain further business.

Also important is the look of your vehicle - keeping it clean may help to improve the image of the company.

Ultimately, remember that you are never 'just the driver'. As the operator-customer interface, you also have a responsibility to preserve and enhance the good image of the company. A helpful and courteous attitude is an important part of your work.

Telematics

Telematics describes a system that collects performance information from a vehicle. Using an on-board computer, aspects from driving style and vehicle efficiency to drivers' hours and load security can be monitored. Global Positioning Systems and communication devices assist with general organisation of operations.

The use of telematics is becoming more popular. It is a system that allows operators to track their fleets in real time. It combines modern communications with information technology in the cab. This allows the operator to

- divert vehicles to a change in delivery point
- manage fuel consumption and costs
- pass latest information to the driver on the best route which avoids known congestion and trouble spots
- monitor the vehicle temperature
- monitor the safety and security of the vehicle and its load.

It can also be used to identify driver habits which can contribute to vehicle running costs, such as a driver who

- changes gear in sequence
- blips the accelerator when changing gear.

Both actions can add to fuel costs.

Freight transport modes

The different ways that goods and materials can be moved are known as 'transport modes'. Freight transport modes include road, rail, sea. air, inland waterway and pipeline. There are several factors that have to be taken into account before the most suitable mode of transport can be chosen.

For example, the shelf-life of a product may determine the best transport mode to use. Some boxes of very expensive and highly perishable seafood, which landed this afternoon at a Scottish port and are required by a customer in France tomorrow morning, may have to be sent by plane. The choice of mode in this example would take into account the needs of distance, short shelf-life and speed of delivery.

Oil from the Middle East countries, on the other hand, because of the sheer size of bulk quantities to be transported, would require different transport modes such as pipelines and large ships to transport the oil to refineries throughout the world.

Different modes may be combined to reduce operational costs. If a vehicle needs to transport a load overseas, for example, it may be cheaper and save time to load it onto a container ship rather than drive a vehicle onto a ferry. Also, there may be a choice of ways to move items - containers may also be transported as rail freight.

Supply chains and logistics

There are many supply chain types, for example

- the food supply chain starts at the farm where animals and crops are grown, moving onto food processing, packaging and final distribution to the shops and supermarkets
- the petro-chemical supply chain starts at the oil well drilling rig where the liquid is extracted and sent for processing into products like fuel and plastic goods for distribution to retail outlets.

Transport modes are the links on which the supply chain depends. The art of making sure the whole of the supply chain is working efficiently is known as Logistics. In the UK, road freight is currently the most popular way of delivering goods to many industrial, commercial and retail premises. Therefore, the professional commercial vehicle driver plays a key role in the operation of UK supply chain logistics.

Types of operators

Haulage companies, and owner-drivers who carry other people's goods for a living, are known as Hire and Reward Operators. These companies may also be referred to as Professional Hauliers, Distribution Companies or Third Party Logistics Suppliers. Such organisations can provide, for example, general haulage services or dedicated customer contracts supplying goods handling, warehousing and transport. Other operators include

- sub-contractors - haulage companies may decide to give their customers' goods to other hauliers to deliver.

This is known as sub-contracting. Many owner-drivers make a living as sub-contractors

- own-account operations - manufacturers and service providers may choose to deliver their own goods and materials using their own drivers and vehicles. This type of transport operation is known as own-account transport
- freight forwarders - these are companies that are known as intermediaries. They act on behalf of importers, exporters or any other company or person. They organise the safe, efficient and cost-effective transportation of products. Many transport and logistics operators also offer freight-forwarding services.

Back-loading

The spare capacity on return journeys from deliveries can be utilised by back-loading. This is achieved by finding loads that need to be moved to a destination along the route of the returning vehicle. These loads could be returns of your own goods, products from your customer or goods from a third party. Back-loading provides better use of fuel by minimising empty running as well as maximising revenue.

A national standard operating licence is required if you carry goods other than your own. The options for back-loads can vary from forming a partnership or joining a supply chain initiative to contacting a return-load specialist. These organisations often use the internet to match loads to

available vehicles and can also be known as "clearing houses". However, specialised vehicles may find it harder to find a return load. If you're involved in carrying different types of loads always be aware of the cross-contamination of products. Some consignments require particularly specialised vehicles, such as in the chemical, fertiliser, cement and paper industries.

Before carrying any load make sure it will not contaminate your vehicle or existing load, which may make it unsafe or dangerous to carry other goods. Be especially careful with vehicles that are used for footstuffs. It's advisable NOT to carry any other types of products on vehicles that are normally used to carry foodstuffs, to avoid the danger of cross-contamination.

Specialised road freight transport operations

Many products require specialist transport operators with specially-designed vehicles to transport them.

Temperature-controlled goods

Frozen foods must be transported at temperatures below freezing point and the use of refrigerated lorries and trailers is essential to ensure the food is delivered in good condition. Drivers will need to be trained to operate refrigeration units as well as in correct hygiene procedures.

The same requirements apply to the movement of chilled and perishable goods, eg fresh flowers, which are transported at controlled temperatures above freezing point.

Some highly dangerous chemicals have to be transported at prescribed temperatures. These chemicals are normally transported in specially-designed, temperature-controlled vehicles and the drivers must be fully trained in their use.

Road tankers and tank containers

Many customers want their goods delivered in large quantities, rather than in bags or drums etc. Tankers and tank containers are an efficient way of doing this. They also help reduce packaging waste and product handling/storage costs.

On a road tanker, the tank (or shell as it is often known) is permanently fixed to the lorry or trailer chassis. The tank container, on the other hand, is normally attached to the vehicle or trailer using twistlock mechanisms and has the advantage of being able to be lifted on or off the vehicle by crane or forklift. This means that the carrying lorry is freed up for other work while the tank container can continue its journey, for example, via ship or train.

Tankers and tank containers can be designed to carry solid materials (granules, powders), liquids or gases. Drivers must be properly trained on how to use the equipment and valves fitted to the particular vehicle being driven.

There are many different types of tank and tank container, for example

- some need to be pressurised to assist in emptying (eg cement tanker)
- some empty themselves just by the effects of gravity (eg petrol tanker)
- some have to be raised like a tipper lorry to empty the contents. Drivers have to make sure that this is done safely on level ground, using any fitted stabilisers to ensure the tank or tank container does not fall over.

You should never fill, transport or unload a tank or tank container unless full training on the specific type of product and loading/unloading procedures have been received. You must also understand the full consequences of spillages and know what action to take in the event of such a situation, with regard to human safety and the environment.

Bulk transport

In general terms, bulk goods are carried in tipper lorries, skips and Intermediate Bulk Containers (IBCs).

The customer may want goods delivered in bulk to gain similar benefits to those mentioned in relation to tanker transportation systems. Many goods cannot be delivered in large quantities using tanks and tank containers; for example solid coal, fertiliser, minerals, scrap and wastes. These must use bulk transport.

Similar to tankers and tank containers, bulk tippers and skips carry large quantities of materials which must be handled with skill and care. Open-top bulk lorries, such as tippers and skips, should be covered to prevent spillages which could cause environmental damage and other dangers to the public and road users.

Transport of livestock

The principal legislation concerned with transporting animals is the Welfare of Animals (Transport) Order 1997. All animal transport vehicles are covered by general provisions regarding vehicle strength, size, ventilation, floor surface and roof suitability. For example, vehicles and trailers should have an anti-slip surface to give animals sufficient grip to prevent falling.

There are further distinctions drawn between vehicles carrying animals on journeys of up to 8 hours and those vehicles used for longer journey times. For longer journeys, there must also be

- sufficient bedding material placed on the floor

- adequate and suitable feed available
- suitable connections available for linking to a water supply during stops
- direct access to animals
- moveable panels to create various compartments as required.

As a driver able to transport animals, you will need to either

- be given specific training by your employer, or prove that you have already done this training previously
- prove that you have equivalent practical experience to care for the animals correctly.

Your operator, as an experienced transporter of livestock, should have all the necessary information and full guidance notes available on all aspects of animal transport, such as

- correct authorisations required for transport of animals
- relevant documentation (Animal Transport Certificates, journey logs which need to accompany the animals)
- specific requirements concerning feeding, watering and rest periods for different animals
- cleaning and disinfection rules
- latest updates on the required driver training courses and competencies.

Manual handling techniques

More than a third of all over-three-day injuries reported each year are caused while manual handling - the transporting or supporting of loads by hand or by bodily force.

To reduce the risk of an injury while manually handling loads

- follow appropriate systems of work which are laid down for your safety
- make proper use of any equipment provided
- inform the relevant person if you identify any hazardous handling activities
- take care to ensure that your activities do not put others at risk.

Good techniques for lifting

When lifting you should:

think before lifting/handling. Plan the lift. Can handling aids be used? Where is the load going to be placed? Will help be needed with the load? Remove any obstruction beforehand. For a long lift, consider resting the load midway to change grip

keep the load close to your waist. Keep the load close to your body for as long as possible while lifting. Keep the heaviest side of the load next to your body. If a close approach to the load is not possible, try to slide it towards your body before attempting to lift it

adopt a stable position. Your feet should be apart with one leg slightly forward to maintain balance (alongside the load, if it is on the ground). Be prepared to move your feet during the lift to maintain stability. Avoid tight clothing or unsuitable footwear, which may make this difficult

get a good hold. Where possible, the load should be hugged closely to your body. This may be better than gripping it tightly with hands only

start in a good posture. At the start of the lift, slight bending of your back, hips and knees is preferable to fully flexing your back (stooping) or fully flexing your hips and knees (squatting)

avoid twisting or leaning sideways, especially while your back is bent. Shoulders should be kept level and facing in the same direction as your hips. Turning by moving your feet is better than twisting and lifting at the same time

keep your head up. Look ahead, not down at the load, once it has been held securely

move smoothly. The load should not be jerked or snatched as this can make it harder to keep control and can increase the risk of injury

not lift or handle more than can be easily managed. There is a difference between what people can lift and what they can safely lift. If in doubt, seek advice or get help

Adopt a stable position

Start in a good posture

put down, then adjust. If precise positioning of the load is necessary, put it down first, then slide it into the desired position.

Good techniques for pushing and pulling

Here are some practical points to remember when loads are pushed or pulled.

Handling devices. Aids such as barrows and trolleys should have handle heights that are between your shoulder and waist.

Force. As a rough guide the amount of force that needs to be applied to move a load over a flat, level surface, using a well maintained handling aid, is at least 2% of the load weight. For example, if the load weight is 400 kg, then the force needed to move the load is 8 kg. The force

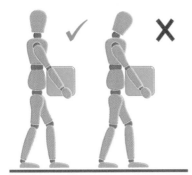

Keep the head up

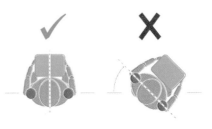

Avoid twisting or leaning sideways

needed will be larger, perhaps a lot larger, if conditions are not perfect (eg wheels not in the right position or a device that is poorly maintained). Try to push rather than pull when moving a load, provided you can see over it and can control steering and stopping.

Slopes. Enlist help from another person if you have to negotiate a slope or ramp, as pushing and pulling forces can be very high. For example, if a load of 400 kg is moved up a slope of 1 in 12, the required force is over 30 kg, even in ideal conditions - good wheels and a smooth slope. **This is above the guideline weight for men and well above the guideline weight for women.**

Uneven surfaces. Moving an object over soft or uneven surfaces requires greater forces. On an uneven surface, the force needed to start the load moving could increase to 10% of the load weight, although this might be offset to some extent by using larger wheels. Soft ground may be even worse.

Stance and pace. To make it easier to push or pull, keep your feet well away from the load and go no faster than walking speed.

Before using any specialist equipment (eg forklift trucks, overhead cranes etc) you must ensure you are fully trained in its use. You should also ensure that any licences or certificates of competence relevant to such equipment are renewed or updated at appropriate intervals as required.

Ergonomic considerations

As important as manual handling is how comfortable you are when driving. Remember that you may be spending some considerable time in the same restricted position - what is comfortable for five minutes may feel very different after ninety minutes. You should check for, and make, any adjustments necessary before you start any journey, more especially if you are to drive an unfamiliar vehicle for the first time.

Never adjust your seat while the vehicle is moving. Before starting the vehicle, you should carefully check the following:

- does the seat position feel comfortable for you and is the seat locked in position
- does the angle of the seat back provide suitable support for good posture
- is the head restraint in the correct position for your safety and comfort
- can you reach all the controls without straining or overreaching in any way
- can you see the road ahead clearly - the seat or steering wheel may also adjust for height
- do any of the mirrors need adjustment to meet your particular requirements
- is the seat belt comfortable and in the right position across your body.

If you find any of the above cannot be adjusted sufficiently to meet your needs, you should speak to your operator or the company health and safety representative for advice.

Diet and driving ability

Medical standards for many common conditions linked to poor eating habits, such as heart disease and diabetes in middle age, are more stringent for LGV and PCV drivers than car drivers. A sensible approach to food, fluid and caffeine intake can benefit your driving performance and safety in the short term and improve your health in the longer term. This will reduce the risk of an early end to your time working as a driver, either from death or disability, or from withdrawal of your driving licence on medical grounds.

Long-term health effects from bad eating habits

One of the key factors for ensuring long-term general good health is a well-balanced diet. A pattern of poor eating habits will increase your risk of developing serious long-term health problems in middle age, such as obesity, diabetes and heart disease. These diseases will increase your risk of sudden incapacity at the wheel, as well as make you more likely to develop serious illness at other times and increase your probability of an early death.

Other factors such as smoking and lack of exercise also increase these risks.

The development of these serious diseases takes many years and your dietary habits in earlier years will contribute to your risk of disease when you are between forty and seventy years of age.

The main ways in which your diet can contribute to future serious ill-health are

- **excessive calorie intake from any source, but commonly from sugars and fat.** This can lead to obesity. Not only does this impair your physical performance but it is also linked to an increased risk of late-onset diabetes, raised blood pressure and heart disease

- **intake of saturated fats.** These are usually the hard fats in butter and lard rather than in oils such as sunflower and olive. Packaged foods will normally give information on the levels present. High levels of intake are associated with an increased risk of arterial disease, leading to heart attack and stroke

- **salt.** While your body needs salt in small amounts, most western diets contain far more than is essential. This can lead to high blood pressure and an increased risk of heart disease and stroke.

It is not always easy to detect the presence of these undesirable components in food. Savoury pies may be very high in both salt and saturated fat but these are hidden by the taste and texture of the pie. Cakes, while seeming sweet, also contain large amounts of fat, which is not apparent.

Soft drinks, when they do not use non-sugar sweeteners, often contain very large amounts of sugar which is hidden by the acidity of other ingredients. Labelling allows you to identify ingredients and to make choices that will help you avoid those which are undesirable.

Proteins are essential components of diet but are not needed in vast quantities by adults, although their presence makes for slow digestion and prolonged satisfaction after eating. However, care is needed to ensure that you do not eat excessive amounts of foods like eggs and cheese.

Protein-based foods should be included as part of a healthy eating plan. However, eating them in large quantities can add extra unnecessary fat or salt to your diet, which can contribute to an increase in cholesterol levels. Recommended protein portion sizes vary according to sources, but a general approximation would be

- 4 oz (100 g) meat, fish or poultry
- approx 1 oz (30g) of hard cheese or nuts
- two whole eggs

Many traditional ways of serving proteins, such as frying, battering and presentation in pies and puddings, can add additional undesirable foods. The addition of fats should be limited to unsaturated ones such as sunflower and olive oils or products such as spreads manufactured from them.

Fibre in fruit, vegetables and unrefined cereals also prolongs post-meal satisfaction and may to an extent be protective against several forms of ill-health. There is a recommendation that five portions of fruit/vegetables/salad should be eaten each day. Eating five portions a day will help towards a healthy balanced diet and contribute to your long-term health.

Diet and performance while driving

Concentration, and therefore safe driving, will be improved by regular meals timed to fit into rest breaks rather than continuous snacking while on the move.

Regular meals are preferable to snacks when trying to control diet as, with the exception of fruit, most snack foods are high in sugar, fat or salt.

Meals based around protein-containing foods (such as meat, fish, eggs, cheese and peas or beans) and slowly-digested calories (such as bread, rice, pasta and vegetables) will keep you satisfied and prevent hunger for longer than those high in sugar which give immediate calories.

When driving through the night or on late-evening or early-morning shifts you need to consider the following points:

• an additional meal is desirable at the beginning and in the middle of the period of work

• at the start of night work, after a period when night-time sleep has been customary, digestion is likely to be less efficient and you may need to adjust the amount and type of food eaten to take account of any feelings of discomfort

• if it is not possible to find a meal other than one containing a high fat content or quick-release calories, it may be better to prepare your own food in advance

• care should be taken to balance eating patterns for the rest of the day to avoid an excessive intake of calories.

Fluid intake

Your fluid requirements will depend, in part, on the temperature of your cab and the physical demands during loading and unloading. You should carry water in case of delays on the journey, especially in summer.

Water is the ideal drink; it quenches thirst for longer than drinks such as tea and coffee, which increase urine production. The only advantage of bottled waters over tap water in developed countries is their convenience. A large amount of hidden sugar, and hence calories, can be consumed in those bottled and canned drinks which are not marked as low in calories or sugar.

The amount of caffeine in purchased hot drinks is very variable. Caffeine from coffee, and to a lesser extent from tea, does not reduce sleepiness; it masks sleepiness and can prolong alertness for an hour or so, usually with a rebound increase in tiredness and sleepiness afterwards. Tea and coffee without sugar provide fluid and caffeine with few calories, although large amounts of caffeine can cause jitteriness and anxiety.

Branded caffeine-containing soft drinks provide a more reliable source, but usually also contain a lot of sugar, so try to go for sugar-free or artificially-sweetened options. Caffeine-rich drinks should be considered a short-term emergency countermeasure rather than being used as a way to prolong the amount of time at the wheel. In addition to what is already mentioned on drinking and driving elsewhere - do not drink and drive as it will seriously affect your judgement and ability.

Remember, if you are feeling sleepy, stop driving and sleep, do not rely on caffeine.

YOU DRIVE FOR A LIVING BUT YOU'D KILL FOR SOME SLEEP?

Tiredness Kills. Make time for a break.
www.thinkroadsafety.gov.uk

section **two**

UNDERSTANDING LARGE GOODS VEHICLES (LGVs)

This section covers

- Understanding LGVs
- Forces affecting your vehi
- Vehicle characteristics
- Vehicle limits
- Vehicle maintenance
- Loads and load restraint

Understanding LGVs

You'll need to study and understand the information given in this book before you can consider taking an LGV driving test. You also need to understand how various kinds of LGVs handle in order to drive them safely.

To drive a lorry safely you must first appreciate the main differences between driving small and large goods vehicles.

These are

* weight
* width
* length
* height
* distance needed to pull up
* distance needed to overtake
* control needed when going downhill
* power needed to climb uphill
* the need to avoid any sudden changes of speed or direction.

Some of these aspects will be obvious from the moment you first start to drive an LGV. Other features will only become apparent after you've gained experience. The essential factor is to recognise that much more forward planning and anticipation is needed to drive an LGV safely.

Whether an LGV is

* laden or unladen
* rigid

* towing a drawbar trailer
* articulated

it's most stable when travelling in a straight line under gentle acceleration. Sudden or violent

* steering
* acceleration
* braking

can cause severe loss of control. All braking should be carried out smoothly and in good time.

Most modern large vehicles are fitted with an air braking system. Older vehicles might have a hydraulic braking system. In the latter case, if you find you need to pump the brakes, stop as safely as you can in a convenient place and check the hydraulic system. Don't drive on unless you're sure that you can stop safely.

Driving new or unfamiliar vehicles

Before driving any vehicle, you should be familiar with all its controls and operating systems. This is especially important if it's

* a new vehicle
* a type which you have not driven before
* one with which you are not familiar.

Erratic handling

Sudden acceleration forward might cause an insecure load to fall off the back of a vehicle. Similarly, if harsh braking is applied

- the load may attempt to continue moving forward
- the tyres may lose their grip on the road surface, causing the vehicle to skid
- the weight of the vehicle is transferred forward causing the front of the vehicle to dip downward.

Any sudden steering movement may also unsettle the load and cause it to move. Any movement of the load is likely to make the vehicle unstable.

All acceleration and braking should be controlled and as smooth and progressive as possible.

Jack-knifing

This is usually more likely to occur with an unladen vehicle.

In the case of an articulated vehicle, severe braking can result in jack-knifing as the tractive unit is pushed by the semi-trailer pivoting around the coupling (fifth wheel). This is even more likely if the vehicle isn't travelling in a straight line when the brakes are applied.

Similar results will occur with a drawbar trailer, where there may be two pivoting points: at the coupling pin and at the turntable of the front wheels of a trailer with two or more axles.

Changing into a lower gear when travelling at too high a speed or releasing the clutch suddenly can produce much the same effect, as the braking effect is only applied to the driven wheels.

For some years now, well-proven systems have been available that reduce the risk of jack-knifing on articulated vehicles.

Trailer swing

This can occur on a drawbar combination (or occasionally on an articulated unit) when

- sharp braking is applied on a bend
- excessive steering takes place at speed
- the brakes on either the tractive unit or trailer aren't properly adjusted.

It follows that all braking, gear changes, steering and acceleration should be smooth and under full control.

Laden articulated flatbed trailer

Drawbar trailer

Articulated refrigerated trailer

Box van

Forces affecting your vehicle

Friction

The grip between two surfaces is due to friction. The grip that rubber tyres have on a road surface produces traction (force), which enables a vehicle to

- move away or accelerate
- turn/change direction
- brake/slow down.

The amount of friction, and hence traction, will depend on

- the weight of the vehicle
- the vehicle's speed
- the condition of the tyre tread
- the tyre pressure
- the type and condition of the road surface
  - anti-skid
  - loose
  - smooth

- weather conditions
- any other material present on the road
  - mud
  - wet leaves
  - diesel spillage
  - other slippery spillages
  - inset metal rail lines
- the rate of change of speed or direction (sudden steering/braking)
- the condition of mechanical components
  - steering alignment
  - suspension.

Sudden acceleration or deceleration can reduce the grip your vehicle has on the road. Under these conditions the vehicle may

- lose traction (wheelspin)
- break away on a turn (skid)
- not stop safely (skid)
- overturn.

Gravity

When a vehicle is stationary on level ground the only force generally acting upon it (ignoring wind forces, etc) is the downward pull of gravity.

On an uphill gradient, gravity will affect a moving vehicle and its load so that

- more power is needed from the engine to move the vehicle and its load forward and upward
- less braking effort is needed and the vehicle will pull up in a shorter distance.

On a downhill gradient the effect of gravity will tend to

- make the vehicle's speed increase
- require more braking effort to slow down or stop
- increase stopping distances.

A vehicle's centre of gravity is the point around which all of its weight is balanced. To keep the vehicle and its load stable this should be arranged to be

- as low as possible
- along a line running centrally down the length of the LGV.

The higher this centre of gravity occurs, the less stable a vehicle and/or its load will be. As a result the vehicle will become more easily affected by

- braking
- steering
- the slope (camber) of a road
- the wheels running over a kerb, resulting in either the load tilting or falling, or the vehicle overturning.

End-tipper vehicles

When a loaded tipper vehicle body (whether tanker, bulk carrier or high-sided open body) is raised to discharge a load, the centre of gravity is raised to a critical position. It's vitally important to ensure that the vehicle is on a level, solid surface before engaging the hoist mechanism.

Ensure that there are no overhead power lines in the vicinity. Keep clear of scaffolding or any other obstructions.

Side-tipper vehicles

Always select the firmest level site available before tilting the vehicle body. Until the load is discharged, all the weight will be transferred to one side. Unless the vehicle is on firm level ground there is a risk of it overturning. Always take the time to check the ground before tipping. Get out and check all around the vehicle. Make sure that it's safe before you tip.

Safety issues

There should be on-site precautions for tipper drivers, warning them of overhead cables and pipework. These can be in the form of goal posts, height gauge posts or barriers. However, it is up to the driver to always check before tilting the body. Such vehicles may have extra safety features such as audible movement alarms and inclinometers. These can warn the driver and others in the vicinity of potental load instability.

It is important for drivers of vehicles with fork lifts, crane mounts, and overhead lifting devices to check the area where the jib will lift and swing, especially when lifting loads in residential areas. You should avoid swinging the lifting device too quickly, as this will cause instability and may cause the vehicle to tip over.

These lifting devices are becoming more common as they reduce loading and unloading time. This leaves the driver less tired from the exertion of loading and unloading, and in better physical condition to drive the vehicle.

Articulated tipper vehicles help lower fuel costs as they can carry a greater load, reducing the amount of journeys that have to be made. As the load is spread over more axles they are safer and cause less damage to roads.

End tipper vehicle

Kinetic energy

This is the energy held by a moving vehicle. The amount depends on the

- mass (weight) of the vehicle, plus its load
- speed of the vehicle.

Kinetic energy must be reduced by the brakes in order to stop a vehicle. The kinetic energy of a stationary vehicle is zero.

An increase in speed from 15 mph to 45 mph (x 3) increases the kinetic energy **ninefold** (3 x 3). If you reduce the speed by half, say from 50 mph to 25 mph, the kinetic energy acting on your vehicle is **one-quarter** of what it was before braking.

As the brakes reduce the speed of a vehicle, kinetic energy is converted into heat. Continuous use of the brakes can result in them becoming overheated and losing their effectiveness, especially on long downhill gradients. This is known as 'brake fade'.

The effort required to stop a fully laden LGV travelling at 56 mph (90 km/h) is so much greater than that needed to stop an ordinary motor car travelling at similar speed. You'll need to allow extra time and space to stop an LGV safely. Don't follow other vehicles too closely – always leave a safe separation distance. In addition, harsh braking should be avoided at all times when driving an LGV.

Momentum

This is the tendency for a vehicle and/or its load to continue in a straight line. It depends on

- mass (weight) of the vehicle plus its load
- speed of the vehicle.

The higher the speed, the greater the momentum and the greater the effort required to stop or change direction.

Centrifugal force

When a vehicle takes a curved path at a bend the force acting upon it will tend to cause the vehicle to leave the road at a tangent to the bend. At low speeds this force will be overcome by the traction of the tyres on the road surface.

If a loaded vehicle takes a bend at too high a speed the centrifugal force acting on it may cause it to become unstable and may also cause the load to become detached and fall off the side. For example, when a vehicle turns through a sharp left-hand bend, the centrifugal force will direct the vehicle or its load off the road to the right.

Forces on the load

If the forces acting on a load cause it to become detached from the vehicle, the load will move in the direction of the force.

While

- accelerating, it will fall off the back
- braking, it will continue moving forward
- tilting, it will topple over
- turning, it will continue on the original path and fall off the side.

There are significant weight and handling differences between a loaded and unloaded vehicle. Factors affected include

- handling
- roadholding
- acceleration
- braking
- fuel consumption.

Stay aware of the feel and handling of your vehicle at all times. If you are on a multi-drop delivery things might change dramatically as goods are delivered and the load distribution changes.

Loss of control

You can ask too much of your tyres if you turn and brake at the same time, especially at higher speeds. Once any or all the tyres lift or slide (that is, they lose traction) you're no longer in control of the vehicle. What happens next will depend on the particular forces that are acting on the vehicle.

When any change is made to a vehicle's motion or direction, the same forces will act on any load being carried. The load needs to be secured to the vehicle so that it can't move.

Shedding loads

There are several differences between driving a large vehicle and driving a smaller vehicle or a car. An unladen vehicle will handle differently from a laden one. Handling will also change depending on the size or type of load carried. Whilst this list is not definitive, the following are common causes for shedding of a load.

- Driver error
  - sudden change of speed or direction
  - driving too fast
- Instability of load
  - unsuitable vehicle
  - badly stowed load
  - movement in load
  - failed restraints
  - unsuitable type of restraint
- Mechanical failure
  - suspension failure
  - tyre failure
  - trailer disengaged
  - wheel loss
- Collision
  - another vehicle
  - a bridge, etc.
  - lamp posts
  - signs
  - signals
  - bollards.

Most of these situations are preventable. You should know the handling characteristics of the vehicle that you're driving and drive in a safe and sensible manner.

Maintaining control

You can't alter the severity of a bend or change the weight of a load. However, you do have control over the speed and braking of your vehicle.

Reduce speed in good time, by braking if necessary, before negotiating

- bends
- roundabouts
- corners.

To keep control you should ensure that all braking is

- controlled
- in good time
- made when travelling in a straight line, wherever possible.

Avoid braking and turning at the same time (unless manoeuvring at low speed). Look well ahead to assess and plan.

The different types of large goods vehicles will each require specific handling. You'll need to bear this in mind if you want to become a professional LGV driver.

Vehicle characteristics

Short-wheelbase vehicles

These

- will bounce more noticeably than some long-wheelbase vehicles when empty. (This can affect braking efficiency and all-round control)
- shouldn't be pushed into bends or corners at higher speeds simply because the vehicle appears to be easier to drive.

Long-wheelbase rigid vehicles

These require additional room to manoeuvre, especially

- when turning left or right
- negotiating roundabouts
- entering or leaving premises.

Typical examples of this type of vehicle are

- removal vans
- box vans
- brick carriers
- bulk carriers (for aggregates, etc)
- eight-wheeler tankers.

Box vans

In addition to the extra space needed when turning, the box type of body, when lightly loaded or empty, is very susceptible to crosswinds on exposed stretches of road.

Roll-over

The type of suspension fitted to a vehicle will influence its resistance to roll-over.

Modern tri-axle semi-trailers fitted with single wheels on each side have extended the tracking width available compared to twin-wheeled units, and hence have improved resistance to roll-over.

Although vehicles equipped with air suspension systems are often considered to possess improved anti-roll stability compared to traditional steel-leaf spring suspension, test results have shown that there are similarities in their level of stability.

Large petrochemical companies include specialised driver training within their training schemes to avoid such incidents happening.

The wave effect

If the drivers of certain tanker vehicles relax the footbrake when braking to a stop, there's a danger that the motion in the fluid load could force their vehicles forward. This is due to the wave effect created in the tank contents, especially where baffle plates are omitted from the tank design. Such tanks are sometimes found on vehicles carrying foodstuffs. Having baffle plates would help to reduce the wave effect but would make it difficult to clean the tanks.

Using walkways

Drivers of tanker vehicles must exercise special care when climbing onto walkways to gain access to tank hatches. Not only is this to avoid injury as a result of slipping off, but also to avoid the danger of overhead cables, pipeways, etc.

Venting

All tanks must be vented according to instructions. This will avoid serious damage to the tanker body as the external air pressure becomes greater than the pressure within the tank.

Dangerous Goods

Drivers of vehicles carrying dangerous goods may need to hold a vocational training certificate. Vehicles carrying certain dangerous goods, and other materials which may pose a hazard, are subject to detailed emergency procedures which must be followed.

The following groups of drivers need to be in possession of (and carry with them at all times) an ADR vocational training certificate, (see Glossary) issued under appropriate UK regulations. This shows that they're licensed by DVLA to carry dangerous goods by road

- drivers of road tankers with a capacity of more than 1000 litres
- drivers of vehicles carrying tank containers with a total capacity exceeding 3000 litres
- drivers of all vehicles carrying explosives (subject to limited exemptions)
- drivers of all vehicles which are subject to the Carriage of Dangerous Goods and use of Transportable Pressure Equipment Regulations 2007.

DVLA will only issue the certificate upon receipt of proof of course attendance at an approved training establishment and passing of examinations set by the Scottish Qualifications Authority. The certificate is valid for five years. Enquiries about courses and certificates should be directed to the Scottish Qualifications Authority (see page 312 for contact details).

As well as having a vocational training certificate, drivers of vehicles carrying dangerous goods must also have the correct driving licence entitlement for the vehicle they are driving.

Compressed gases

Drivers of vehicles carrying compressed gases, especially at low temperatures (eg liquid nitrogen, oxygen, etc), must comply with regulations relating to the transport of such materials.

Plates and markings

Vehicles carrying dangerous or hazardous goods need to have markings on them which will clearly identify the items. This could, for example, help the emergency services deal with any incident quickly and safely. The symbols on the back or sides of a vehicle should relate to the type of material that the vehicle is, or will normally be, carrying.

As the driver, you **MUST** make sure the correct symbol or mark is clearly visible on your vehicle. If any vehicle displaying a warning symbol is involved in an incident, serious consequences could result. You should be aware of what each symbol means (see page 326 for plate examples).

More information on limits and regulations relating to the carriage of dangerous goods can be found in Section Three.

Classifications

Dangerous or hazardous goods are divided into nine classes, as follows:

- Class 1   - Explosives
- Class 2   - Compressed gases
- Class 3   - Flammable liquids
- Class 4.1 - Flammable solids
- Class 4.2 - Spontaneously combustible
- Class 4.3 - Dangerous when wet
- Class 5.1 - Oxidising agents
- Class 5.2 - Organic peroxides
- Class 6.1 - Toxic
- Class 6.2 - Infectious substances
- Class 7   - Radioactive
- Class 8   - Corrosives
- Class 9   - Miscellaneous.

There are also a number of other products, classified as obnoxious, which are not covered in the list above. These include animal waste, hospital waste, refuse, pressurised gases or liquids and asbestos.

When driving a vehicle carrying hazardous or dangerous goods, make sure you have with you all the necessary protective clothing, safety equipment and any documentation relevant to the class of goods being carried.

Always follow all safety instructions, procedures and training provided by your operator. If you are in any doubt, check with your operator to be sure you have had the most appropriate training and that your certificate is up-to-date. (Also see page 177 for information on carrying dangerous goods through tunnels.)

Fire or explosion

In the case of vehicles carrying dangerous goods, all safety precautions must be strictly followed, especially where there's a risk of fire or explosion.

The electrical systems of vehicles carrying petrochemicals and other highly inflammable materials are modified to meet stringent safety requirements. No unauthorised additions or alterations must be made to such vehicles. Any defects must be reported immediately.

The appropriate fire-fighting equipment must be available and drivers trained in its use.

Articulated car transporters

These vehicles have unique characteristics and require a high standard of driving.

The overhang created by the top deck swings through a greater arc than the cab of the tractor unit, particularly when negotiating turns. This means that there's a risk of collision with

- traffic signals
- lamp-posts on central refuges
- traffic signs
- walls and buildings.

Items such as mirror projections can also come into contact with

- pedestrians
- street furniture
- other vehicles.

You should plan ahead and take an appropriate avoiding line on approach to turns when driving these vehicles. Before driving any large vehicle, you should identify specific overhangs and projections and make sure you use good all-round observation at all times. You should also be checking for any rear-end sweep.

The stability of these vehicles also needs to be considered. It's a case of last on, first off, so the lower deck may be clear of vehicles while there may be several still on top. The centre of gravity is substantially shifted in such cases.

You should be aware of the height of your vehicle at all times, especially if you're carrying vans.

Demountable bodies

This type of vehicle is similar to a container, except that the body is fitted with legs which can be lowered to enable the carrier vehicle to drive under or out.

Care needs to be taken to ensure that the

- legs are secured in the down position before the vehicle is driven out
- legs are secured in the up position before the vehicle moves off
- height is correct and the body is stable before driving the carrier vehicle underneath
- surface is firm and level before demounting the body.

The legs are usually secured with a locking pin and safety clip or similar device. If the legs or securing devices are damaged in any way, leave the box on the vehicle chassis and report the defect.

Another type (often an open, bulk high-sided body) is fitted with skids and is winched up onto the carrying vehicle. Apart from the dangers of overloading, care must be taken when operating such winches.

The construction of these vehicles often means that the centre of gravity can be higher than normal when conveying a loaded skip. Take this into account, especially when cornering.

Double-decked bodies

These vehicles are constructed to give increased carrying capacity to box van or curtain-side bodies. They're frequently used in the garment distribution sector.

Care must be taken to ensure that when the vehicle is in transit the lower deck isn't left empty while a load remains on the top tier. Such a shift in the centre of gravity will result in the high-sided vehicle being even more vulnerable in high winds and, therefore, more likely to overturn.

Refrigerated vehicles

When driving refrigerated or reefer vehicles carrying suspended meat carcasses, care must be taken to avoid the pendulum effect when cornering. Always reduce speed in good time.

The internal temperature of the van or trailer should be checked periodically to ensure it is correct. Ensure there is enough fuel in the fridge fuel tank for the journey, when it is independent of the main tank.

If the fridge unit fails, make sure you have details of who to contact. Depending on how many drops/deliveries you have left you may need to decide if it is better to make your drops and get the fridge fixed later.

When driving refrigerated vehicies, or when loading/unloading, care should be taken to ensure the doors are closed. Leaving them open will increase the temperature in the vehicle. Also take care when working inside the body as the floor may be wet, icy or slippery.

Vehicle limits

The transport industry is subject to an extremely large number of regulations and requirements relating to

- drivers
- operators
- companies
- vehicles
- goods.

It's essential that you keep up-to-date with all the changes in road transport legislation that affect you.

The first thing you'll need to know about is your vehicle. The various aspects to consider are its

- weight (restrictions)
- height (clearances, restrictions, etc)
- width (restrictions)
- length (clearances, restrictions)
- ground clearance (low-loader or dual-purpose trailers only).

You'll also need to know the speed limits that apply to your vehicle and the speed at which it will normally travel.

Before moving any large vehicle, you should familiarise yourself with its limits, restrictions and clearances. Also be aware of any overhangs or mirror projections which may come into contact with street furniture, pedestrians or other vehicles. Use good all-round observation at all times.

The plate showing the maximum gross weight could be located in one of several places, i.e in the vehicle cabin, under the body panel or on the trailer chassis.

Weight

It's essential that you're aware of, and understand, the limits relating to any vehicle that you drive. (Definitions of terms relating to weight limits can be found in the glossary of terms in Section Seven of this book).

Weight limits in many cases refer to the gross vehicle weight (GVW) or the maximum authorised mass (MAM). You can drive heavier vehicles if engaged in inter-modal operations between road and rail terminals. These are subject to a number of conditions

- the number of axles
- tyre specifications
- axle spacings
- road-friendly suspension.

Also, special documentation is required to cover such movements between rail-head and road depot.

Road-friendly suspension generally means that an axle is fitted with air suspension, or a suspension regarded as being equivalent to air suspension (EC directive 96/53/EC(a)). At least 75 per cent of the spring effect is caused by an air spring (that is, operated by compressed air or compressible fluid). If this sounds complicated it's intended to illustrate that the law relating to weight limits is complex.

Accurate information is required to ensure that the vehicle complies with the law and also that the driver isn't committing any offence.

The Vehicle and Operator Services Agency (VOSA – formerly the Vehicle Inspectorate and Transport Area Network) and also the police and some local authorities make spot weight checks on vehicles.

Roadside checks frequently reveal contraventions of many weight limit regulations. Once identified, the police or VOSA may escort a vehicle and its driver to the nearest official weighbridge. Both driver and operator are liable to prosecution if a vehicle on a public road is found to be overloaded (also see page 158 for more information on safety of loads on vehicles). Any co-driver travelling in the passenger seat would not be liable to prosecution.

It's essential that all limits are complied with in order to avoid overloading, and possible prosecution. Overloading your vehicle past its weight limits also means that the engine needs to work harder and, as a result, will use more fuel.

Weight restrictions normally apply to the plated weight of a vehicle. When tractor units of articulated LGVs are being driven without a trailer they're still subject to a number of regulations. These relate to

- lighting regulations
- roads subject to weight limits
- lanes from which LGVs are banned on multi-lane motorways.

Regulations also include axle weight limits applying to the tractor unit, which must not be exceeded when the vehicle is loaded.

It's essential you ensure that the load is distributed correctly and safely, either on or in your vehicle. This means that loads are built up against the headboard or front wall of the body in order to reduce movement in transit. When loading your vehicle, ensure that the front axle or axles aren't overloaded (see page 97-99). Heavy items should be placed at the bottom with lighter items on top. In addition, heavy items should also be distributed evenly along the length of the vehicle.

When your vehicle is fully loaded, you should make certain checks before commencing your journey to be sure there is no danger of overloading. There are certain visual indicators which may be present and you can look for these by making

- a visual check of the vehicle suspension
- a body check for any excessive leaning
- checks for tyres touching/rubbing together or spray suppression equipment touching the ground.

If you notice any of these, or are in any doubt whatsoever, you should take your vehicle to the nearest weighbridge for confirmation before commencing your deliveries. Drivers are allowed to do this. They are then allowed to drive to a place where they can take off some of the load if the vehicle is found to be overloaded.

Articulated units and part loads

To increase stability and reduce the risk of the trailer wheels lifting when turning, it's preferable to have part-loads (such as an empty single International Standards Organisation (ISO) container) located over the rear axle(s).

Whatever goods vehicle you drive you should study the Department for Transport publication *Code of Practice: Safety of Loads on Vehicles*.

Recovery vehicles

Always make sure that axle loading limits aren't exceeded when a recovery vehicle removes another LGV by means of a suspended tow. This is sometimes overlooked.

Height

If you're the driver of any vehicle where the overall travelling height of the vehicle, its equipment and load (including any trailer) is more than 3 metres (9 feet 10 inches) you **MUST** ensure that

- the overall travelling height is conspicuously marked in figures not less than 40 mm high in such a manner that it can be read in the cab from the driver's seat. It should be marked in feet and inches, or in feet and inches and in metres

- any height indicated isn't less than the overall travelling height of the vehicle.

A height notice isn't required on a particular journey if you're carrying sufficient

information in documents about the route or choice of routes. This should include the height of bridges and other overhead structures to allow you to complete your journey without any risk of a collision with an overhead structure. You must then travel on the route described in these documents.

When en route, remember your vehicle height can change for a variety of reasons. For example, adjustment of the fifth wheel, trailer loaded, unloaded or reloaded, diminishing loads etc. Avoid short cuts to save time as this could lead you to a low bridge. Stop and seek advice on an alternative route if you

- are diverted from your planned route
- realise that your route is obstructed by a bridge lower than the height of your vehicle.

Road traffic signs

If your vehicle is higher than the dimension shown on a circular road sign at a bridge, you are legally required to stop and not pass the sign.

If your vehicle is higher than the dimension shown on a triangular road sign at a bridge, you should not pass the sign unless you know that you will be seeking access to premises before you reach the height restriction.

Warning devices

If a vehicle and any trailer drawn by it has a maximum height of more than 3 metres (9 feet 10 inches), a visual warning device should warn any driver if the highest point of the equipment exceeds a predetermined height when the vehicle is being driven.

The predetermined height must not exceed the overall travelling height by more than 1 metre (3 feet 3 inches) unless the equipment has a mechanical locking device that can lock it in a stowed position. In addition, the equipment needs to be fixed in that position by the locking device when the vehicle is being driven.

The requirement for height notices, route information or warning devices won't apply if on a particular journey you're highly unlikely to encounter any bridge or overhead structure which isn't at least 1 metre (3 feet 3 inches) higher than the maximum or overall travelling height of the vehicle.

Overhead clearances

Drivers of any vehicle exceeding 3 metres (9 feet 10 inches) in height should exercise care when entering roofed premises such as

- loading bays
- depots
- dock areas
- freight terminals
- service station forecourts
- any premises that have overhanging canopies

when passing underneath

- bridges

- overhead cables
- overhead pipelines
- overhead walkways
- road tunnels

or when negotiating

- level crossings.

Electric Cables

Overhead electricity lines crossing public roads will normally be clear for a vehicle of 5 metres (16 feet 6 inches) in height (6.1 metres (20 feet) on DfT designated high vehicle routes). As high voltage electricity can "jump" across a gap, the wire will be positioned higher than this to allow for a safe electrical clearance. This clearance **MUST NOT** be compromised.

When transporting a high load, contact the local electricity company for advice regarding the amount of advance notice which needs to be given to the electricity authorities concerned (at least 19 days). You should inform them of the load, routes, etc. See your local telephone directory for details.

The power supply conductors for railways and tramways on public roads will normally allow clearance for a vehicle of 5 metres (16 feet 6 inches) in height unless the signage on the approach indicates otherwise. At level crossings where the safe height is less than 5 metres (16 feet 6 inches), a height barrier will be provided in the form of a wire supporting bells. If your vehicle will not pass under this barrier, it's not safe to pass under the electrical line. You **MUST** obey the safe height warning road signs and you **MUST NOT** continue forward if your vehicle touches any height barrier or bells.

Telephone wires

If your load exceeds 5.25 metres (17 feet 6 inches) in height, the telephone companies must be notified.

Street furniture

When planning the movement of such vehicles and loads the local Highways Authority will need to be contacted where overhead gantry traffic signs or suspended traffic lights are likely to be affected by loads over 5 metres (16 feet 6 inches).

Low bridges

Every year around 800 incidents occur involving vehicles or their loads hitting railway or motorway bridges. Some of these bridge strikes are due to drivers relying totally on their satnav system and not reading the traffic signs and the road ahead. You should still plan your route before your journey. An impact with any

bridge can have serious consequences. An LGV, or any part of its load, colliding with a railway bridge could result in the bridge being weakened. This could also inconvenience rail traffic or create the potential for a major disaster.

These factors are in addition to the costs involved in making the bridge safe, re-aligning railway tracks, and the general disruption to road and rail traffic.

You should always plan your route in advance and read any signs. Never rely on a satellite navigation system alone, as even those designed for large vehicles may have out-of-date or incomplete information at any given time.

The headroom under bridges in the UK is at least 5 metres (16 feet 6 inches) unless marked otherwise. Where the overhead clearance is arched, this normally means only between the limits marked. If your vehicle collides with a bridge you must report the incident to the police. If a railway bridge is involved, report it to the **railway authority** as well by calling **0845 711 4141.**

Do this immediately to avoid a possible serious collision or loss of life.

Give information about

- the location
- the damage
- any bridge reference number (found on a plate bolted to the bridge or wall).

THIS IS BRIDGE SPC2/61

Templars Way

Sharnbrook

In the event of any road vehicles striking this bridge please phone

THE RAILWAY AUTHORITY on

0845 711 4141

as quickly as possible. The safety of trains may be affected

Know your height

You **must** know the height of your vehicle and its load. Don't guess and, if in doubt, measure it. Also, don't ignore

- traffic signs
- road markings
- warning lights, bells or other audible alarms.

Effects of a bridge strike

Striking bridges is potentially dangerous and expensive. You could

- be killed or seriously injured
- cause death or serious injury to another road user

Height guide	
Metres	Feet/Inches
5.0	16 6
4.8	16
4.5	15
4.2	14
3.9	13
3.6	12
3.3	11
3.0	9 10
2.7	9

- lose your job
- suffer serious economic loss
- cause serious disruption to the community.

Your company may lose their operator's licence and they will also be liable for the costs of bridge damage and examination.

Don't take chances. If you aren't sure of the safe height, stop and call the authorities. Always

- plan your route
- slow down when approaching bridges
- know the overall vehicle/load height
- keep to the centre of arched bridges
- wait for a safe gap to proceed if there's oncoming traffic.

Don't rely on satellite navigation systems alone, even those specifically designed for large vehicles.

Width

As the driver of an LGV you must be aware of the road space that the vehicle occupies. This is particularly important where width is restricted because of parked or oncoming vehicles. Look out for signs showing restrictions.

Traffic calming measures are becoming much more common. Don't get into a situation where you're forced to reverse or turn.

Wide loads

Loads projecting over 305 mm (12 inches) beyond the width of the vehicle or those over 2.9 metres (9 feet 5 inches) but less than 3.5 metres (11 feet 5 inches) require side markers and notification to the police. Wide loads that are over 3.5 metres (11 feet 5 inches) but less than 4.3 metres (14 feet 1 inch) require side markers, police notification and an attendant.

Wide loads that are 4.3 metres (14 feet 1 inch) to 5 metres (16 feet 6 inches) are also subject to the following speed limits

- 30 mph on motorways
- 25 mph on dual carriageways
- 20 mph on all other roads.

Wide loads between 5 metres (16 feet 6 inches) and 6.1 metres (20 feet) require

- side markers
- police notification
- an attendant
- Department for Transport approval

and are subject to the above speed limits.

Side marker boards must comply with regulations so that they show clearly on either side of the projection to the front and to the rear. All marker boards must be independently lit at night.

Overall Width Limits

Metres	Feet/Inches		
2.75	9	4	Locomotives
2.6	8	5	Refrigerated vehicles and trailers*
2.55	8	4	Motor tractors
2.55	8	4	Motor cars
2.55	8	4	Heavy motor cars
2.55	8	4	Trailers*
2.3	7	6	Other trailers

* Subject to certain conditions

Long, low vehicles

For drivers of long, low vehicles there is a risk of grounding the vehicle at some railway level crossings. A warning sign is displayed, with instructions to contact the railway controller. The vehicle must be stopped where indicated, and a phone call made to the number displayed or by using the dedicated telephone provided.

The driver must follow the instructions of the railway controller, and call back once the vehicle is safely clear of the crossing.

Large or slow vehicles

At some railway level crossings, drivers of large or slow vehicles which might take an abnormally long time to cross, must contact the railway controller before crossing. The contact with the railway controller is the same as for long, low vehicles.

Length

Locations where length restrictions apply are comparatively few but they include

- road tunnels
- level crossings
- ferries
- certain areas in cities

Drivers of long rigid vehicles, either with or without drawbar trailers, or articulated LGVs must be aware of the length of their vehicle especially when

- turning left or right
- negotiating roundabouts or mini-roundabouts
- emerging from premises or exits
- overtaking
- parking, especially in lay-bys
- driving on narrow roads where there are passing places
- negotiating level crossings.

They must be particularly aware of the risk of grounding, for example on a hump bridge, which will be indicated by appropriate traffic warning signs.

Maximum Length Limits

Metres	Feet/Inches	
12	39 4	Rigid vehicles
16.5	54	Articulated vehicles*
18.75	61 6	Vehicle and trailer combinations**
18	59	Articulated vehicles with low-loader semi-trailer manufactured after 1 April 1991 (not including step-frame low-loaders)
2.55	8 4	Heavy motor cars
2.55	8 4	Trailers*
2.3	7 6	Other trailers

Car transporter semi-trailers

Metres	Feet/Inches	
12.5	41	Kingpin to rear
4.19	13 8	Kingpin to any point at the front

Other semi-trailers

Metres	Feet/Inches	
12	39 4	Kingpin to the rear
2.04	6 7	Kingpin to any point at the front
14.04	46	Composite trailer
12	36 4	Drawbar trailer with four or more wheels, and drawing vehicle is more than 3,500kg MGW
7	23	Other drawbar trailers

* Maximum length limit for vehicles designed to carry exceptionally long indivisible loads is 27.4 metres (89 feet 9 in)

** See *Construction and Use Regulations* (The Stationery Office) for details covering road trains.

Vehicle maintenance

Preventative maintenance

Ensuring that the daily walk-round checks are carried out will enable you to find any defects that could become a problem and cause the vehicle to break down or be driven whilst illegal. The time taken to complete a thorough check will be less than that required to organise a repair or replacement while out on the road. Follow manufacturer's guidelines for service intervals; in addition to this, being aware of components wearing out or requiring replacement will help prevent costly breakdowns for your company.

Neglecting the maintenance of vital controls and fluids such as brakes, steering and lubricants is dangerous; they need to be checked regularly. The consequences are too great to risk driving a vehicle with defective parts. Having your vehicle serviced according to its maintenance schedule helps the engine work more efficiently, thereby saving fuel and reducing the effect on the environment by cutting emissions.

Technical support

Traffic Commissioners and the **Vehicle and Operator Services Agency (VOSA)** will provide advice and assistance to operators on safety inspection intervals. VOSA offers a brake performance check service, headlight alignment and an emission check at all of its full-time heavy goods vehicle testing stations.

You can contact your local trading standards officer for a list of weighbridges currently in calibration.

Daily checks

You also need to check the following regularly to ensure your vehicle is well maintained and not in need of attention. Check

- there are no fuel or oil leaks including missing or broken fuel caps
- the security and condition of your battery
- tyres (tread depth, condition) and wheel fixings
- debris between double wheels
- spray suppression equipment
- steering
- excessive engine exhaust smoke
- brake hoses
- coupling security (if applicable)
- brakes.

See also the daily walk-round checks on page 153; when completed they will help you notice if any part of your vehicle needs maintenance. Always refer to the handbook for your individual vehicle before carrying out any maintenance tasks and follow any safety guidance it may contain.

When a defect, such as a faulty fog lamp, is found on a walk-round check, you should make a record of the defect and have it rectified before going onto the public highway.

Construction and functioning of the internal combustion engine

There are two main types of internal combustion engine

- spark ignition (petrol) – the fuel and air mixture is ignited by a spark
- compression ignition (diesel) – the rise in temperature and pressure during compression causes spontaneous ignition of the fuel and air mixture.

During each revolution of the crankshaft there are two strokes of the piston: the piston travels both up and down the engine cylinder. Both types of engine can be designed to operate using a two-stroke or four-stroke principle. Almost all modern goods vehicles use the diesel four-stroke principle.

The four-stroke operating cycle

Induction stroke

The open inlet valve enables the piston to draw in a charge of air when travelling down the cylinder. With spark ignition engines the fuel is usually pre-mixed with air.

Compression stroke

Both inlet and exhaust valves close and the piston travels up the cylinder. As the piston approaches the top, ignition occurs. Compression ignition engines have the fuel injected towards the end of the compression stroke.

Expansion or power stroke

Combustion created throughout the charge raises the pressure and temperature and forces the piston down. At the end of the power stroke the exhaust valve opens.

Exhaust stroke

The exhaust valve remains open, the piston then travels up the cylinder and remaining gases will be expelled. When the valve closes, residual exhaust gases will dilute the next charge.

Diesel fuel system

Compression ignition (commonly called diesel) engines are now almost universally used for large goods vehicles and passenger-carrying vehicles.

The fuel injection system, operated by the accelerator pedal, controls the amount of fuel delivered to the engine. This varies the engine speed by delivering fuel in a fine spray at high pressure in a precisely controlled amount.

Air is drawn into the combustion chamber, or more usually forced in under pressure via a turbocharger or supercharger. A turbocharger is an exhaust gas-driven turbine while a supercharger is a mechanically-driven turbine. The power and torque are increased and maintained over a wider engine speed range than the normally aspirated engine. Both result in improved engine performance.

Never use poor quality diesel fuel. This may lead to increased wear of the injection pump and early blockage of fuel injector nozzles. In winter the composition of diesel fuel is altered by the use of additives to lower the temperature at which waxing or partial solidifying of the fuel occurs. If waxing happens the engine may not even start or, if it does, it may run unevenly or stop.

Winter grade fuels should be perfectly satisfactory in all but very severe conditions. Electrically powered fuel line heating systems are often fitted.

Open the water drain valve, usually fitted to the base of the fuel filter, at least at the intervals recommended by the vehicle manufacturer.

Bleeding of fuel systems

It may become necessary to bleed the fuel system to remove any trapped air if

- the engine is new or has been renovated
- the fuel system has been cleaned or the filter changed
- the engine has not been run for a long time
- the vehicle has been driven until the fuel tank is empty.

Engine lubrication system

The engine uses a pressure-fed, full-flow, wet sump system. The oil filter, which is normally disposable, contains a bypass valve, which operates if the filter becomes blocked. A pressure relief valve controls the oil pressure; this is housed in the oil pump housing. The oil pump is driven directly from the engine.

Oil is drawn from the sump to the oil pump via a wire mesh pre-filter. The oil circulates from the pump through the main filter, which collects sediment from the oil.

The oil then passes to the engine bearings and other moving parts and, having completed its circle, the oil drains back into the sump.

Always use the recommended type and viscosity of lubricant as suggested by the manufacturer. The oil should also be changed at the recommended intervals. Friction and wear will reduce the life expectancy and the performance of an engine. Friction increases when there is direct metal-to-metal contact between sliding parts. Lubrication helps prevent such contact, by reducing wear from friction and heat on working parts within the engine. A film of lubricant covers the various surfaces to keep them apart and maintain fluid friction rather than dry friction.

Lubrication prevents corrosion of the internal components in the engine. It removes the heat generated in the bearings or caused by combustion and absorbed by metal components. It is also able to seal piston rings and grooves against combustion leakage.

Checking oil levels

You need to check the oil frequently: make sure the vehicle is parked on a level area not on a slope. Check the oil while the engine is cold for a more accurate result. If your vehicle is fitted with automatic transmission there may be an additional dipstick for transmission oil level checks.

You should not run the engine when the oil level is below the minimum mark on the dipstick. Don't add so much oil that the level goes above the maximum level, this creates excess pressures that could damage the engine seals and gaskets and cause oil leaks. Moving internal parts can hit the oil surface in an over-full engine causing possible damage and loss of power.

If the oil pressure warning light on your instrument panel comes on when you're driving, stop and check the oil level as soon as it is safe to do so. If the level is satisfactory, there may be a more serious problem such as failure of the oil pump, which would lead to severe engine damage.

Lubrication oil – engine

The oil in your engine has to perform several tasks at high pressures and temperatures up to 300°C. Lubrication resists wear on moving surfaces and combats the corrosive acids formed as the hydrocarbons in the fuels are burnt in the engine. Engine oil also helps to keep the engine cool. Use the lubricant recommended in the vehicle handbook.

Lubrication oil – gearbox

Most vehicles have a separate lubricating oil supply for the gearbox; it is especially formulated for gearbox use. Follow the instructions in the vehicle handbook.

Engine coolant

It is generally recognised that using an approved coolant solution containing an anti-freeze additive throughout the year will give you the best protection. Coolants ensure the cooling system will be protected from freezing in cold weather. In addition to the anti-freeze agent, coolant contains a corrosion inhibitor which reduces oxidation and corrosion in the engine and prolongs the life of the cooling system. The anti-freeze additive is an inhibitor called ethylene glycol that has a boiling point of 195°C compared to water at 100°C. The coolant solution is usually diluted with the same volume of water to give maximum protection.

Check the coolant level frequently; if you need to top up regularly it might indicate a leak or other fault in the cooling system that will require checking. Never remove the radiator cap to refill when the engine is hot, always allow the engine to cool before adding further diluted coolant. Don't overfill the system, as the excess will be expelled as soon as the engine warms up.

Transmission system

All transmission systems are vehicle-specific and you should check the vehicle handbook. However, to help you drive in the most efficient way, most vehicles are colour-coded on the rev counter (sometimes called tachometer). This gives an easy guide to the optimum use, with green showing the section giving adequate torque/power

and optimum fuel efficiency. As a general rule you should normally keep the rev counter within the green band when driving.

Other sections may also be colour-coded, but you should refer to your vehicle handbook as variations occur, depending on the manufacturer. As a general guide

- Green band - normal use, adequate power and optimum fuel efficiency
- Amber band - occasional use when accelerating firmly
- Blue band - optimum use of engine braking
- Red band - keep out, driving within this section could damage the engine.

If the fuel is regulated by an engine management system, as it is on most modern vehicles, you do not need to press the accelerator to give additional revs when turning the ignition to start the engine. This causes excessive fuel injection and will waste fuel.

A manual transmission system is made up of the clutch, gearbox and driveshafts. The torque is transmitted from the engine to the road wheels via the clutch and gearbox. The normal form of clutch is referred to as a friction clutch.

The clutch

This temporarily disconnects/connects the drive between the engine and gearbox. It enables the drive to be taken up gradually.

The three main components of a clutch are the driven plate, sometimes referred to as the clutch plate or friction plate, plus the pressure plate and release bearing. The driven plate is clamped between the pressure plate and the engine flywheel by spring pressure.

The engine creates the turning motion or torque, which is transmitted from the crankshaft to the flywheel. The driveshaft, attached to the friction plate, transmits the torque to the gearbox. Depressing the clutch pedal operates the release bearing to relieve the spring clamping pressure and free the driven plate.

The life of a clutch can be prolonged by careful use and avoidance of slipping or riding the clutch. Replacement should be carried out before the driven plate becomes too worn, as further use could cause the flywheel to become scored.

The gearbox

The purpose of the gearbox is to

- control the torque (driving force) being transmitted by the engine
- provide a means of reversing the vehicle
- provide a position for neutral.

The gears contained in the gearbox allow the driver to vary the speed of the road wheels corresponding to any particular engine speed. This also results in varying the tractive effort, which is applied through the tyre to the road, to overcome the resistance to the movement of the vehicle during moving off from rest, accelerating and hill climbing.

It is common for multiple gear ratios to be used in the gearboxes of LGVs and there is widespread use of semi-automatic and automatic gearbox systems to assist the driver and improve vehicle performance. In many systems there is no need for a normal clutch pedal and vehicle movement from rest is achieved in response to movement of the accelerator pedal. Gear changing may be controlled by the driver (semi-automatic), controlled hydraulically or, increasingly, by the use of electronic systems, to change gear according to the requirements of the vehicle use situation. Using as high a gear as possible will improve fuel economy.

The constant-mesh box is gradually being replaced with synchromesh transmission.

All manufacturers now use range changers and splitter boxes to change between the high- and low-range ratios. These use either the single-H pattern layout (also referred to as four-over-four) or the double-H (also referred to as the four-beside-four). The gearshift layout may vary according to the make of vehicle, and you are advised to use the vehicle manual for guidance on the gear layout.

When the vehicle is cold you may have difficulty selecting a gear on a synchronised box but once the box has had a chance to warm up, gear changing will be easier.

Older vehicles were fitted with gearboxes which required a driver to double-declutch when changing gear (see page 320). On modern vehicles fitted with synchromesh transmission there is no need to double-declutch when changing gear, as this can waste fuel and cause unnecessary extra wear.

Types of gearboxes

A two-speed axle is an alternative reduction gear fitted to the rear drive axle which doubles the number of available gears. The operating mechanism is fitted to the gear lever, and is electrically operated.

Splitter box

The splitter box, like the two-speed axle, is electrically operated but the gears are split in the gearbox rather than at the

rear drive axle. Its operation is the same as the two-speed axle: a switch is fitted to the gear lever and it is possible to operate the switch and select a gear which is half a ratio higher or lower.

Range changer

The range changer is generally air operated, the gears are split in the gear box. Effectively you can change through the gears twice, once in low range then again in the high range.

Unlike the two speed axle and the splitter box, the gears may not be independently split. When reversing with this type of gear box, it must be in the low range.

Electronic power shift

There are several similar systems that use a semi-automatic gearbox. They are simple to use, and the gear shift lever is very small with a splitter switch and a function button. The shift control is pushed forward to move forward, pulled backward for downshift and pushed left for neutral. An alarm will sound if an attempt is made to change down when the engine speed is too high.

Electrical system

Much progress has been made regarding the systems within vehicles, so that most mechanical units are now controlled by electricity. The wiring requirements are so extensive in some vehicles that a system called 'multiplexing' is used. This system is computer controlled and uses a cable carrying electronic messages to switch equipment on or off. A power bus cable carries the main electric current to operate the equipment.

LGV and PCV vehicles commonly use 24 Volt lead/acid batteries to provide the power to start the vehicle. Once the engine is running, the alternator takes over and provides the electrical power needed whilst also recharging the battery. The alternator generates electrical current and is usually directly driven by the engine via a belt.

A controlled current is directed to the battery which enables it to remain charged and provide current for the other electrical systems of the vehicle, such as the lighting system.

Fuses of varying ratings, dependent on the power consumption, protect the different circuits within the vehicle. They prevent excess current from overloading the system, which may cause electrical fires. It is advisable to carry spare fuses, but make sure that you use the correct rating and find out why the fuse blew before replacing it.

Care should be taken when checking batteries, as explosive gases build up and the dilute sulphuric acid used as an electrolyte will burn skin. Always follow manufacturers' recommendations when dealing with batteries.

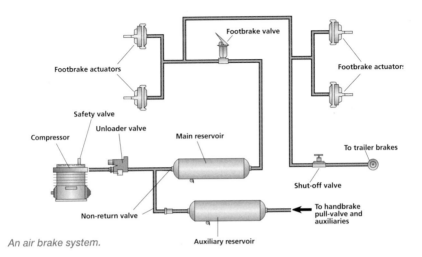

An air brake system.

Braking system

Applying the brakes

Planning and anticipation of road hazards should remove the need for harsh braking. Harsh or heavy braking can result in a vehicle's wheels locking, leading to a loss of vehicle control, particularly on slippery road surfaces (for example, wet, icy or snow-covered). It also increases a vehicle's fuel consumpton and the likelihood of the load shifting.

In an emergency braking situation you may need to brake heavily. If your vehicle is equipped with an anti-lock braking system (ABS)* and you're unlikely to be able to stop the vehicle before reaching an obstruction apply maximum force to the brake pedal, maintaining this force. You shouldn't pump the brake pedal as this will reduce the effectiveness of the ABS system.

If your vehicle doesn't have ABS, wheel lock can be controlled during heavy deceleration by cadence braking, that is, rapid pumping of the brake pedal.

*Note

ABS is the registered trade mark of Bosch (Germany) for Anti Blockiersystem.

Types of brakes

There are three types of braking systems fitted to LGVs

- the service brake
- the secondary brake
- the parking brake.

The service brake is the principal braking system used and is operated by a foot control. It's used to control the speed of the vehicle and to bring it safely to a halt. It may also incorporate an anti-lock braking system (ABS).

The secondary brake may be combined with the footbrake or the parking brake control. This brake is provided for use in the event of the service brake failing.

The secondary brake normally operates on fewer wheels than the service brake and therefore has a reduced performance level.

The parking brake is usually a hand control and may also be the secondary brake. It should normally only be used when the vehicle is stationary. The parking brake must always be set when the driver leaves the driving position. It's an offence to leave any vehicle unattended without applying this brake.

LGVs are also frequently equipped with endurance braking systems (commonly called retarders).

Anti-lock braking systems (ABS)

ABS is only a driver aid. It doesn't remove the need for good driving practices, such as anticipating events and assessing road and weather conditions. You still need to plan well ahead and brake smoothly and progressively.

Anti-lock braking systems employ wheel speed sensors to anticipate when a wheel is about to lock. Just before the wheels lock, the system releases the brake and then rapidly re-applies it. This may happen many times a second to help maintain braking performance and prevent the wheels from locking. This means that you can continue to steer the vehicle during braking.

Anti-lock braking systems are in common use on LGVs, and are required by law on some. You'll need to know which vehicle combinations are required to have an ABS fitted by law. Care needs to be taken to ensure that the braking system on the tractive unit or rigid towing vehicle is compatible with the braking system on the semi-trailer or trailer.

Checking ABS

It's important to ensure that the ABS is functioning before setting off on a journey. Driving with a defective ABS may constitute an offence.

Modern anti-lock braking systems require electrical power for their operation. Multi-pin connectors are required to carry the electrical supply to operate the trailer brakes. The satisfactory operation of the ABS can be checked from the warning signal on the dashboard. A separate signal for the trailer is provided on the dashboard, although in some cases a signal on the trailer headboard will operate instead. The way the warning lamp operates varies between manufacturers, but with all types of signal it should be displayed when the ignition is switched on and should go out when the vehicle has reached a speed of about 10 km/h (6 mph).

Endurance braking systems

Commonly referred to as retarders, these systems provide a way of controlling a vehicle's speed without using the wheel-mounted brakes. This can be particularly useful when descending long or steep hills as a vehicle's speed can be stabilised without using the service brakes. Also, by using this system instead of the foot brake, brake lining life is extended. While retarders generally apply the brakes in a more progressive way, you still need to be aware that the wheels could lock under certain conditions.

Retarders operate by applying resistance, via the transmission, to the rotation of the vehicle's drive wheels. This may be achieved by

- increased engine braking

- exhaust braking

- transmission-mounted electromagnetic or hydraulic devices.

Braking generates heat in the brakes and, at high temperatures, braking performance can be affected. The retarder leaves the service brake cool for optimum performance when required.

Using an exhaust brake is also beneficial to fuel economy. When the exhaust brake is applied, fuel delivery to the combustion chamber is halted. The vehicle is driven

forward by its own momentum, so there is no need for fuel to be burnt. In addition, by making the engine work as a compressor, the combustion chamber is hotter than it would be if the driver were simply to take his foot off the accelerator and depress the footbrake. As a result, when fuel is injected back into the combustion chamber, it will atomise more efficiently than in a cooler chamber.

The system may be operated with the same foot pedal as the service brakes (an integrated system) or by using a separate hand or foot control (an independent system). Retarders normally have several stages of effectiveness depending on the braking requirement. With independent systems the driver has to select the level of performance required.

When driving on slippery surfaces care must be exercised when operating retarders if drive wheel locking is to be avoided. Some retarders are under the management of the ABS system to help avoid this problem.

Connecting a system

It's vitally important that you understand the rules which apply to connecting and disconnecting the brake lines on either an articulated vehicle or a rigid vehicle and trailer combination. You'll be asked to demonstrate this during your practical driving test.

There are two brake configurations that you may encounter – either the three-line or the two-line system. A three-line system comprises

- Emergency **red** line
- Auxiliary **blue** line
- Service **yellow** line

A two-line system has only an emergency and a service line.

Two-line vehicles and two-line trailers are obviously compatible, as are three-line vehicles and three-line trailers. A two-line motor vehicle can be connected to a three-line trailer – the trailer auxiliary line being left unconnected.

When connecting a three-line motor vehicle to a two-line trailer it's important that you follow the vehicle manufacturer's advice as to what to do with the third (blue) line. Failure to follow the manufacturer's instructions could render the combination dangerous.

When coupling a modern motor vehicle, fitted with automatic sealing valves in the 'suzie' lines (see glossary on page 324) ensure that the trailer is equipped to activate them. Some older vehicles may be equipped with taps, or hand-operated valves. If these are fitted you must ensure that these are opened after coupling the 'suzies' and closed before uncoupling them.

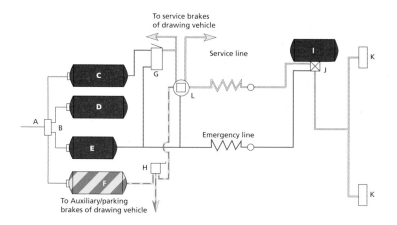

A – Supply from compressor	E – Service reservoir (trailer)	I – Trailer reservoir
B – Multi-protection valve	F – Parking/Auxiliary reservoir	J – Relay emergency valve
C – Service reservoir (front)	G – Dual foot valve	K – Single diaphragm actuators
D – Service reservoir (rear)	H – Hand control valve	L – Trailer control valve (or triple relay valve)

Example of an acceptable two-line connection: two-line vehicle drawing a two-line trailer

There have been a number of fatal incidents due to trailer brakes releasing as the air lines were connected. It is a mistake to believe that disconnecting the air lines engages the trailer parking brakes; on some systems it is only the emergency brake that is applied and this will release as soon as the air line is re-connected or over time as air pressure is lost from the system. Before connecting or disconnecting any brake line, ensure that the trailer parking brake has been correctly applied. This precaution **MUST NOT** be overlooked.

Safety

Air brake systems are fitted with warning devices that will be activated when air pressure drops below a predetermined level. In some circumstances there may be sufficient pressure to release the parking brake even though the warning is showing.

In these cases the service brake may be ineffective. You should never release the parking brake when the brake pressure warning device is operating.

Towing vehicles are equipped with braking lines for attachment to a trailer. On modern vehicles these lines are fitted with automatic sealing valves rather than manual taps. When a trailer is coupled to a towing vehicle it's important to check that the brakes of the trailer function correctly. If they don't, remedial action must be taken **before** the vehicle is driven. Failure to do so could result in the loss of braking effectiveness on the whole combination.

Inspection and maintenance

You aren't expected to be a mechanic; however, there are braking system checks that **are** your responsibility.

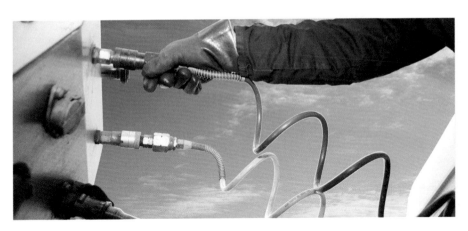

Ensure all air systems are up to operating pressure

Action in the event of brake failure

When driving vehicles fitted with either full air brakes or air-assisted hydraulic brakes, in the event of loss of air pressure, there would be a warning light and/or buzzer to alert you with sufficient reserves of air pressure remaining to allow you to pull up safely.

In the event of total loss of air pressure on a full air-brake system the brakes could be locked on. You may find yourself stuck in a position that causes an obstruction to other traffic. The brakes can only be released when air pressure is restored.

Types of braking system

Large vehicles mainly have full air-braking systems, or air-assisted brakes (hydraulic system with air assistance). Smaller vehicles have hydraulic braking systems (sometimes called a hydraulic vacuum servobrake circuit).

Hydraulic brakes

With hydraulic brakes, if the brake pedal travel increases or reduces this could indicate a system malfunction.

For vehicles fitted with hydraulic brakes and air-assisted brakes, you should check

- the brake fluid level as part of your daily walk-round check
- the brake fluid warning light if fitted.

Before you move off you should press the brake pedal to get a feel for it. If it is too hard, it suggests a loss of vacuum or that the vacuum pump is not working. If the brake pedal gives too little resistance and goes down too far, it suggests a loss of fluid or that it is badly out of adjustment.

If there are any problems, you should get the system checked by a qualified mechanic before moving off.

In addition test the brakes every day as you set out. Choose a safe place to do this. If you hear any strange noises or the vehicle pulls to one side, consult a qualified mechanic immediately.

Air reservoirs

Air braking systems draw their air from the atmosphere, which contains moisture. This moisture condenses in the air reservoirs and can be transmitted around a vehicle's braking system. In cold weather this can lead to ice forming in valves and pipes and may result in air pressure loss and/or system failure. Some air systems have automatic drain valves to remove this moisture, while others require daily manual draining. You should establish whether your vehicle's system reservoirs require manual draining and, if so, whose responsibility it is to make sure that it's done.

You should also make a physical check of the air system, ensuring air lines are serviceable, and listen for leaks while the engine is switched off. You could also empty the air tanks by pumping the footbrake, then restart the engine and recharge the system. If you still suspect a problem, seek expert help and do not start the journey.

Warning systems

Before each journey make sure that all warning systems are working. Brake pressure warning signals may be activated automatically when the ignition is turned on (as for an ABS), or may require that you use a 'check' switch provided on the driving controls.

Never start a journey with a defective warning device or when the warning is showing. If the warning operates whilst you're travelling, stop as soon as you can do so safely and seek expert help. Driving with a warning device operating may be very dangerous and is an offence.

Tyres

All tyres on your vehicle and any trailer must be in good condition. They need to be checked weekly for damage or wear and they must be at the correct pressure. Follow manufacturers' recommendations for the correct pressure required. Neglecting tyre pressures is a major cause of tyre failure: check your tyre pressures when the tyres are cold, that is, before the vehicle is used.

Ensure that all tyres are suitable for the loads being carried. Heavy goods vehicle and passenger-carrying vehicle tyres have codes indicating the maximum load and speed capability. These must be suitable for the vehicle's particular conditions of use.

The life of a tyre will depend upon the load, inflation pressure and the speed at which the vehicle is driven. Under-inflated tyres will increase wear of the outer edge of the tread area of the tyre. Over-inflated tyres will distort the tread and increase wear in the centre of the tread area of the tyre.

Radial ply tyres have textile cords, arranged radially across the tyre almost at right angles to the width of the tread. The tyre walls are quite supple and a rubber covered steel mesh belt, which runs around the tyre underneath the tread rubber, braces the tread area. The belt keeps the tread in flat contact with the road to improve traction and grip.

81

Keeping tyres correctly inflated will help prevent failure and also improve fuel consumption.

Check wheels and tyres for balance to avoid uneven wear. When a wheel and tyre rotate they are subject to centrifugal forces. If the mass of the wheel and tyre is dispersed uniformly then the wheel is balanced. Balance weights are used to rectify any imbalance.

Commercial vehicles with tubeless tyres use metal valve stems fitted to the wheel rim. Either an O-ring or a flat-flanged rubber washer makes the sealing airtight. Vehicles fitted with tube tyres have an adaptor, which is moulded to a rubber patch and vulcanised to the inner tube. The valve-stem casing is then screwed on to the tube adaptor.

Changing a tyre

Great care must be taken when changing the tyre of a large vehicle; you would normally call out a professional tyre fitter. If you are forced to change a tyre you should

- select a firm flat surface
- check that the parking brake is applied
- ensure the passengers or other personnel are clear of the area in which you are working
- check the wheel is not damaged and that another tyre can be fitted to it
- deflate the tyre before attempting to remove the wheel
- not loosen or unscrew the clamping nuts if they are connected to divided wheel rims
- take care not to damage the flanges and locking rings when taking the tyre off.

Fitting a new tyre

As a driver, it is unlikely that you will ever have to fit a new tyre. However, it is still useful for you to be aware of the procedure involved.

Having checked the condition of the wheel before replacing with a tyre of the correct size, you should

- renew the complete valve whenever a tubeless tyre is being replaced

- fit the wheel to the tyre whilst the wheel is lying flat on the ground. This will enable the tyre to fit the rim and obtain a good airtight seal

- inflate commercial tyres in a cage or similar safety cell

- inflate to 1 bar level with the valve core removed

- insert a valve core

- inflate to manufacturer's recommendation

- fully tighten wheel nuts, to the torque recommended by the vehicle manufacturer, using a calibrated torque wrench. Tighten the wheel fixings gradually and alternately diagonally across the wheel. Recheck the torque after about 30 minutes if the vehicle remains stationary or after 40 to 80 km (25 to 50 miles), if used.

Power tools are not recommended for tightening wheel fixings. It is recommended that pressure gauges are checked frequently for accuracy.

When leaving building sites or other areas with loose debris, check between the tyres for bricks or other large objects that could damage your tyres or following traffic should they fall out.

Fitting wheels

As a driver you're unlikely to have to change a wheel. Many companies will only allow specialist fitters and breakdown organisations to change wheels. However, the following information may be useful.

- Never attempt to change a wheel by yourself on a motorway, dual carriageway or in a busy location.
- Be aware of the danger of other traffic.
- Ensure the vehicle is parked on level, firm ground.
- The jack or lifting device should be suitable for the height and weight of the vehicle.
- When re-fitting the wheel, fully tighten the wheel nuts to the torque recommended by the manufacturer, using a calibrated torque wrench.
- Where possible get someone to assist you.

Coupling system

The coupling system, often referred to as the fifth wheel, is a device used to connect the tractor unit to a trailer. It permits articulation between the units. Guidance on the correct way to uncouple or recouple a unit can be found in Section Five, 'Preparing for the Driving Test'. Follow this advice for a safe and successful completion of this procedure.

Maintenance

A fifth wheel must be maintained properly to ensure safety. It requires regular lubrication and inspection. Draw-bar units should have the eyelet checked to ensure there is no damage or wear. Heavy duty grease with a lithium or calcium base should be used for all lubrication.

Maintenance of the fifth wheel should be carried out every 10,000 km (or 1 month). To do this uncouple the tractor and clean the fifth wheel mechanism, rubbing the plate and kingpin. Inspect the fifth wheel for damage and defects. Regrease with clean grease.

Loads and load restraint

When securing a load you need to take into account

- the nature of the load
- the suitability of the vehicle
- the stability of the load
- the type of restraint
- protection from weather
- prevention of theft
- prevention of damage to the load
- ease of delivery.

The object is to ensure a secure load and a stable vehicle when

- braking
- steering

even in emergency situations.

The failure of tyres on the vehicle or trailer shouldn't cause the load to become insecure. This is particularly important when stowing loads such as wooden pallets, hay, etc, which are usually stacked high on flat-bed vehicles.

Any load must be carried so that it doesn't endanger other road users at any time. It should be

- securely stowed, with the load centre of gravity as low as possible
- evenly distributed, so that excessive stress is not applied to the restraints

- within the weight limits permitted for your vehicle
- within the size limits for the vehicle (unless clearly marked or proceeding under a special movement order under escort).

You also need to consider how the weight of the load could affect the handling of the vehicle during transportation.

You should ensure that all devices for securing the load are effective, that all

- ropes, chains and straps are secure
- sheets are fastened down
- nets are securely fastened
- container locking handles are secured
- doors, drop sides and tailgates are fastened
- doors and curtains are secure and unable to blow about, whether open or closed
- hatches on tank vehicles are closed to prevent spillage.

You should also prevent

- material falling from bulk cement vehicles
- any nets covering skip loads being lost.

Types of load

A load may consist of large heavy pieces of machinery but that doesn't mean it will stay in place throughout a journey. Fatalities have occurred through such items falling from a vehicle or shifting under braking or cornering. Loads should always be secured solidly and carefully.

When making a decision about the type of restraints to be used, consider what might happen if you have to brake hard and swerve to avoid an incident. Your vehicle might have to negotiate

- road works
- a construction site
- a lorry park

where uneven surfaces may cause it to tilt.

Large plant and machinery

Carrying large machinery and plant vehicles, excavators, diggers etc, requires specialist knowledge and usually specially-adapted vehicles. General rules and safety

precautions include

- stowing equipment to give the lowest overall height
- butting the wheels or tracks against chocks and/or front and rear bulkheads (chains are the preferred type of lashings)
- preventing forward, rearward and sideways movement
- securing buckets and arms to prevent independent movement
- relieving hydraulic pressure by operating all controls with the engine switched off.

When loading a digger or other machine onto a low-loader trailer, you need to ensure that the weight of the main part of the machine is distributed evenly between the axles. On a digger the arm should be kept as low as possible with the bucket folded underneath and secured to prevent movement. The load should be restrained against forward, backward and sideways movement by chain or webbing lashings. All lashings should have some form of tensioning device.

Metal loads

Metal loads can take various forms, but can be broadly divided into nine categories:

- long sections
- flat sheets
- large units and castings
- coils
- scrap vehicles
- scrap metal
- machinery and tools
- steel for concrete reinforcement
- combination of the above, ie mixed loads

All types of metal loads should be handled with care and have sufficient lashings in firm contact with the top surface of the load. If the load is stacked, it should be kept as low as possible with heavier items at the bottom. No layer should be larger than the one below.

In general small heavy items, eg small castings, must be securely restrained and carried on sided vehicles which are higher than the load and strong enough to withstand the forces generated by motion. Loads such as a heavy steel section or scrap metal should be secured to the vehicle by chains.

Care should be taken to ensure chain links do not damage the load, or that any lashings are not damaged by sharp edges on the load. Corner protectors and sleeves should be used as necessary.

Some items such as coils of wire may come ready strapped to a pallet, but remember that such strapping is only sufficient to secure the coil to the pallet. It will be necessary to further secure the entire unit to the vehicle - securing just the pallet will be insufficient.

Scrap metal can be a very diverse load. Loose items of scrap can be carried in sided vehicles with no additional means of restraint, provided that the headboard, sideboards and tailboards are higher than the load. Scrap vehicles can be difficult to transport because of the way that

movement, caused by their own tyres and suspension, can affect stability. Chain or webbing lashings with tensioning devices should be used to secure them.When transporting machinery and tools larger pieces of equipment should be placed in contact with a headboard.Smaller items and tools should be boxed and secured to the vehicle body with anchored restraints.

Excavators, plant and other types of heavy machinery should be secured using suitable chocks, straps and chains as appropriate. Do not rely on the weight of the machine alone.

Bundles of concrete-reinforcing mesh should have the lashings carefully located between the cross-wires so there is no danger of damage to the lashing from the ends of the cross-wires. Bundles with smaller cross-sectional areas should be on top of the load, and placed so there is no overhang. Bundles of reinforcing bar must be secured in a manner suitable to individual shape and size, and the load planned to avoid any instability.

The restraints may need reconfiguration after delivery of a part-load. While it is essential to take into account any loading/unloading patterns when configuring a load, it is of vital importance that every part of a mixed load be suitably restrained.

Timber loads

Timber is a live commodity which can lead to independent movement of part of a load, if inadequately restrained. Any load should be placed against the headboard where possible. Bulk-packaged sheets are usually strapped or wired at each end, and these straps should be checked for security, with further restraint used if any damage or insecurity is noted.

Loose timber, generally made up into standard sets, should be loaded to a uniform height. Light loads, eg for retail deliveries, can be carried on sided vehicles but the load height should not exceed the height of the headboard, sides or tailboard. If it does, additional lashing must be used. In general, chain or webbing lashings are recommended and should be placed at points where the load is rigid. Large, heavy packs of timber should be secured by ratchet straps.

Timber can settle on a vehicle, so all types of restraint should be regularly checked and retightened as necessary. Any loose ends of timber at the rear of the vehicle should be secured with rope or webbing to minimise whip.

Round timber should be stacked along the length of the vehicle. Shorter logs should be positioned in the middle to ensure maximum safety. The outer logs must extend past the ends of the securing uprights by at least 300 mm (12") and there should NOT be any gaps between them.

Logs should be laid top to tail for even balance, with each pile lashed together. The lashing should be secured by a suitable device. Staples can be used in conjunction with chains.

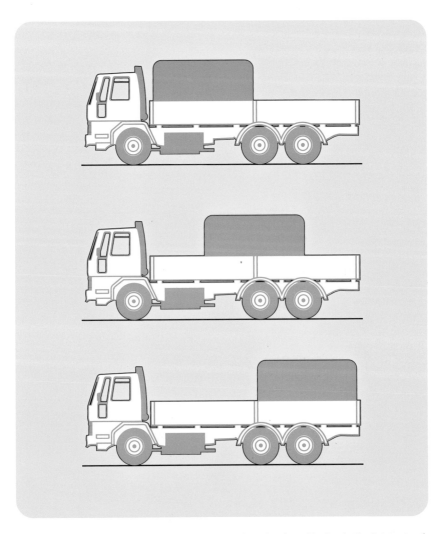

Load positioning - the above is only a basic guide to load positioning in the interests of safety. Different types of load may require slightly different positioning. There are many factors to consider carefully when loading, including type, weight, height, shape and volume of the load as well as airflow round the vehicle. Loading issues are very complex. For more detailed guidance, refer to the DfT Code of Practice entitled "The Safety of Loads on Vehicles".

Some rounded timber loads, particularly logs or trees, can spread sideways. It is important that vehicles are fitted with side stanchions which reach the height of the load, and which should be capable of resisting any outward movement of the load. The top middle log should be the highest point of the load. This should prevent movement and limit the effect the load has on the vehicle's handling.

Loose bulk loads

Loose bulk loads are those which do not readily lend themselves to any form of packaging, eg sand, ballast etc. These are usually carried in open-bodied vehicles. This category also includes such things as waste skips. Before lifting a full skip, a sheet or net should be secured over the contents to prevent items falling off.

Particular care should be taken with granular or flaked materials which could settle or compact in transit. There can be a danger of small quantities of material

being blown from the top of the load compartment or falling through gaps in bodywork. The load compartment should be covered if there is a risk of this and the type of cover will depend on the nature of the load.

When it is raining or snowing, certain loads can get wet and become very heavy. This is most likely to happen with open tipper lorries and sheeted and netted loads. Examples of loads affected are sand, ballast, etc, but other load types can also be affected.

Dry sand, ash and metal-turning swarf are especially susceptible to being blown away, and should be covered by suitable sheeting. Mesh netting is suitable for loads such as builders' waste. With loaded skips, the driver cannot control what is placed inside but is responsible for ensuring safe carriage of the skip and its contents. A sheet or net should be secured over the skip prior to loading onto the lorry, to prevent the contents from spilling onto the road.

Loose loads within a container should be checked periodically as these can move within the container while vehicles are travelling up and down steep gradients, placing overload stresses on axles.

Palletised loads

Palletised loads have two main problems to be considered - the stability of the load on its pallet and the security of the pallet to the transporting vehicle. The strapping used to secure the load to the pallet is intended merely to keep load and pallet together.

It is not sufficient to just restrain the pallet during transit. Both load and pallet should be secured to the vehicle. Before loading, pallets should be examined for any damage or weakness. They should not be used if there is any doubt that they are strong enough to withstand the load.

Pallets should be positioned so that the load is balanced across the vehicle. If load space is not fully utilised, pallets should be placed along the centre line of the vehicle, front to back, and closed up to one another to further restrict any movement.

The best way to secure palletised loads is to use nets and straps. However, the chosen method will depend on the vehicle type and size, relevant anchorage points and load size and weight. Whatever method is used, lashings should be positioned to prevent movement of the pallets in any direction. Vertical and tipping motions can be prevented by a lashing placed across the top of the pallet load. Empty pallets should still be restrained and secured, as the wind can easily blow them from vehicles.

High loads

Particular dangers need to be considered here, for example where there are bridges or other structures across roads. Any vehicle fitted with high-level equipment capable of exceeding a height of 3 metres (9 feet 10 inches) must be fitted with a visual warning device which tells the driver if the equipment has been left in an extended position.

There are other types of load not mentioned above, eg plate glass, which are often carried by specialist vehicles such as those with side frames attached so the glass can stand up against the side of the vehicle within the frame.

Ultimately, the most important common factor with any load is that, as the driver, it is your responsibility to ensure that the load is adequately, suitably and safely restrained throughout its journey.

Follow any instructions provided by your operator, and ensure your vehicle is adequate for the task, with sufficient and appropriate restraints available to secure the load you are required to carry.

Loading methods

It is not possible to suggest loading methods for all types of load in view of the diversity involved. However, the list below gives some general advice in brief. Whenever loading or unloading, the engine should be switched off in order to save fuel and in the interests of safety.

Rolls, drums, cylindrical loads - these should be placed with the axis across the vehicle if possible, so that the rolling tendency will be to the front or rear. Lashings should be used over each layer (plus sheeting to provide extra down-force on lighter loads, eg cardboard tubes) and chocks provided to prevent backward movement. There are alternative loading procedures for example if the length of cylinders is less than twice their diameter, in which case they can be placed on end. However, lashings must be used to prevent sideways movement in addition to the usual cross-lashings. If drums need to be kept upright, it is best to secure them with straps. Tubular steel would be best restrained using chains or webbing straps with tensioning devices.

Boxes - these should be tightly placed so they are prevented from moving in any direction, interlocking if possible and loaded to a uniform height. There should be at least one lashing for each row of boxes.

Sealed sacks - these should be laid on their backs, with alternate layers at 90 degrees (right angles) to one another. The load should be of uniform height, with at least one cross-lashing for each sack length. Loads of sacks should be sheeted if possible.

Material packed in plastic sacks and loaded onto pallets may be liable to slip unless shrink-wrapped or secured by banding. However, material in canvas sacks may well remain totally stable.

Open sacks - for example those for coal delivery, should be loaded to uniform height with cross-lashings for each layer and be sheeted overall to prevent loose materials being lost from the vehicle.

Empty sacks - these can be hazardous if they fall from a vehicle in motion. They should be securely restrained to the vehicle platform.

Loose bricks - both bulk mass and individual items should be restrained and the load height should not exceed the height of the surrounding body. They may require purpose-made restraint systems.

Metal cages - These often have wheels or castors, which may not always have immobilisers. Cages should be restrained by using a load restraining bar to immobilise them in transit. Load restraining bars can also be used as a safety measure to immobilise other types of part load if necessary.

Mixed loads - each part of the load should be secured by cross-lashings in a manner suitable to a load of its type. Longitudinal lashings must be adequate for the total load weight and separators must be used so that no part of the load can move forward independently.

For maximum stability, the load should be placed to keep the centre of gravity as low and as near to the vehicle's centre line as possible along both the vehicle's length (longitudinally) and width (laterally). Also, the load should be spread to give an even weight distribution over the whole floor area.

- Heavy articles should form the base and central part of the load.
- Light crushable articles should form the top and sides of the load.

- Different-sized containers should be loaded with the smaller items placed centrally, and the larger items forming the outer walls of the load. Avoid projections beyond the vehicle sides.

- Irregular shapes should be kept to the upper part of the load if it is not possible to place them centrally.

- Dangerous substances should be placed to segregate any which may interact together. Protect from rain, handle and stow carefully to reduce the risk of damage to vulnerable containers. Load so that labels can be easily read. Make sure you have gained the necessary vocational training certificate if you are going to handle hazardous substances.

(More information on mixed loads can be found on page 87 under Metal loads.)

Plastic containers - these can become slippery if damp and care must be taken when loading, securing and sheeting, especially if dangerous substances are involved.

Bales - eg hay or cloth. One suggested loading pattern is as follows:

- the first two tiers to be loaded crosswise and the centre five bales secured to the vehicle

- third tier to be loaded lengthwise and each bale secured individually to the vehicle

- if a fourth tier is necessary, it should be no more than two rows of bales, loaded lengthwise, with the front and rear bales secured to the vehicle

- the whole load should be covered with sheeting if appropriate.

Dual-purpose trailers - these have been developed incorporating

- a belly tank installed along the centre of the trailer for transporting fluids

- a flat-bed deck above the tank for the conventional carriage of goods.

In such instances care must be taken not to rupture the tank below.

Load shift

During a journey loads may shift - you may notice leaking liquid or hear noises which could indicate cargo moving inside your vehicle. If you suspect a problem pull up at the nearest safe and suitable place and inspect the load.

Be very careful when opening doors or curtains. Stay aware of your own safety at all times and follow any specific safety instuctions given by your operator. The problem may be a minor one that you can easily and safely rectify yourself before continuing your journey. However, in more serious situations, seek advice and or/assistance. Don't resume your journey until the problem has been rectified.

Anchorage points

It is common practice to use the rope hooks, which are bolted or welded to the underside of side rails/outriggers on most platform vehicles, as the anchor points for the load restraint system. However, rope hooks are not subject to constructional standards so they vary in strength, size and material content. They should not be used to anchor loads, as they are rarely designed to withstand forces exceeding 1-1.5 tonnes. Many are so weak that they can be distorted by use of the ratchet buckle which tightens webbing straps.

Load anchorage points should be rated at capacities of 0.5 tonne, 1.0 tonne, or 2.0 tonne and beyond, and the capacity of each point should be indicated on the vehicle. Depending on the size of the vehicle and its load capacity, sufficient load anchorage points should be provided (with a minimum of three on each side) so that the sum of the capacity of the anchorage points on both sides of the vehicle should not be less than the maximum rated load of the vehicle.

Vehicles being carried piggy-back must always have some form of chocks applied to their wheels, in addition to a restraint. Never merely rely on a handbrake holding them in place. Each individual trailer should be secured to the one on which it rests and should also be secured independently to the carrying vehicle.

95

Headboards and front bulkheads

In most circumstances a headboard, when present, can be treated as part of the load restraint system. It should be capable of withstanding a horizontal force, uniformly distributed over its vertical area, which is equal to at least half the vehicle payload. It should be no less than the width of the cab, and equal to the width of the loading platform.

The height should be sufficient to obstruct forward movement of the load the vehicle is designed to carry, unless adequate load restraint is provided by other means.

For loads such as metal bars, beams or sheet metal, the headboard must be adequately reinforced to resist damage from individual load elements.

Tubular loads such as scaffolding poles, lamp standards, extrusions, girders, etc, may all move forward with some force if emergency braking occurs. In such cases the headboard on the vehicle or semi-trailer can be demolished, with fatal results. The load being carried should always be in contact with the headboard, for maximum benefit and for reasons of safety.

Calculation of payload

Maximum permitted gross axle weights are determined by axle spacing and tyre equipment. The payload is the maximum load you can carry and this can be calculated as detailed overleaf.

The Maximum Authorised Mass of the vehicle (MAM) minus the kerbside weight, the weight of the crew and any drivers' equipment, equals the payload. Always remember that the kerbside weight does not take into account the weight of the crew and extra equipment, such as fridges and televisions, etc. When loading the vehicle to - or near to - its capacity, the vehicle may need to be weighed with crew and extras, to ensure it is not overloaded.

Example - for a vehicle with a MAM of 40 tonnes and with the kerbside weight plus the weight of the crew and any extra equipment of 10 tonnes, the maximum payload able to be carried would be 30 tonnes.

For definition of weights, refer to the Glossary.

Calculation of axle load

The formula for calculating axle loads is

$$\frac{P \times D}{W} = FAL$$

where
P = payload
D = distance from centre of load to rear axle
W = wheelbase
FAL = front axle load

In the image below, the following figures are relevant:

- the payload carried is 10 tonnes

- the distance from the centre of the load to the rear axle is 2 metres

- the wheelbase is 5 metres

The calculation is $\frac{10 \times 2}{5} = 4$ tonnes

This means that 4 tonnes of the 10-tonne payload are being imposed on the road through the front axle. The balance of the payload (6 tonnes) is therefore being imposed on the road through the rear axle.

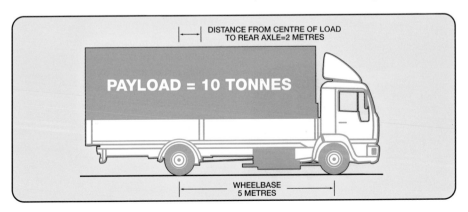

DISTANCE FROM CENTRE OF LOAD TO REAR AXLE=2 METRES

PAYLOAD = 10 TONNES

WHEELBASE 5 METRES

These figures only reveal how much of the payload is being imposed on the road. The operator must add axle kerb weights (eg empty vehicle weight) to those figures to get a true figure of the total weight being imposed on the road by the entire loaded vehicle.

If you suspect that your vehicle is overloaded, take it to the nearest weighbridge to check. Also see pages 58-9 for more information on vehicle weight.

Diminishing payload

An area of concern is the diminishing load problem on a payload comprising two or more deliveries. The same formula is used to ascertain axle loading. Any loads put on a vehicle where the centre of the load is behind the rear axle will act as a counterweight to the front axle.

Two or three sections of a load could be placed on a vehicle in such a manner as to cause the front axle to be overloaded. A fourth section could be placed on the vehicle with the centre of the load behind the rear axle. Use of the formula would give

the weight being lifted off the front axle. This could result in the front axle now being within the axle plated weight but when that section was off-loaded the front axle would revert to being overloaded.

Although the total weight of the load decreases, the distribution of the load means that the weight left is not spread over the axles evenly. For example, unloading from the back will increase the weight on the front axle. Care should be taken to redistribute part loads during multidrop journeys.

Axle weight limit

Permitted individual axle weights are shown on the vehicle plate. Operators have a responsibility to ensure vehicles operate safely and legally and that maximum weights shown on the plates are not exceeded.

Using lifting axles

The more tyres a vehicle has in contact with the road, the greater the friction between vehicle and road (rolling resistance). Using a lifting axle where appropriate can reduce rolling resistance which helps save fuel. However, you need to make sure that the weight limits on the remaining axles are not exceeded. You should lower the lifting axle when your vehicle is laden (assuming it doesn't deploy automatically).

Self-steering axles

These are fitted on the rear of trailer bogies or multi-axle vehicles and follow a similar course to the front steering axle. The rear axle is therefore able to follow the curve of the road as the front of the vehicle turns. Some are free to move independently, others have hydraulic assistance. They can reduce tyre scrub, increase tyre life and improve fuel consumption. There must be some method of locking them when the vehicle is reversing.

Consequences of overloading an axle

In addition to damage to the road surface, too much weight over the axle could lead to

- reduced braking power and therefore an increase in stopping distance
- increased likelihood of brake fade
- less vehicle stability
- steering becoming heavy, if the affected axle is a steering axle
- tyres overheating and failing
- legal consequences and possible prosecution.

If an enforcement officer finds that a vehicle is overloaded, this can result in a prohibition notice. This notice will prevent the driver from continuing the journey until the weight is corrected. Correcting the problem may involve the goods being redistributed (in axle overload cases) or unloaded to bring the weight down.

The driver will then be issued with a 'removal of prohibition notice' to continue the journey. In some cases the driver may be issued with a 'direction to drive notice'

which allows them to travel to a specified place to off-load.

Legislation imposes fines of up to £5000 for each offence, eg each overloaded axle plus any overloading on the total weight. If the vehicle is dangerously overloaded, the driver could face a dangerous driving charge, with a maximum penalty of two years in prison.

Other offences which also carry a maximum fine of £5000 include

- refusal to allow vehicle to be weighed
- obstruction of an officer

If an overloaded vehicle results in someone being killed, both driver and operator could face a prison sentence for Manslaughter or Death by Dangerous Driving.

Use of gearbox ratios

You should use your gears depending on the load carried and the profile of the road. For example

- when driving a fully laden vehicle you may need to use all the gears, for example when going uphill, as this requires more power. Using most or all of the gears will make optimum use of the available power
- when driving an empty or partially-loaded vehicle, less power is required from the engine so it may be possible to miss out some gears
- when driving downhill, it may be necessary to hold a lower gear to

increase the engine braking. This reduces the need to use the brakes, and so reduces the likelihood of brake fade.

Safety factors relating to vehicle loads

Drivers should wear suitable personal protective equipment which employers are required to provide where there is a risk to their health and safety. This should be worn at all times where necessary during loading, carriage or delivery of goods.

Hydraulic lorry loaders and cranes have helped reduce the number of incidents that occurred during loading or unloading of the vehicles. These help drivers by reducing over-exertion and fatigue so they are better prepared to drive the vehicle. They also reduce loading and unloading time. When using a lorry-mounted crane or fork-lift truck to load and unload, be aware of any overhead obstructions. See page 44 for more advice.

Regulations require drivers of

- tankers carrying dangerous goods
- tanker container vehicles
- vehicles carrying dangerous goods in packages

to hold Vocational Training Certificates issued by DVLA. You must attend and pass an approved course set by the City and Guilds. They are valid for five years before needing to be renewed by attending a refresher course. These certificates must be carried when driving the relevant vehicle.

It is an offence to drive a dangerous goods vehicle unless you are the holder of a valid certificate.

Further information and advice on load safety and loading equipment can be found in the Code of Practice entitled Safety of Loads on Vehicles, which is available from The Stationery Office.

Two codes of practice cover the use of lorry loaders as cranes

1. *Code of Practice for Safe Use of Cranes. Lorry Loaders* (BS 7121-4) – this is published by the British Standards Institute and is available from

British Standards Institute
389 Chiswick High Road
London W4 4AL
Tel: 0208 996 9001
Email: info@bsi-global.com
Website: www.bsi-global.com

and also from The Stationery Office.

2. Lorry loaders: the *Code of Practice for Installation, Application and Operation* – this is published by the Association of Lorry Loader Manufacturers and Importers of Great Britain (ALLMI) and is available to purchase from

ALLMI
Second Floor Suite,
9 Avon Reach
Monkton Hill
Chippenham, Wilts SN15 1EE
Tel: 01249 659150
Fax: 01249 464675

Weather conditions

In bad weather, rain can increase the weight of certain loads and take the vehicle over its legal weight. Handling, stability and braking could be affected to a dangerous level. This is most likely to occur with open tippers or flat-beds. Loads most at risk include

• sand

• rubble

• hay bales

Types of restraint

It's important that the correct anchoring points are employed irrespective of the type of restraint being used. Remember, however, that the hooks fitted under some decks are only intended for fastening sheeting ropes.

Straps

These are generally made of webbing and are frequently used to secure many types of load. Ensure that all straps, tensioners, etc, are kept in good, serviceable condition. If a load has sharp edges, straps with suitable sleeves and corner protectors can be used.

Battens and chocks

Large, heavy objects such as metal ingots, castings, fabrications, etc, should be chocked by nailing battens to the vehicle or trailer deck.

Chains

If there's any danger of either the weight of the load being too great for ropes or straps, or the load having sharp edges that would shear ropes or straps, then chains must be used together with compatible tensioning devices. Chains are the best method of securing scrap metal to vehicles/trailers or a scissor lift onto a flat bed vehicle.

Chains will provide added security when tree trunks or logs are being carried. Don't rely solely on vertical stanchions to hold the load. However, chains of the split-link type, or those made of iron and other unsuitable materials, should not be used as they are less reliable than solid link or steel chains.

Ropes

Traditionally, ropes have been the commonest method of securing both a load and sheets. Ropes may be of fibre or modern man-made materials, such as nylon, polypropylene, etc.

When using ropes, the ends should be spliced or otherwise treated to prevent fraying. The rope should be of at least three-strand construction, with a minimum normal diameter of at least 10 mm. There should be an attached label or sleeve on which the manufacturer should have indicated the maximum rated load for the rope. Knots and sharp bends will reduce the effective strength which, in ropes made of sisal or manila, can be further affected by water saturation. Wet ropes should always be allowed to dry naturally.

Whatever type of rope is used, you should gain experience in the correct methods of securing the load. The knots used are known in the trade as 'dolly knots' (see illustration on page 326). These can only be released when required (and not otherwise). Additionally, you should ensure that the proper tension is applied and that only the correct securing points are used.

Ropes are totally unsuitable for some loads, such as steel plates, scrap metal, etc.

When using wire ropes, it is recommended that the diameter should not be less than 8 mm, and the rope should be completely rust-free. If there are any broken wires or strands, **DON'T USE THE ROPE**.

Nets

Nets are sometimes used around loads as an additional means of helping contain items. They should be fastened down securely to avoid the possibility of them coming loose and creating a potential danger.

Sheeting

If sheeting is used – whether tarpaulin, plastic, nylon or any other material – it must be secured in such a way that it doesn't become loose and create a hazard to other road users.

When starting to cover a load with more than one sheet you should start with the rear-most sheet first, working forward. This type of overlap will reduce the possibility of wind or rain being forced under the sheeting as the vehicle travels along. This protection is especially important in bad weather conditions, and when carrying loose sand etc, to prevent the load from being blown away. The same principle should be applied to folds in the sheeting at the front or sides of the vehicle so that wind pressure will close any gaps rather than open them.

In order to secure the sheets onto a load you'll need to use the same type of knots used when restraining loads (dolly knots). These remain taut in transit but can be released with the minimum of effort.

All spare sheets and ropes must be tied down securely when not in use, so that they don't fall into the road or cause damage or injury to other vehicles and road users. When travelling with an empty vehicle, **all** restraints should be stowed securely.

You should check your load and securing devices periodically to ensure nothing has moved or become loose. A loose load could make your vehicle unstable and this could be dangerous for other road users.

Hanging loads

Hanging loads will move in response to vehicle momentum and change of direction. Fixed, hinged stops can help restrict movement of a load, such as hanging meat carcasses, when in transit.

Curtain sides

The manufacturers of vehicles fitted with curtain-side bodies may be satisfied that a high degree of protection is given by the material used in their construction. This, however, doesn't relieve the driver of the responsibility for ensuring that a load is properly stowed and secured so that it won't move while in transit. This is particularly important where there may be a 'multi-drop' load of varying materials, some of which may come under the hazardous materials classification. Unless the curtains are specifically designed for the purpose, they must NOT be used for load restraint, only containment. Curtains mainly protect against the weather and provide a

level of security. Any rips or tears in a curtain should be repaired immediately. The torn material can flap about, thereby

* creating wind resistance (drag)
* increasing fuel consumption.

Take notice of warnings of poor weather conditions broadcast on the radio, especially if your vehicle is empty. Under such conditions it's often safer to secure both curtain sides at one end of the vehicle, cutting down the wind resistance and removing the likelihood of being blown over or off the road. Make sure they are tied securely so they don't come loose and flap around during high winds, which could be a hazard to other road users. When the vehicle is fully loaded, keeping the curtains tightly closed reduces wind resistance and helps to save fuel.

Irrespective of vehicle type, once on the road it is your responsibility as the driver to ensure that the load remains secure. In the particular case of curtain-sided vehicles,

this would normally be confined to a periodic visual inspection of the curtains and a check of the tensioning straps.

If you notice that one side of the curtain is bulging, you must stop as quickly and safely as possible. The curtain might be the only support to a slipped load, so do not open it before checking. Enter the compartment by the rear door (or by carefully opening the opposite curtain if it shows no sign of bulging). Be aware of your own safety at all times.

Once the situation has been assessed a judgement can then be made to either continue the journey if a minor bulge is evident or, in the event of a more serious situation, to seek advice and/or assistance.

Container lorries

International Standards Organisation (ISO) cargo containers should only be carried on vehicles or trailers equipped with the appropriate securing points, which are designed to lock into the container body.

Such vehicles may be intended for carrying

• a single 12-metre (40 feet) container

• one or two 6-metre (20 feet) containers

• larger numbers of smaller, specially designed units

Whatever type of container is carried, all locking levers (twistlocks) must be in the secured position during transit. When emptying a container, you should be aware that some of the load may have moved during transit and be resting against the rear doors. Take great care when opening them for your own safety.

Steel ISO containers shouldn't be carried on flat-bed platform vehicles where there are no means of locking the container in position. Never rely on the weight of the container and its contents to hold it in place on a flat deck.

Ropes are totally inadequate to hold a typical seagoing steel container in place. Skeletal vehicles or trailers that have a main

ENSURE TWISTLOCKS
DISENGAGE BEFORE
LIFTING CONTAINER
DEC00071

chassis frame with outrigger supports, into which the ISO container can be locked, are safer and more secure.

Ferry operations

When a vehicle is carried on a ship, the vehicle and load will be subject to forces due to the rolling and pitching motions of a seagoing vessel. It is important to note that a restraint system suitable for road use may be inadequate at sea.

The securing of the vehicle to the ship is also important. Vehicles should be fitted with lashing points that are of adequate strength to withstand forces likely to be encountered at sea. These lashing points should be easily accessible to deck crews.

More information can be found on the Department for Transport Marine Directorate's *Roll-on, Roll-off ships - Stowage and Securing of Vehicles - Code of Practice*, and The Department of Trade *Merchant Shipping Notice M849 or BS EN 29367*, giving guidance on securing vehicles on ships and an indication of forces likely to be encountered at sea.

Unloading

If your vehicle is fitted with equipment for lifting and/or removing heavy loads, one of your main responsibilities prior to lifting is to ensure the vehicle is parked on firm level ground. This will help eliminate any possibility there might be for the load to become unstable during lifting. When using

a lorry-mounted crane, stabilisers should **always** be used. Avoid swinging the crane too quickly during loading and unloading as this will cause instability and may cause the vehicle to tip over.

Certain vehicles are fitted with stabilisers, for example

- those with a hydraulic lifting arm system for moving skip containers
- those with crane mounts for delivering bagged or strapped loads such as sand or bricks
- recovery trucks which have hoists for lifting and moving other vehicles.

If your vehicle is fitted with stabilisers, then you should make sure all are in contact with firm level ground and locked in position. The safety and stability of the load itself should then be checked before any unloading begins. Also take care when using lifting gear, especially where there are overhead cables and pipework in the area - see page 44 for more advice on this subject.

section **three**
LIMITS AND REGULATIONS

This section covers

- Environmental impact
- Drivers' hours and records
- Operator licensing - the driver's responsibilities
- Driving in Europe
- Carriage of illegal immigra
- Your health and conduct
- Your vehicle
- Your driving

16'-0"

Oncoming
vehicles
in middle
of road

Environmental impact

Transport is an essential part of modern life, but we cannot ignore its environmental consequences – local, regional and global.

There's increasing public concern for the protection of our environment. As a result, many motor vehicle manufacturers are devoting more time, effort and resources to the development of environmentally-friendly vehicles.

Considerable research and effort is taking place to develop more efficient vehicles. The following explains the effects of pollution and what you, the driver, can do to help. (You will also find further information on eco-friendly driving skills in the next Section).

Motor vehicles account for most of the movement of people and goods.

The increased number of vehicles on the roads has damaged the environment; it has resulted in

- changes to the landscape
- air pollution, causing
  - human health problems, in particular respiratory disease
  - damage to vegetation
- building deterioration
- bridge weakening
- changes to communities
- the using up of natural resources
- disruption of wildlife.

When planning your route and delivery schedule, remember that local authorities can impose delivery restrictions to improve the local environment and quality of life. For example, this could mean preventing deliveries being accepted or despatched during the night or early hours which would help reduce noise disturbance to nearby residents.

A local traffic authority can also make Traffic Regulation Orders (TROs) to restrict rights to use a public highway.

Exhaust emissions

Fuel combustion produces carbon dioxide, a major greenhouse gas, and transport accounts for about one-fifth of the carbon dioxide we produce in this country.

MOT tests now include a strict exhaust emission test to ensure that all vehicles are operating efficiently and causing less air pollution.

Diesel engines

These engines are more fuel efficient than petrol engines. Although they produce higher levels of some pollutants (nitrogen oxides and particulates), they produce less carbon dioxide (a global warming gas). They also emit less carbon monoxide and fewer hydrocarbons.

Alternative fuels

To improve exhaust emissions even further, ultra low sulphur diesel or city diesel fuels can be used. These have been formulated so that the sulphur content is very low. Sulphur is the main cause of particulates in exhaust emissions, and it also produces acid gases. The lower the content of sulphur in fuel, the less the damage to the environment.

Compressed Natural Gas (CNG)

While there are improvements in the quality of exhaust emissions produced, some of the technical disadvantages relate to the size and design of the fuel tanks required.

Electricity

Trials have been taking place with electric vehicles for a number of years, but it is only recently that advances have been made in overcoming the problems of battery size and capacity.

Fuel cells

These operate like rechargeable batteries and produce little or no pollutants, but have greater range and improved performance than most battery electric vehicles.

Hybrid vehicles

These offer the advantages of electricity without the need for large batteries. The combination of an electric motor and battery with an internal combustion engine gives increased fuel efficiency and greatly reduced emissions.

Hydrogen

This is another possible fuel source for road vehicles that is being studied. However, technical problems include storage of this highly inflammable gas.

Liquid Petroleum Gas (LPG)

This consists mainly of methane, produced during petrol refining. Vehicles can run on LPG alone or both LPG and petrol (known as dual fuel). Benefits include low cost, lower emissions and reduced wear and tear to engine and exhaust systems. Disadvantages include cold start problems and valve-seat wear.

Methane

Because of the naturally occurring renewable sources of this fuel, it is also being considered as a possible alternative to diesel oil which is a finite resource.

Solar power

Needing only daylight to function, solar vehicles are small, light, slow and silent.

They produce no emissions at all; however, they are very expensive as yet and improvements are needed so they can store energy for use in the dark.

Fuel consumption

Fuel consumption can depend on the design of your vehicle.

- Cab-mounted wind deflectors can effectively lower wind resistance created by large box bodies, together with lower side-panel skirts.
- Tipper bodies with prominent strengthening ribs on the outside can be plated-over to give improved performance.
- A fly sheet tightly fastened over the top of tipper bodies (especially when empty) can reduce the drag effect.

Further information and publications can be found on the following website: **www.energysavingtrust.org.uk/fleet**

Diesel spillages

Because of the extremely slippery characteristics of diesel fuel, care must be taken at all times to avoid spillages. Not only is diesel fuel dangerous to anyone stepping onto it (especially getting down from a vehicle cab) but it also creates a serious risk to other road users, particularly motorcyclists.

Take care when refuelling and ensure that all

- filler caps
- tank hatches

are properly closed and secure at all times. If at any time you notice your fuel filler cap is missing, you **MUST** get it replaced before continuing.

Don't be tempted to overfill your fuel tank as this can contribute to fuel leaks. For more advice see page 216-7 (fuel consumption) and page 219-20 (maintaining your vehicle).

Road-friendly suspension

Reference has already been made to the requirement that some form of road-friendly suspension be fitted to vehicles which are intended to carry increased weights (see page 58). By replacing springs with some form of compressible material (usually air) a reduction in vibration caused by the impact of LGV wheels on road surfaces will reduce the damage to

- the road surface
- adjacent structures
- under-road services (gas, water, etc)
- bridges.

These systems can, in some instances, be fitted retrospectively to vehicles. However, this does mean that the vehicle will usually have to be equipped with additional compressed air storage tanks, creating some additional weight.

An increasing number of manufacturers are making use of the benefits that road-friendly suspension gives in reducing damage to goods in transit.

Specialised semi-trailers used to carry fragile goods have no rear axles as such. When loading takes place

- the hollow trailer body is positioned to surround the racks holding a fragile load (eg glass)
- the body is lowered into place
- the load is secured
- the body is raised into the travelling position.

The whole process is carried out by controlling the sophisticated road-friendly suspension system on each trailer wheel assembly.

Audible warning systems

As an LGV driver it's up to you to recognise the effects your vehicle, and the way in which it's driven, can have on the environment around you.

Reversing your vehicle can cause a hazardous situation. There may be pedestrians in the area that you'll need to warn. There are different types of audible warning device which give a signal to others around the vehicle that it's reversing, such as a

- bleeper
- horn
- recorded verbal message, etc.

These must not be allowed to operate on a road subject to a 30 mph (48 km/h) speed limit between 11.30 pm and 7 am.

Take care when setting any vehicle security alarm system. You only want such an alarm to sound when it's necessary – not by mistake.

Remember, using an audible warning device doesn't take away the need to practise good, all-round effective observation. If you think that you're unable to reverse safely you **must** get someone to help you.

Dangerous goods

The Carriage of Dangerous Goods by Road Regulations 1996 (CDG Road) as amended by the Carriage of Dangerous Goods Amendments Regulations 1999 cover the rules for vehicles, operators and drivers. This is otherwise referred to as the ADR Regulations. Explosives and radioactive materials are covered in a separate regulation. More information on the different classes of dangerous goods can be found in the previous Section.

Any quantity of dangerous goods transported in a tank or tank container must adhere to these regulations. Packaged dangerous goods rules are dependent on the transport category of the goods, the size of the containers and total load carried. Rules relate to safe parking of vehicles carrying dangerous substances: make sure you are aware of them if driving these types of vehicles.

Hauliers transporting goods must now comply with international standards. These regulations became law under the

Carriage of Dangerous Goods and Use of Transportable Pressure Vessels Regulations 2004, Statutory Instrument SI2004 no. 568.

The carriage of almost all dangerous goods in Britain must now meet the international ADR standard. This means that all dangerous goods vehicles must carry, at the minimum

- a wheel chock
- two warning signs or lamps
- fire extinguishers
- high visibility jackets and torches for the crew.

Operators will need to demonstrate the availability of this equipment at roadside checks, although they are not part of the ADR annual vehicle inspection. Vehicles carrying all UN1202 diesel, heating oil and gas oil will be particularly affected by the regulations.

The main requirements you should be aware of when transporting dangerous goods by road are that

- the sender of the goods must provide the vehicle operator with information in writing about the load in the form of a declaration confirming the goods are in a fit condition for carriage
- the vehicle operator must provide the driver with documents containing details about the goods prior to loading. The details must include emergency information.

111

These documents must be kept in the cab during transportation of the goods.

Always comply with any loading, stowing or unloading instructions. Certain dangerous goods may have to be segregated or are not permitted on the same vehicle.

Keep all vehicle marking placards that give information clean and clearly visible on your vehicle; they should be covered up or removed if no dangerous goods are being carried. The driver of any such vehicle should ensure they have adequate training or instruction to understand the requirements associated with carrying a dangerous load.

The following groups of drivers need to be in possession of a vocational training certificate showing that they're licensed by DVLA to carry dangerous goods by road

- drivers of road tankers with a capacity of more than 1000 litres
- drivers of vehicles carrying tank containers with a total capacity exceeding 3000 litres

- drivers of all vehicles carrying explosives (subject to limited exemptions)
- drivers of all vehicles which are subject to the Carriage of Dangerous Goods and Use of Transportable Pressure Equipment Regulations 2007.

DVLA will only issue the certificate upon receipt of proof of attending a course at an approved training establishment and passing examinations set by the Scottish Qualifications Authority.

The certificate is valid for five years. **Enquiries about courses and certificates should be directed to** *Scottish Qualifications Authority* (see page 312 for contact details).

As well as having a vocational training certificate, drivers of vehicles carrying dangerous goods must also have the correct driving licence entitlement for the vehicle they are driving.

What YOU can do to help

You have a part to play in helping to reduce the impact road transport has on the environment.

You should

- plan routes to avoid busy times and congestion
- anticipate well ahead
- avoid the need to make up time

- cover bulky loads with sheets to reduce wind resistance
- switch off the engine when stationary in queues for a long time
- drive sensibly and always keep within the speed limit (good driving habits save fuel)
- use the appropriate gear and avoid over-revving in low gears
- avoid rapid acceleration or heavy braking as this leads to greater fuel consumption and more pollution. Driving smoothly can reduce fuel consumption by about 15 per cent as well as reducing wear and tear on your vehicle
- check your fuel consumption regularly
- use air conditioning sparingly – running air conditioning continuously increases fuel consumption.

Keep your vehicle well maintained

You should

- have your vehicle serviced as recommended by the manufacturer. The cost of a service may well be less than the cost of running a badly maintained vehicle. Make sure your garage includes an emissions check in the service
- make sure the engine is operating efficiently. Badly adjusted engines use more fuel and emit more exhaust fumes
- make sure filters are changed regularly

- make sure that your tyres are properly inflated. Under-inflated tyres increase fuel consumption and can be dangerous. Over-inflated tyres tend to wear unevenly and so need to be replaced more frequently
- make sure brakes are correctly adjusted
- make sure diesel injectors are operating efficiently
- make sure that you send oil, old batteries and used tyres to a garage or a local authority site for recycling or safe disposal if you do any of your own maintenance. Don't pour oil down the drain. It's illegal, harmful to the environment and could lead to prosecution.

Select for economy or low emissions

- Consider using ultra-low sulphur fuel, such as city diesel, as it reduces harmful emissions of particles.
- When replacing tyres, consider buying energy-saving types which have reduced rolling resistance. These increase the fuel efficiency and also improve your grip on the road.

Members of the public are encouraged to report any vehicle emitting excessive exhaust fumes.

Traffic management

Continuous research has resulted in new methods of helping the environment by easing traffic flow.

Traffic flow

The strict parking rules in major cities and towns help the traffic flow. The Red Routes in London, also present in other major towns and cities, are an example of this and have cut journey times and improved traffic flow considerably (see page 161-2).

Speed reduction

Traffic calming measures, including road humps and chicanes, help to keep vehicle speeds low in sensitive areas. There are also an increasing number of areas where a 20 mph (32 km/h) speed limit is in force.

Rural area parking

Avoid parking your vehicle on the grass verge in rural areas. The weight will cause damage to the verge, which may even collapse under the vehicle's weight. This could mean your vehicle might become stuck, or even roll over. Also, as you drive away, mud and debris can be deposited on the road surface.

Further information on environmental issues can be found at:

www.defra.gov.uk/environment/index.htm

or

ETA Services Ltd
68 High Street
Weybridge KT13 8BL

Tel: 01932 828882
Fax: 01932 829015.

Drivers' hours and records

Goods drivers' hours of work are controlled in the interests of road safety, drivers' working conditions and fair competition. A European regulation sets maximum limits on driving time and the minimum requirements for breaks and rest periods. These are known as the EC rules. Drivers who break the rules are subject to heavy fines and could lose their licence to drive LGVs. Altering drivers' hours records with intent to deceive, or tampering with tachographs, can lead to a prison sentence. Similar penalties apply to those who permit such offences. (See pages125-8 for new working time regulations information.)

EC rules

The EC rules apply to vehicles used for the carriage of goods, including any trailer or semi trailer, where the maximum permissible weight (MPW) exceeds 3.5 tonnes. They apply to national and international journeys throughout the European Union, and are also consistent with the rules adopted by many countries beyond. Tachographs must be used under the EC rules.

Drivers of light goods vehicles with a maximum permissible weight of 3.5 tonnes or less are not required to keep daily records but must comply with the legal limits required on maximum daily driving and daily duty time under the UK domestic drivers' hours rules.

Where a light goods vehicle of 3.5 tonnes or less (which is exempt from the EC rules due to its weight) has a trailer attached, bringing the combined weight over a maximum permissible weight of 3.5 tonnes, then EC rules will apply. Exceptions to this may arise due to the nature of the operations on which it is engaged. If none of the exemptions apply, then a tachograph must be fitted and used to monitor the hours worked under the EC rules.

Exemptions

The following are exempt from EC drivers' hours and tachograph rules. In most of these cases, domestic rules apply

- vehicles with a maximum authorised speed not exceeding 40 km/h (just under 25 mph)

- vehicles owned or hired without a driver by the armed services, civil defence services, fire services, and forces responsible for maintaining public order when the carriage is undertaken as a consequence of the tasks assigned to these services and is under their control

- vehicles, including vehicles used in the non-commercial transport of humanitarian aid, used in emergencies or rescue operations

- specialised vehicles used for medical purposes

- specialised breakdown vehicles operating within a 100 km radius of their base

- vehicles undergoing road tests for technical development, repair or maintenance purposes and new or rebuilt vehicles which haven't yet been put into service
- vehicles or combinations of vehicles with a maximum permissible mass not exceeding 7.5 tonnes used for the non-commercial carriage of goods
- commercial vehicles, which have a historic status according to the legislation of the Member State in which they are being driven and which are used for the non-commercial carriage of passengers or goods.

In addition to the exemptions above, which apply to all EU member states, the following derogations have been implemented in the UK

- vehicles used or hired, without a driver, by agricultural, horticultural, forestry, farming or fishery undertakings for carrying goods as part of their own entrepreneurial activity within a radius of up to 100 km (from the base of the undertaking
- vehicles owned or hired, without a driver, by public authorities to undertake carriage by road which do not compete with private transport undertakings
- agricultural tractors and forestry tractors used for agricultural or forestry activities, within a radius of up to 100 km from the base of the undertaking which owns, hires or leases the vehicle

- Vehicles or combinations of vehicles with a maximum permissible mass not exceeding 7.5 tonnes, used
  - by universal service providers as defined in Article 2 (13) of Directive 97/67/EC of the European Parliament and of the Council of 15 December 1997 on common rules for the development of the internal market of community postal services and the improvement of quality of service to deliver items as part of the universal service, or
  - for carrying materials, equipment or machinery for the driver's use in the course of his/her work.

Within a 50 km radius from the base of the undertaking, and on condition that driving the vehicles does not constitute the driver's main activity

- vehicles operating exclusively on islands not exceeding 2,300 sq km in area, which aren't linked to the rest of the national territory by a bridge, ford or tunnel open for use by motor vehicles
- vehicles used for the carriage of goods within a 50 km radius from the base of the undertaking and propelled by means of natural or liquefied gas or electricity, the maximum permissible mass of which - including the mass of a trailer or semi-trailer - does not exceed 7.5 tonnes

- vehicles used for driving instruction and examination with a view to obtaining a driving licence or a certificate of professional competence provided that they are not being used for the commercial carriage of goods or passengers
- vehicles used in connection with sewerage, flood protection, water, gas and electricity maintenance services, road maintenance and control, door-to-door household refuse collection and disposal, telegraph and telephone services, radio and television broadcasting, and the detection of radio or television transmitters or receivers
- specialised vehicles transporting circus and funfair equipment
- specially fitted mobile project vehicles, the primary purpose of which is use as an educational facility when stationary
- vehicles used for milk collection from farms and the return to farms of milk containers or milk products intended for animal feed
- vehicles used for carrying animal waste or carcasses which are not intended for human consumption
- vehicles used exclusively on roads inside hub facilities such as ports, interports and railway terminals
- vehicles used for the carriage of live animals from farms to local markets and vice versa or from markets to local slaughterhouses within a radius of up to 50 km

- vehicles operated by the Royal National Lifeboat Institution (RNLI)
- vehicles manufactured before 1 January 1947
- vehicles propelled by steam
- vehicles used for the provision of ambulance services by or at the request of an NHS body
- vehicles used to transport organs, blood, equipment, medical supplies or personnel by or at the request of an NHS body
- vehicles used by a local authority to provide services for old persons or for mentally or physically handicapped persons
- vehicles used by HM Coastguard and lighthouse services
- vehicles used for maintaining railways by the British Rails Board, or any holder of a network licence which is a company wholly owned by the Crown, Transport for London (or a wholly owned subsidiary), a Passenger Transport Executive or a local authority
- vehicles used by British Waterways Board when engaged in maintaining navigable waterways.

Additionally, drivers who are members of the Territorial Army or Cadet Corps instructors have limited exemption from daily and weekly rest requirements in certain circumstances. Further details can be obtained from VOSA (see page 313 for contact details).

Analogue Tachographs

When driving within the EC rules, drivers' hours and rest periods are recorded by means of a chart that's inserted into a tachograph. A tachograph is a device that records hours of driving, other work, breaks and rest periods. It can also record the distance covered and the speed at which the vehicle travels.

The tachograph should be properly calibrated and sealed by an approved vehicle manufacturer or calibration centre. These must be checked at a Department for Transport (DfT) (or DVA in Northern Ireland) approved calibration centre every two years and recalibrated every six years. A plaque either on or near the tachograph will say when the checks were last carried out.

If there's anything wrong with the tachograph it should be replaced or repaired by a DfT-approved centre as soon as possible. If the vehicle can't return to base within seven days of failure of the tachograph or of the discovery of its defective operation, the repair must be carried out during the journey. While it's broken you must keep a written manual record either on the charts or on a temporary chart to be attached to the charts.

Charts

You must carry enough charts with you for the whole of your journey. You'll need one for every 24 hours. You should also carry some spares with you in case the charts become dirty or damaged or if your chart is retained by an Authorised Inspecting Officer. Your employer is responsible for giving you enough clean charts, of an approved type, for the tachograph installed in the vehicle.

You, the driver, must ensure that the correct information is recorded on the charts. You must enter on the chart

- your surname and first name (you should do this before departure)

- the date and the place where use of the chart begins (before departure) and ends (after arrival)

- the registration number of the vehicles driven during the use of the chart (this should be entered before departing in a different vehicle)

- the odometer reading at the start of the first journey and at the end of the last journey shown on the chart (and the readings at the time of any change of vehicle)

- the time of any change of vehicle.

Recording information

The tachograph will start recording onto the chart as soon as it's inserted.

You must ensure that the time recorded on the chart is the official time of the vehicle's country of registration and that the mode switch is in the appropriate position. The modes are shown as symbols.

- Driving (this is automatically recorded on some tachographs)

- Other work

- Periods of availability (POA) (only when length is known in advance)

- Break or rest

Under 'other work' you should include time spent on vehicle daily walk-round checks, attending training courses, loading and unloading and travelling (when requested by the employer) to join or leave the vehicle.

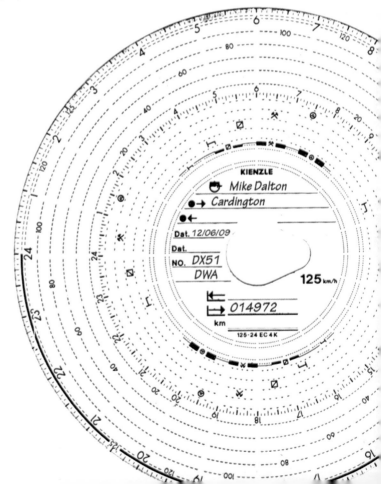

If you're driving more than one vehicle in one day you must take your chart with you and use it in the next vehicle. If for some reason the equipment in the other vehicle isn't compatible, you should use another chart.

If you are working away from the vehicle and cannot leave a chart in the tachograph (ie, because the vehicle is likely to be used by someone else), or you have left a chart in but have changed work mode whilst away from the vehicle, you must make a manual entry on the reverse of the chart; ie, OW 09.15–10.20. If your chart is dirty or damaged you should start another and then attach it to the damaged one.

Ensure that all the information for the day is entered on your chart(s). The obligation to record the complete information correctly falls on you, the driver, as well as on the operator. There are heavy fines imposed for the misuse or falsification of charts.

Chart inspections

Your tachograph records must be available for inspection at the roadside by the enforcement authorities. You must carry the record sheet (and print-outs) for the current day and for the previous 28 days. (Note: you should also carry and be able to produce your digital tachograph driver card if one has been issued to you). You will be committing an offence if you don't, even if you are pulled over while driving a vehicle equipped with an analogue tachograph.

If your records are kept by an enforcement officer you should ask the officer to endorse the replacement chart with his or her name and telephone number. The officer should also state the number of charts retained. Alternatively, he or she may provide you with a receipt.

To ensure that all records are kept up-to-date and available for inspection by enforcement staff, you must give the completed charts to your employer within 42 days. This requirement must be complied with even when a driver changes employer. If you are working for more than one employer, you must provide each with sufficient information to make sure the rules are being met.

The law says that employers must keep the tachograph record sheets and printouts (where applicable) in chronological order and in a legible form for at least one year from the date of their use. They must be submitted to enforcement officers as required. Also, if a driver requests it, employers must provide copies of the records as well as, if requested, copies of downloaded data from the driver card. There are various methods of storing the charts (eg on pegs, in envelopes, in folders, etc, and either under vehicle registration or under each driver's name).

Working time records

The law says that employers must keep a record of the hours worked by all employees including mobile workers (see glossary on page 322). This can be in a very simple form, such as through the normal payroll system. These records should be stored/filed for at least two years after the end of the period covered. Employers must be able to give employed drivers and other workers copies of the records of hours worked if requested.

Digital Tachographs

Digital tachographs convert the signal into encrypted electronic data stored in both the vehicle unit and the **driver smart card**. The vehicle unit records the vehicle movement as well as the drivers who use the vehicle. The driver smart card records all the driver's activities as well as details of the vehicle driven. Digital tachographs have to be calibrated before use and every two years from the previous calibration or after each repair, whichever is the earlier. Also if tyre sizes are changed. A plaque either on or near the tachograph will say when the last calibration was carried out. Digital tachographs became mandatory on all new LGVs 'in-scope' of EU drivers' hours rules on 1st May 2006.

The digital tachograph records all movement of the vehicle along with a record of driver(s) and crew who have inserted their card into the tachograph when driving or conducting other duties. Unlike the analogue tachograph, which will only record activity onto a paper chart, the digital tachograph will record the date, time and duration of all driving activity irrespective of whether a driver smart card has been inserted into the tachograph. This information can be printed off and produced if requested by an enforcement officer. The printout record can be manually corrected if the card or equipment malfunctions or if the rules are breached due to an unforeseen event.

The tachograph also records within its own memory a record of events and faults such as driving without a driver card inserted, speeding, power disconnections, security breach attempts etc, as well as a detailed speed trace for the last 24 hours of actual driving. Downloading and storing of data should be carried out frequently enough for the operator to be able to monitor the driver's hours and record-keeping and at least as frequently as regulations require.

As with analogue tachographs, if the digital tachograph becomes faulty, drivers may continue to use the vehicle, but must make a manual temporary record on the printout (or the paper roll if a printout is unavailable). This should contain data enabling the driver to be identified (driver card number and/or name and/or driving licence number) including their signature, plus all information for the various periods of time, which can no longer be recorded or printed out correctly by the recording equipment.

The driver should take a print at the start and end of the day. They can continue to drive without a driver card for a maximum of 15 calendar days. If they do not have a replacement card by then they must cease driving vehicles equipped with digital tachographs.

Driver Smart Cards

These are a 'must have' – a driver cannot legally drive a vehicle 'in-scope' of EU Drivers' Hours Regulations equipped with a digital tachograph unless he or she has first been issued with a driver smart card. Driver cards for digital tachographs are issued by the Driver and Vehicle Licensing Agency (DVLA), Swansea and DVA in Northern Ireland. Replacement and exchange cards can be collected from a local DVLA office or a VOSA testing station. In Northern Ireland, the cards are issued by the Driver and Vehicle Agency (DVA), previously known as DVLNI. The card, like a driving licence, belongs to the Secretary of State for Transport.

The driver smart card is intended to prevent drivers' hours offences. Cards are personalised to the driver and include

- identification information
- expiry date
- driving licence number
- photograph of the driver
- copy of the driver's signature
- unique issue number of the card.

Information is held electronically on the card chip as well as being printed on the card. If, on reporting for work and intending to drive a vehicle equipped with a digital tachograph, you find you have left your card at home, you should return home to collect it.

Drivers are not allowed to have more than one valid driver smart card issued to them. Cards are valid for a maximum period of five years. You should receive a reminder about three months before the expiry date. However, it is your responsibility to make sure that you apply for a new card at least 15 days before the old one expires.

The driver smart card should be inserted into the digital tachograph whenever the driver takes charge of a vehicle equipped with one. The tachograph will then prompt the driver to manually enter a record of any work activities undertaken since the card was last removed from a digital tachograph. Where the driver conducts both 'in-scope' and 'out-of-scope' driving, this also can be recorded by a manual entry.

The driver smart card allows for a record normally spanning a period covering 28 days on which driving and other activities have been recorded (this is based on 97 activity changes per day). The card will start to overwrite the earliest records once full so it is a legal requirement that data is downloaded from driver smart cards and stored before this occurs.

Drivers, when in charge of a vehicle, are currently required to be able to provide records of their activities covering the current day and the previous 28 days, ie driver smart card together with any analogue charts.

Irrespective of whether a driver has driven a digital tachograph equipped vehicle during this period, if he/she has been issued with a driver smart card they must carry the card at all times when driving to enable inspection and checking of the data record by VOSA (DVA in NI) or the police.

Lost or stolen driver smart cards

As a professional driver, you have a responsibility to report any loss or theft of your driver smart card to DVLA. This must be done within seven days. (In Northern Ireland, report to the Driver and Vehicle Agency (DVA) formerly DVLNI). You can apply for a replacement card by phone if no details have changed on the card. You can make payment by Visa, Eurocard, Mastercard, Maestro or Delta.

Replacement and exchange cards can be collected from a DVLA local office or VOSA Testing station, when advised that the card is ready. In Northern Ireland, replacement and exchange cards must be collected and signed for by you in person at a Local Vehicle Licensing Office or DVA test centre and you must state the most convenient location for card collection.

If your card is lost, stolen or faulty, you must take a print at the start and end of each day, showing start and end times. On both prints you need to list manual entries showing periods of driving, rest, breaks, other work and availability. You also need to add your

- name
- licence number or driver card number
- signature.

You can do this for a maximum of 15 calendar days. If you do not have a replacement card by then, you must cease driving vehicles equipped with digital tachographs.

Company Cards

These are used as keys by vehicle operators to lock-in data recorded when the vehicle is being used by their drivers – doing so enables them to readily identify their own data and prevents unauthorised persons from being able to see or download their data. The card also acts as the key which enables them to download data from the tachograph. Without the company card and suitable equipment and/or access to support services an operator will not be able to properly manage data.

Workshop Cards

A Workshop Card is issued only to qualified fitters who have successfully completed a training course that has been approved by VOSA. It should be used in the same way as a Driver Card, during digital tachograph related road tests, to enable this to be recorded together with the calibration or check. This will then form a complete record of the activities relating to a vehicle, which can be downloaded at a later time.

The loss or malfunction of a card, because of the security implications, must be notified immediately to VOSA, and a replacement card will be issued through a VOSA office. A workshop card must not be used as a company card and, as this would be recorded by the vehicle unit, any such abuse or any other illegal use would probably lead to the card being withdrawn.

Workshop cards will be issued to the holders of company cards only under the strictest conditions, with the consequences of illegal use fully explained.

Control Cards

These are used by VOSA (DVA in NI) enforcement officers or the police. An enforcement officer or examiner can use this card to download information from a digital tachograph. You must stop when requested to do so by such officers. Any person who fails to comply with, or obstructs, a vehicle examiner during the course of their duties, can be fined up to a maximum of £5000.

Tampering

Drivers who are convicted of forging, using or altering in any way, the seal of the tachograph with intent to deceive, can be fined up to the statutory maximum of £5000 or be imprisoned for a term not exceeding two years.

The penalty for tampering with tachographs/data, or falsifying record sheets/driver cards, is 2 years imprisonment or the statutory maximum fine (currently £5000), or it can be both.

EC drivers' hours

'Driving' means being at the controls of a vehicle for the purposes of controlling its movement, whether it's moving or stationary with the engine running.

New drivers' hours regulations

A new EU regulation on drivers' hours (Regulation (EC) No 561/2006) was introduced on 11 April 2007. It aims to simplify and clarify the rules and update the exemptions and national deviations. For more information and details of all changes, visit **www.transportoffice.gov.uk** (use **www.businesslink.gov.uk/transport** from April 2009.)

Daily driving

A day is defined as any period of 24 hours beginning when you start other work or driving after the last daily or weekly rest period. The maximum daily hours you may drive is nine. This can be increased to 10 hours twice a week. The daily driving period must be between two daily rest periods, or a daily rest period and a weekly rest period.

daily rest period	4.5 hours driving	45 mins break	4.5 hours driving	45 mins break	1 hr driving	daily rest period

Unforeseen events

Providing road safety is not compromised, a departure from the rules may be permitted. This is only to enable a driver to reach a suitable stopping place. The stopping place should be chosen to ensure the immediate safety of persons, the vehicle or its load.

Drivers must ensure that tachographs are annotated accordingly (on the back of an analogue tachograph chart or on a printout or temporary sheet if using a digital tachograph). The reasons for exceeding driving hours **MUST** be recorded while at

this suitable stopping place. Repeated and regular occurrences could indicate that employers are not scheduling work correctly. Examples of the reasons for such events are

- delays caused by severe weather
- road traffic incidents
- mechanical breakdowns
- interruption of ferry services
- any event likely to cause, or which is already causing, danger to people or animals.

This concession is only to enable drivers to reach a suitable stopping place - not necessarily to complete their planned journey. Drivers and operators would be expected to reschedule any disrupted work to remain in compliance with EU rules. To avoid exceeding drivers' hours when experiencing traffic delays on a motorway, exit at the next junction and find a suitable place to take a break.

During a journey on which the vehicle has been driven on a public road, any driving off the public roads now counts as driving time and should be recorded as such. However, if no driving has been carried out on a public road then it counts as other duty and should be recorded as other work.

Breaks

You must ensure that you take an uninterrupted break of 45 minutes immediately after four and a half hours of driving.

daily rest period	4.5 hours driving	45 mins break	4.5 hours driving	daily rest period

This break may be split into a break of at least 15 minutes followed by a break of at least 30 minutes, each distributed over the driving period. A break MUST be at least 15 minutes to be a qualifying break and the second break MUST be at least 30 minutes to comply with EU rules. A 45-minute break (or split breaks totalling 45 minutes) is required before getting back behind the wheel. During any break you must not drive or undertake any other work. For example:

daily rest period	2 hrs driving	15 mins break	2.5 hrs driving	30 mins break	4.5 hours driving	daily rest period

Employers must schedule work to enable drivers to comply with EC rules on drivers' hours. However, providing road safety is not jeopardised, and to ensure the safety of persons, vehicle or load, a driver may depart from the rules in order to reach a suitable stopping place. Reasons for doing so must be recorded on the back of the tachograph record sheet. This should not be a regular or repeated occurrence, as it would indicate that work was not being correctly scheduled.

Planned breaches of the driver's hours are not permitted. If you are using a digital tachograph you must take a print of your activities and note the reasons on the back of the print.

Daily rest periods

A regular daily rest period means any period
of rest of at least 11 hours.

Alternatively this may be taken in two
periods, the first of which must be an
uninterrupted period of at least 3 hours and
the second an uninterrupted period of at
least 9 hours.

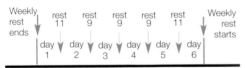

A reduced daily rest period is any period of
rest of at least 9 hours but less than 11 hours.
This reduced daily rest period cannot be
taken more than three times between any
two weekly rest periods.

If you're taking your rest period when
accompanying a vehicle on a ferry or train, a
regular daily rest period may be interrupted
not more than twice by other activities not
exceeding one hour in total. However, the
driver must have access to a bunk or
couchette during that rest period.

Weekly driving

A week means the period of time from
0000 hours on Monday to 2400 hours on
the following Sunday.

Mon 00:00	day 1 9 hrs	day 2 10 hrs	day 3 9 hrs	day 4 10 hrs	day 5 9 hrs	day 6 9 hrs	Sun 24:00

There is a weekly driving limit of 56 hours
and you must not exceed 90 hours in any
two consecutive weeks.

Weekly rest periods

A regular weekly rest period is any period
of rest of at least 45 hours. In any two
consecutive weeks you must take either two
regular weekly rest periods or one regular
weekly rest period and one reduced weekly
rest period of at least 24 hours.

If you take a reduced rest you must add the
period of time by which it was reduced to a
daily or weekly rest period of at least nine
hours before the end of the third week
following the week in question.

A weekly rest period that begins in one week and continues into the following week may be added to either of these weeks.

Sat 08:00 ——————— 45 hours ——————→ Sun 24:00 Mon 05:00

Any period of compensatory rest taken away from base can be taken in a stationary vehicle as long as it has suitable sleeping facilities for each driver.

Weekly rest 33 hrs | Week 1 | Week 2 | Week 3 | Week 4 | Sunday 24:00

Compensation of 12 hours must be paid back by 24:00 on Sunday of the third week following the week of reduced rest.

Catching up on reduced rest

If you've reduced your daily and/or weekly rest periods the compensatory rest must be added to another rest of at least nine hours. You can request to take this at either your base or where your vehicle is based. Rest taken as compensation for the reduction of a weekly rest period must be taken in one continuous block.

Two or more drivers (Multi-manning)

If the vehicle is used by two drivers (multi-manning) each driver should ensure their card is inserted into the correct slot. The driver needs to insert their card into slot 1 and the second person's card goes into slot 2.

The system records availability and time for the driver in the passenger seat who is not currently driving. When the drivers change then the cards are swapped over. By selecting the 'crew' option the system will recognise that the vehicle is being used in a multi-manning capacity.

Multi-manning means that drivers' duties can be spread over 21 hours so that the duty time of the drivers can be extended. During each period of 30 hours, each driver must have a rest period of not less than nine consecutive hours. There must always be two or more drivers travelling with the vehicle for this rule to apply. A driver may take a break while another driver is driving, but not a daily rest period.

The internal clock of a digital tachograph is set to Universal Time Coordinated (UTC). The time display can be set to display any time the driver chooses, however all data recorded to the VU or card will be in UTC.

UTC is effectively the same as Greenwich Mean Time (GMT) so it must be remembered that, during British Summer time, UTC time will be one hour behind BST. Any manual inputs for activities not recorded on a driver card **MUST** take account of the one-hour time difference during British Summer Time.

Domestic drivers' hours

The domestic rules apply to most goods vehicles that are exempt from EC rules.

Driving limits

You must not drive for more than 10 hours in any one day. This limit applies to the time actually spent driving. Off-road driving counts as duty rather than driving time.

Daily duty

You must not be on duty for more than 11 hours on any working day. You're exempt from the daily duty limit on any working day when you don't drive. You will also be exempt from this limit if you don't drive for more than 4 hours on each day of the week.

Exemptions

- Drivers of vehicles used by the armed forces, the police and fire brigades, or those vehicles used for flood protection.

- Drivers who always drive off the public road system.
- Private driving.

Drivers of goods vehicles, including dual-purpose vehicles or those not exceeding 3.5 tonnes MPW, are exempt from the duty limit, but not the driving limit where they are used by

- doctors
- dentists
- nurses
- midwives
- vets.

Vehicles used for any inspection, cleaning, maintenance, repair, installation or fitting

- by a commercial traveller
- by the AA, RAC or RSAC
- for cinematograph or radio and television broadcasting

are included among the exemptions. The domestic rules also allow for events needing immediate action to avoid danger to life or health of people or animals, and for the prevention of serious disruption to essential services or for danger to property.

Keeping records

You must keep a written record of your hours of work on a weekly record sheet, which is available from commercial printers. If you're driving a vehicle in excess of 3.5 tonnes MPW which carries parcels on postal services you must use a tachograph.

Mixed EC and domestic driving

It's possible that you may drive under EC rules and domestic rules during a week or even one day. You can choose to drive under EC rules for the whole of the time. If you use a combination of both sets of rules you must ensure that EC limits are not exceeded when driving vehicles on EC work.

You can't use the time driving under EC rules as off-duty time under the domestic rules; driving under EC rules counts towards the driving and duty limits under the domestic rules. Similarly, you can't claim driving and other work under domestic rules as rest time for EC rules. Remember, any EC driving in a week means that you must take daily and weekly rest periods.

Rules on Working Time

Drivers subject to the UK domestic drivers' hours rules are affected by four provisions under the Horizontal Amending Directive (HAD), introduced on 1 August 2003. These are:

- a requirement to limit hours to no more than an average 48 hour week (although individuals will be allowed to 'opt-out' of this requirement, if they want to)
- an entitlement to 4 weeks paid annual leave
- health checks for night workers
- an entitlement for adequate rest.

The reference period for calculating the 48-hour average working week is normally a rolling 17-week period. However, this reference period can be extended up to 26 weeks if representatives from both sides of industry can agree to do so.

Self-employed drivers are not subject to the HAD, but they may be affected by the road transport directive in 2009.

Drivers subject to EU drivers' hours and tachograph rules are required to adhere to separate working time provisions under the Road Transport (Working Time) Regulations, which came into force in March 2005. The following are the main provisions of the UK's implementing regulations:

Weekly Working Time - must not exceed an average of 48 hours per week (calculated over the reference period of 17 weeks). A maximum working time of 60 hours can be performed in any single week, providing the average 48-hour limit is not exceeded.

Night Work - will be limited to 10 hours working time in a 24-hour period, where any work is carried out during the night time period 0000 - 0400 hrs. The 10-hour limit may be exceeded if this is permitted under a collective or workforce agreement. Night work means any work performed during night time.

Breaks - When driving is being carried out, the break provisions under EU drivers' hours rules (EC/561/2006) take precedence. However, drivers are not permitted to work for more than 6 consecutive hours without a break. Where working hours total between 6 & 9 hours a day, a break of at least 30 minutes is required. A further 15 minute break is required (45 minutes in total) if total working hours exceed 9 hours. Break periods can be divided, but their duration must be at least 15 minutes long. During a 9-hour shift, at least 30 minutes of break must be taken.

Rest - Same as EU (561/2006) or AETR drivers' hours rules.

Record keeping - Records need to be kept for two years after the period in question.

As stated previously, the reference period for calculating the 48 hour week is normally 17 weeks, but it can be extended to 26 weeks if this is permitted under a collective or workforce agreement. There is no 'opt-out' for individuals wishing to work longer than an average 48 hour week, but break periods and periods of availability (POA) will not count as working time.

Periods of Availability

Generally speaking, a period of availability is waiting time, the period and duration of which is known about in advance by the mobile worker. (For definition of 'mobile worker' see Glossary on page 322). This must be known before departure or just before the start of the period in question.

To meet the requirements of being a POA, a mobile worker should not be required to remain at their workstation (eg cab) but may

do so if they wish or need to do so for security or safety reasons. However they must be available to

- answer calls to start work
- resume driving on request.

Mobile workers do not need to be formally notified about a POA and its duration. It is enough to know about it in advance, for example if

- someone (who does not have to be their employer) has told them
- they have arrived too early for their allocated slot
- they always experience a delay at one of their regular customers.

There are no requirements as to the minimum and maximum length of a POA.

Changes to POA - If having been told in advance that the POA is to be, for example, 60 minutes duration, but this becomes extended to 90 minutes, then only the first 60 minutes would qualify as a POA with the remaining 30 minutes being other work. This is only applicable if the mobile worker is not notified in advance of the additional 30 minutes of waiting.

If having been told the POA is to be 60 minutes but the mobile worker is then told to start work after only 30 minutes, then only 30 minutes would qualify as a POA with the other 30 minutes being recorded as either driving or other work.

Examples of a POA - Situations when a period of time could be recorded as a POA (provided the 'known in advance' precondition is met) can be

- time when accompanying a vehicle being transported by boat or train
- time spent waiting at frontiers
- when driving or travelling as part of a team, time spent sitting next to the driver while the vehicle is in motion - unless the mobile worker is taking a break or performing any other work (eg navigation). This time (or a part of it) could also be counted as a break - but would need to be recorded as such
- waiting for someone to load or unload their vehicle, if they know about the length of the delay at the start of the period because
  - someone has told them
  - they have arrived too early for their slot
  - they always experience a delay at one of their regular customers
- where a mobile worker reports for work but is informed that they are not required to undertake any duties for a specified period (although they need to remain on site to answer calls and be ready to take up work)
- if the vehicle breaks down and the mobile worker is told how long it will take to be rescued.

Examples of situations where a period of time should NOT be recorded as a POA are

- where a driver is diverted due to a road closure, he/she would still be driving so the period could not be counted as a POA
- delays due to congestion (ie stuck in a traffic jam) would not count as a POA because the driver would be stopping and starting the vehicle
- if a mobile worker is monitoring activity by others (eg petrol at filling station, or the unloading of the lorry) - this time would count as working time rather than a POA.

These are examples only. Further information on periods of availability can be found on
www.dft.gov.uk/pgr/freight/road/workingtime/ or contact VOSA (see page 313).

Operator licensing - the driver's responsibilities

Goods vehicle operator licensing

In Great Britain, users of most commercial goods vehicles weighing over 3.5 tonnes must have a goods vehicle operator's licence. This applies even if they use a hired vehicle or only use the vehicle for one day.

The licence authorises an operator to use a maximum total number of motor vehicles and trailers from a specific operating centre or centres where the vehicles are normally kept when not in use.

You need to

- satisfy the traffic commissioner that your operating centre(s) is/are suitable

- list information about the vehicles which will be kept there.

- provide evidence that you are entitled to use the operating centre if you do not own it.

There are three types of Operator's licence

- Restricted, which allows an operator to carry his/her own goods in connection with his/her business

- Standard National, which allows an operator to carry his/her own goods and goods for other people for hire or reward in Great Britain

- Standard International, which allows an operator to carry his/her own goods

and goods for other people for hire or reward, both in Great Britain and on international journeys.

Each vehicle operating under these licences must display a disc in the windscreen. The discs are colour-coded

- orange for Restricted

- blue for Standard National

- green for Standard International.

Licence applications are made to statutorily independent Traffic Commissioners, who are appointed by the Secretary of State for Transport. Great Britain is divided into six Traffic Areas (for contact details of the Traffic Area Offices, see pages 310-311).

An operator must hold a licence in each Traffic Area where an operating centre or centres exist. A free guide for operators summarising the legislation is available from Traffic Area Offices.

If you wish to appeal against a Traffic Commissioner's decision or require further details of the appeals procedure, a free booklet can be obtained from

The Transport Tribunal
48-49 Chancery Lane
London WC2A 1JR
Tel: 020 7947 7493.

The booklet is also available from your local Traffic Area Office.

Northern Ireland operations

Northern Ireland has a separate system administered in the province by the Road Transport Licensing Division of the Driver and Vehicle Agency (DVA). It is not necessary for operators in the province to obtain a short term 'O' licence before entering Great Britain. Holders of current 'O' licences or Northern Ireland Road Freight Operator Licences are permitted to carry goods in each country.

The driver's responsibility for the receipt, carriage and delivery of goods

The driver is responsible for the contents of their vehicle and needs to ensure that it is loaded correctly for stability and ease of access. The goods should be delivered to the appropriate persons at the agreed time within the deadlines set. Always allow sufficient time to get to the individual premises but do not allow a deadline to make you exceed the speed limits for the area or conditions.

The goods should arrive in the condition they were in when collected or loaded onto the vehicle. Do not let lack of attention cause damage to the goods during loading or unloading. The goods should be delivered in accordance with any agreed conditions set for that contract. Operators can limit their liability for any lost, delayed or damaged goods by issuing conditions of carriage.

Encouraging customers to check (where possible) and sign for handover of goods will prevent incorrect deliveries. Any required paperwork should be kept to enable work records to be maintained. If a customer is not around to check and sign for a delivery the delivery note and goods should be returned to the depot.

It is good practice for a carrier to sign a receipt or consignment note acknowledging acceptance of the goods to be carried. A signed receipt for delivery of the consignment should also be obtained from the consignee. The absence of such documents can complicate the situation under any dispute involving incorrect goods or damage in transit.

Know the regulations

In addition to the rules and regulations that apply to drivers' hours, vehicles and loads, you should be sure that you comply with any regulations which affect your

- health
- conduct
- vehicle
- driving
- licence
- safety.

It's essential that you know and keep up-to-date with the regulations and the latest official advice.

Driving in Europe

Driving in Europe

When driving in Europe you must carry your national driving licence, insurance certificate and vehicle registration document. You will also need to carry your passport with you at all times - many countries require visitors to do so as a valid form of ID. Other documentation may also be required for some countries.

International carriage of goods by road

Any goods being carried for hire or reward on international journeys under the provision of the Convention on the Contract for the International Carriage of Goods by Road (CMR) must be recorded on CMR consignment notes. These consignment notes confirm that carriage is being undertaken in agreement with the CMR Convention. There are four copies:

- red - kept by the consignor (sender)
- blue - for the consignee
- green - travels with the vehicle
- white with black border - retained by the originator.

Usually the carrier completes the CMR note. However, most of the information relates to the consignor therefore it is a good idea for them to complete the documents. When the goods have been delivered the consignee is asked to sign the CMR form.

Under the CMR convention the carrier is responsible for any loss or damage to the goods, after taking over and before delivering them. The rules regulate the responsibilities and potential liabilities of the carrier when engaged in international transport for hire or reward. The convention does not apply to

- any carriage performed under the terms of any international postal arrangements
- any funeral consignments
- any furniture removal.

Where it is necessary to divide the consignment, separate consignment notes can be made for the individual parts of the consignment.

This Convention applies to every contract for the carriage of goods by road, when the place taking over of the goods and the place designated for delivery, as specified in the contract, are situated in two different countries. One of these countries must be the contracting country, irrespective of the place of residence and the nationality of the parties.

Consignment notes for own-account carriage by road

Own-account operators are not required to use CMR consignment notes for international journeys. Any journey that can be shown as on own account, not for hire or reward, need only have a simple consignment note.

Customs procedures and documentation

Since 1993 goods being shipped to EU countries are no longer classified as exports. They are known as despatches as long as they are of EU origin and in free circulation within the EU. They are classed as having Community status, can be transported between EU member states and are no longer subject to Customs procedures. These goods require an invoice, a transport document or a completed copy 4 of the Single Administration Document (SAD).

Carriage of illegal immigrants

Customs requirements for exports outside the EU

A declaration of entry must be made to HM Revenue and Customs if exporting to non-EU countries (with certain exceptions).

Road hauliers may be liable for penalties if they bring illegal immigrants into the UK in their vehicles. Each individual responsible person (eg the vehicle owner, hirer and driver) may receive a penalty of up to £2000 for each illegal immigrant carried.

The legislation requires road hauliers to operate an effective system to protect their vehicles against the carriage of illegal immigrants. It is only by operating an effective system that penalties can be avoided in the event that illegal immigrants are carried.

An effective system comprises three separate areas - vehicle security, vehicle checking and documentation.

Vehicle security

The vehicle owner should ensure that the outer fabric of the vehicle does not permit unauthorised access (for example through cuts or tears) and that they can be properly secured. They should provide security devices, depending on the type of vehicle.

- Hard-sided vehicles (eg box trailers) - the rear doors and any external storage compartments should be secured with an integral lock, padlock or seal. All locks and padlocks should be robust and maintained in working order. Seals should be numbered and spares should be provided in case it becomes necessary to re-secure the vehicle during its journey.
- Soft-sided vehicles (eg tilt and curtain-sided trailers) - a security (TIR) cord should be provided, in good condition, with a padlock or seal to join the cord after fitting. Any external storage compartments should be treated as above.

TIR procedures

TIR stands for "Transport Internationale Routiers" which, when translated, means International Road Transport. It is an international transit system allowing goods to travel across one or more international borders with the minimum of customs involvement.

In order to ensure that goods may travel with a minimum intervention en route and yet offer maximum safeguards for Customs administrations in all countries of transit, the TIR regime contains five basic requirements or principles. TIR can be used in the EC for movements which

- begin or end in a non-EC country
- are destined for an EC Member State via a third country, or
- consist of consignments for split delivery to destinations in the EC and in non-EC countries.

You cannot use TIR for transit movements that are entirely within the EC.

Seals

One of the most important features of the TIR system is that containers and vehicles must be sealed by Customs. The seals will be checked at Customs offices en route and at the office of destination to ensure that they have not been broken or tampered with.

Before removing the seals, Customs at the office of destination will check that the seals applied to the container or vehicle are intact and are as described.

If you discover that an official seal has been tampered with or broken you must notify Customs immediately. If the breakage is found on your own premises, you should report the facts to your local control office. If it is found on a vehicle or container in which you are carrying goods under

Customs control, then you should report to Customs at your destination as soon as you arrive there. If there is also extensive damage to the vehicle or container and/or the goods, report to your nearest Customs office at once.

In all cases the Customs officer may ask you to explain how any seal breakage and damage occurred. In all cases of unauthorised seal breakage you must obtain a Customs officer's permission before you remove or unload the goods originally secured by that seal.

An accident or other unforeseen incident that occurs during a transit operation must be brought to the attention of Customs at the first opportunity. Wherever possible, prior authorisation must be obtained from Customs if seals have to be broken or the goods need to be transferred from one vehicle to another. An account of the incident must be noted on the transit declaration, then both goods and declaration must be presented to the nearest Customs authority. When Customs are content that the operation may continue they will reseal the goods and endorse the declaration accordingly.

Vehicle checking

An effective system must provide for checking of the vehicle at appropriate times during its journey to the UK. You, as the driver, will normally be responsible for checking the vehicle. You should check the vehicle at the following times:

Final loading - check the interior of the vehicle when the vehicle is loaded before departure for the UK. This includes checking of any external storage compartments if they are fitted. If you are collecting cargo from different places, this check should be at the final loading point. If you are not able to carry out this check, you should get confirmation in writing from the person responsible for the final loading that there are no unauthorised persons within the vehicle. Immediately after this check, the vehicle (including any external storage compartments) should be secured with appropriate devices

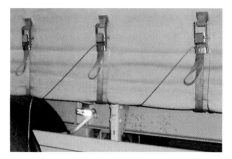

During the journey - you should check that the vehicle's security has not been breached after any stops made whilst travelling to the port of embarkation, particularly if the vehicle has been left unattended. Physically examine security cords, seals and locks for any signs of tampering. The underside of the vehicle should also be checked as would-be illegal immigrants sometimes hide on vehicle axles or in storage areas beneath vehicles

Final check - where the immigration control for traffic travelling to the UK operates in a control zone outside the UK, penalties can be imposed if illegal immigrants are found in vehicles at any time within the control zone (currently operating at Calais, Coquelles and Dunkirk). If you are using these routes, a final check must be carried out before entering the control zone.

If you are travelling through other ports, the final check should be made immediately before boarding the ferry for the UK. The final check should include the security cord (if fitted) and any locks or seals. Also check the underside of the vehicle, its roof and wind deflector (if fitted). If you haven't been able to secure the vehicle properly, the final check should include a thorough manual check of the vehicle's interior

Checks provided by port operators - make use of vehicle checks provided by port operators. These are not foolproof, however, and may not always detect the presence of illegal immigrants. You are responsible for carrying out the final vehicle check.

Documentation

The operator should provide you with a document including

- instructions on how to secure the vehicle
- when and how to check the vehicle
- advice on what to do if illegal immigrants are suspected of being in the vehicle, or if the vehicle's security is breached or compromised.

This document must be carried with the vehicle so that it may be produced immediately for immigration officers, if requested. This should also include a checklist, which acts as a reminder for you to carry out the checks required and enables you to keep a record of the checks you have carried out. This will help to show that an effective system was operated in the event that illegal immigrants are carried (see page 140 for example checklist).

Methods of entry

There are several common ways in which access is gained to vehicles. Some are listed below.

- Unauthorised entry is often gained to soft-sided (including curtain-sided) vehicles because a security cord, properly joined with a seal or padlock, is absent, and to hard-sided vehicles because its doors are not locked or sealed.
- Security cords can be cut and rejoined. Physically checking the cord by pulling on it will usually bring this to notice.
- Seals and padlocks can be broken and rejoined. This can often be revealed by physically checking the seal or padlock.
- Entry gained by cutting the canvas side or roof of the vehicle can be identified through proper checking (particularly at the final check).
- Some illegal immigrants hide beneath vehicles, for example on an axle or in panniers; consequently, checking these areas is vital.

The above examples are not exhaustive. Intending illegal immigrants will look for any possible means of entering a vehicle which can often be achieved in no more than a few minutes.

> **Remember,** it is only by properly operating an effective system that penalties can be avoided if illegal immigrants are carried.

Company name _____ **Vehicle number** _____

Loaded at _____ **Trailer number** _____

Date _____

CHECK	After Loading	1st Stop	2nd Stop	Final CHECK [3]	Extra
Date					Check if time between 3rd party-check + embarkation > 15 min
Vehicle/Trailer inside	Yes / No				
Tilts & Roof checked for damage	Yes / No	Yes / No	Yes / No	Yes / No	Yes / No
External compartments checked	Yes / No	Yes / No	Yes / No	Yes / No	Yes / No
Below vehicle checked	Yes / No	Yes / No	Yes / No	Yes / No	Yes / No
TIR cord tight and in place and checked [1]	Yes / No	Yes / No	Yes / No	Yes / No	Yes / No
Seal in place and checked [2]	Yes / No	Yes / No	Yes / No	Yes / No	Yes / No
Padlock in place and checked [2]	Yes / No	Yes / No	Yes / No	Yes / No	Yes / No
Seal/Padlock number					
Cabin check	Yes / No	Yes / No	Yes / No	Yes / No	Yes / No
'3rd Party' check e.g. CO2, PMMW)				Yes / No	Yes / No
Time checked					
Driver's signature					

[1] The TIR Security Cord should be checked physically for evidence of tampering, in particular for signs that it has been cut and rejoined.

[2] Seals and padlocks should be checked physically to ensure they have not been cut or broken and repaired. If a padlock is difficult to open or close this may suggest it has been tampered with.

[3] If travelling through Calais, Coquelles or Dunkirk, the final check should be carried out before entering the UK Control Zone. If using another port, the final check should take place immediately before boarding the ferry.

140

Your health and conduct

Many collisions happen due to inattention and distraction, as well as failure to observe the rules of the road. These are published in an easy-to-understand format in *The Highway Code*. The DSA publication *Driving - the essential skills* also gives very useful information about best driving practice.

This is in addition to the specialist advice available for goods vehicle drivers given in this book.

Health issues

Even apparently simple illnesses can affect your reactions. You should be on your guard against the effects of

- flu symptoms
- hay fever
- a common cold
- tiredness.

Worries or lack of concentration can also affect your driving ability so always take care whenever you drive.

Fatigue and mental ability

Much research, into the effects of fatigue and sleep-related vehicle incidents (SRVIs), has been undertaken on behalf of the Department for Transport. This research has shown that about 40% of SRVIs are probably work-related as they involve commercial vehicles. These incidents are more likely to result in serious injury than the average road incident, because they often involve running off the road or into the back of another vehicle, and are worsened by the high speed of impact (ie no braking beforehand).

There is a particular risk when driving between 2 am and 7 am because this is when the body clock is in a daily trough. There is another, smaller, trough between about 2 pm and 4 pm. It has been shown that SRVIs are more evident in male drivers up to 30 years of age who often deny or ignore that they are suffering the effects of sleep loss or sleepiness.

It has been shown that sleepy drivers are normally aware of their sleepiness. However, there is always the possibility that drivers who are already mildly sleepy, because of previous sleep disturbance or insufficient sleep, are more vulnerable to any additional sleep loss and perhaps may not easily perceive an **increase** in sleepiness. If you begin to feel sleepy, stop in a safe place before you get to the stage of fighting sleep. Sleep can ensue more rapidly than you would imagine.

The most effective countermeasures to sleepiness are caffeine and a short (about 15 minutes) nap or doze. The two combined - caffeine (in the form of a caffeinated drink, for example, two cups of caffeinated coffee) followed by a nap - are particularly effective. This is because caffeine takes 20-30 minutes to be absorbed and act on the brain, hence the opportunity for a nap. However, this should be considered as a temporary measure only.

Fatigue can lead to reduced concentration and can also impair your reaction time. To avoid fatigue, it is important to take proper rest before starting duty and to take adequate rest breaks during driving and between duty periods. Always take planned rest breaks and, if necessary, take more rest than is required by law.

Falling asleep

Falling asleep whilst driving accounts for a significant proportion of vehicle incidents, particularly under monotonous driving conditions. Incidents where vehicles have

- left the road
- collided with broken-down vehicles, police patrol officers and other people on the hard shoulder of motorways

have been attributed to the problem of drivers falling asleep at the wheel.

Be on your guard against boredom on comparatively empty roads or motorways, especially at night. Always

- take planned rest breaks
- keep fresh air circulating around the driving area
- avoid allowing the driving area to become too warm
- avoid driving if you aren't 100 per cent fit
- avoid driving after a heavy meal.

Whenever you drive, if you start to feel tired, stop at the next lay-by or pull off the motorway (or slip road) as soon as it is safe and legal to do so. Walking around in the

fresh air can refresh you in the short term but this is no substitute for adequate rest. The introduction of

- air-suspension driver's seats
- floating cab suspension
- air suspension on vehicles
- quieter, smoother diesel engines
- more widely adopted sound-proofing materials

has produced a comfortable cocoon environment where you'll spend most of your working day. This can easily cause tiredness.

Effects of shift work

Working shifts can affect rest and sleep cycles. It's tempting to continue as usual when at home, eg undertaking domestic duties or socialising. However, you need to ensure you don't complete them at the cost of rest/sleep. Be flexible - you may need to change times/days when jobs are done.

Shifts that mean your routine differs from those of friends and family can leave you feeling isolated. It's important to make the effort not to lose contact with them. Things you can do to help include

- talking to them about shift work
- making them aware of your schedule so they include you when planning social activities
- planning mealtimes, weekends and evenings together and making the most of your free time

- inviting others who work similar shifts to join you in social activities.

Drugs

Drug abuse has now reached the point where well known multinational companies have introduced random drug testing for their drivers. Those drivers who fail such tests may face instant dismissal.

It should be obvious that you must not take any of the drugs that are generally accepted as banned substances whilst driving. These include

- amphetamines (eg diet pills)
- methylamphetamines (MDMA)
- benzodiazepine (tranquillizers)
- methaqualone (sleeping pills)
- barbiturates (sleeping pills)
- propoxyphane
- phencyclidine (Angel Dust)
- cannabis
- cocaine

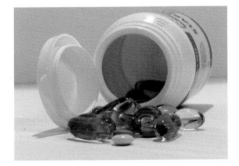

Check whether any medication will cause drowsiness

- heroin
- morphine/codeine.

Unlike alcohol (the effects of which last for about 24-48 hours) many of the effects of drugs will remain in the system for up to 72 hours.

Off-the-shelf remedies, even everyday cold or flu remedies, can cause drowsiness. Read the labels carefully. If in doubt, consult either your doctor or pharmacist. If still in doubt, don't drive.

Alcohol

It's an offence to drive with more than

- a breath alcohol level in excess of 35 µg per 100 ml
- a blood alcohol level in excess of 80 mg per 100 ml.

Be aware that alcohol may remain in the body for around 24-48 hours. Your reactions may be reduced, and the effects will still be evident the next morning so you could fail a breath test. Your body tissues actually need up to 48 hours to recover, although your breath/blood alcohol levels may appear normal after 24 hours.

If you're convicted of a drink–driving offence while driving an ordinary motor vehicle, a driving ban will result in you losing your LGV entitlement and your livelihood.

Remember, don't drink if you are going to drive.

143

Smoking in work vehicles

Following the introduction of legislation during 2006 and 2007, you must not smoke in vehicles used for work purposes in certain prescribed circumstances. Separate regulations apply to England, Wales and Scotland. Your vehicle will also need to have no smoking signs displayed inside the cab area.

Further information can be found on the following websites:

www.smokefreeengland.co.uk

www.clearingtheairscotland.com

www.smokingbanwales.co.uk

Smoking restrictions also apply to all work premises.

Seat belts

It is compulsory for drivers and passengers, in vehicles constructed or adapted to carry goods, to wear their seat belts while making deliveries or collections when travelling over 50 metres.

If children are travelling as passengers in the vehicle, they must wear a child restraint appropriate to their size. The only exception is for an occasional short journey, when, if a child restraint is not available, then an adult belt must be worn.

The number of passengers should not exceed the number of seats fitted with seat belts and child restraints.

Remember, where seat belts are fitted they must be worn.

Health and safety

It has been estimated that up to a third of all road traffic incidents (RTIs) involved somebody who was at work at the time. This may account for over 20 fatalities and 250 serious injuries every week. Incidents involving goods vehicles account for less than 8% of all deaths and injuries caused by road traffic incidents.

The total value of prevention of UK road traffic incidents in 2005 was estimated to be £17,851m. This figure represents the total value, to the community, of the benefits of incident prevention, and includes the following

- costs of ambulance and hospital treatment
- human costs representing pain, suffering, loss of life
- loss of output.

Companies can suffer substantial downtime and staff may need time to recover, which leads to more vehicles off the road and lost business. Road safety is of paramount importance and it is the responsibility of all drivers to try to reduce the number of incidents on the road.

Incidents at work

Incidents at work are not restricted to road traffic incidents. The haulage and distribution industry has a high rate of other types of incident. Excluding road traffic incidents, over a five-year period, studies show that 60 employees were killed, 5000 were seriously injured and 23,000 suffered injuries severe enough to keep them off work for three or more days.*

Almost all deaths at work arise from one of the following

- being struck by a moving vehicle
- falling loads
- falls from vehicles.

Many major injuries happen during loading and unloading and are caused by

- slips and trips
- collapsing or overturning vehicles
- being struck by moving or falling objects
- falls from less than 2 metres
- manual handling.

Manual handling and slips and trips account for two thirds of other reportable injuries.

Parking a vehicle on soft ground for loading and unloading is particularly dangerous. The ground may shift under the weight, causing the vehicle to become unstable or roll over.

Drivers very often need to work at height on a vehicle and falls from vehicles are some of their most common injuries. Managers should consider the following points when trying to minimise the risks

- reducing the need for people to work at height or providing equipment for safe access such as scaffolds, handrails, access steps, gantries and platforms.

*Health and Safety in Road Haulage, published by HSE.

- positioning the load so that items to be unloaded first are the most accessible will reduce the need to climb onto the load

- allowing enough time to complete loading and unloading. This will reduce the risk of slips, trips and falls as drivers will be less rushed

- providing training in how to avoid slips and trips

- ensuring incidents and defects with safety equipment are reported and rectified

- ensuring safe handling of loads at sites of delivery and collection by communicating with clients and suppliers before arrival

- ensuring that appropriate cleaning equipment is provided as well as waste disposal to keep the area tidy. Diesel spills, oil and grease may be picked up on the soles of footwear and spread to other surfaces, making them slippery. Contaminants need to be removed so there must be safe access for cleaning and maintenance

- considering the effects of weather conditions. Falls may be caused by high winds, rain, snow and ice. These conditions can make surfaces slippery and affect balance

- being aware that yards may have potholes and uneven surfaces.

Deliveries and Collections

Deliveries and collections can be dangerous activities. Injuries may result from manual handling, being hit by a vehicle or from falling. Reasonable steps should be taken to prevent incidents. These involve communication between the supplier, haulage company and the person receiving the load (the 'dutyholders'). These parties have a responsibility to inform one another, decide on appropriate safety measures and ensure they are put into practice. Such measures may include

- wearing high-visibility clothing

- designating a responsible person who will be in overall charge of the loading and unloading of visiting vehicles

- knowing what to do if a load has shifted

- ensuring the correct methods of loading and unloading, including the correct equipment, are used

- training drivers in general safety plus what to do if a site does not conform to acceptable safety standards. A driver should be able to recognise a dangerous practice and refuse to load or unload

- encouraging drivers to report any incidents and telling them who to contact

- use of platforms with slip-resistant surfaces, handrails and access steps that remain with the vehicle

- work restraint systems that make it impossible for a worker to get into a dangerous position from which they could fall, such as a harness and lanyard.

To ensure safety, it's important to observe speed limits imposed by the company when driving on site.

Falls from vehicles

Every year 700 people die or are seriously injured falling from vehicles. To minimise the risk of falling from a vehicle

- when entering the vehicle, always open the door fully, use both grab rails to enter the cab, making sure all the steps are used.
- when exiting the cab, turn around and use grab rails with both hands, making sure all steps are used
- don't jump from the lorry or load. Use any steps provided, ensuring that they are safe for you to use
- always use all equipment provided to avoid work at height. If work at height is unavoidable then use fall arrest systems, if possible, especially when roping and sheeting
- keep the lorry tidy - avoid creating tripping hazards
- wear suitable footwear for the job
- ensure steps and work areas are well lit
- use edge protection on tail lifts (where it is fitted)
- do not walk backwards near the rear or side of the vehicle bed
- only use equipment such as ropes, straps, curtains, sheets, nets etc, if you are sure they are well-maintained and in a good state of repair.

To help improve the working environment, you should report any

- damaged or broken sheeting devices

- damaged, loose or inadequate steps and handholds
- slippery surfaces, for example those that are oily or greasy.

Many more activities have become the subject of Health and Safety regulations. These include

- limits to the weight of objects that should be lifted manually, eg loading packages
- provision of protective clothing
  - reflective jackets
  - boots
  - gloves
  - warm clothing
  - hard hats

where appropriate to the nature of the work.

Asbestos

During vehicle maintenance, drivers should be aware of the dangers to health from asbestos dust, especially when dealing with components known to contain this material, such as

- brake shoes
- clutch plates
- tank or pipe lagging.

Safe working practice

Extra care must be taken when working

- near or over inspection pits (danger of falling)
- in refrigerated vehicles which may have wet or slippery floors

- under hydraulically raised tipper bodies (danger of being crushed – use props)
- near engines emitting exhaust fumes (breathing problems)
- with solvents or degreasing agents (lung and skin problems)
- close to vehicle batteries (risk of burns or explosion)
- at the rear of a vehicle fitted with a tail-lift mechanism (foot injuries)
- in or near paint spray shops (lung problems from vapour).

Before you open your cab door, check all round for safety to ensure you do not hit other people, obstructions or vehicles. Also, make sure you have checked that the parking brake is properly applied before either leaving, or working near, your vehicle.

First aid at work

There are regulations governing the provision of adequate first aid facilities and first aiders on any work premises. The extent of what needs to be provided depends on the number of staff, type of business, risk assessments, etc.

Examples of the various risk factor levels are shown below:

Low risk areas - shops, offices, libraries

Medium risk areas - light engineering and assembly work, food processing, warehousing

High risk areas - most construction sites, slaughterhouses, chemical manufacture, extensive work with dangerous machinery or sharp instruments.

There should be first aid facilities of some form in every work place or, at the very least, a first aid kit available. All staff should be aware of where this is located. The minimum first aid provision on any work site is

- a suitably stocked first aid box
- an appointed person to take charge of first aid arrangements and to keep the first aid box suitably stocked.

The appointed person should be available at all times when people are at work on the site, but should not attempt to give first aid for which they have not been trained. There are several short courses available which include particular details surrounding first aid at work. Also, anyone can take a first aid course (see page 228 for details of various course providers).

Many small injuries occur in the work place - these can be very minor, and most do not require hospital treatment. However, to avoid the risk of infection, any wound should be cleaned and properly covered at the first opportunity, especially if

- the work area is dirty or dusty
- the work involves
  - using machinery or tools
  - handling of goods (ie manual loading/unloadng)
  - working with foodstuffs
  - dealing with livestock
  - using chemicals or other possible contaminants.

If, while on site, you incur a minor injury such as a cut or graze, or are helping someone else who has incurred such an injury, you need to take certain precautions to protect yourself as well as the person you are helping. To minimise the risk of infection, you should

- wash and dry your hands before giving any treatment
- protect yourself by wearing disposable gloves
- carefully and gently clean the cut or graze and surrounding skin to remove any dirt and surface debris
- gently pat the area dry

- cover the area with a sterile dressing. You should not use adhesive plasters as these can cause skin irritation.

Record-keeping

The company or site should have an accident book or some other method of logging and recording details about injuries such as

- name and job of injured person
- date, place and time of incident
- details of injury/illness and any treatment given
- what happened to the casualty immediately afterwards (eg back to work, home, hospital)
- name and signature of person dealing with the incident.

You should always ensure that any book or log is properly completed so that a record exists, should complications develop from the injury at a later date. The data recorded can also help identify accident trends and possible areas for improvement in the control of health and safety risks.

Personal protection

Even if the activities involved in collection, transport and delivery of your payload have no requirement for such things as headgear, ear protection or safety glasses, two of the most important and essential safety items for use at all times are

- a hi-vis jacket or vest to maximise your visibility
- protective footwear to guard feet against drop or crush injuries.

Protective footwear

Footwear is an important consideration in the prevention of incidents at work. Steel toecaps help to protect drivers from falling objects and slip-resistant shoes help prevent slips, trips and falls. It is also important to clean mud etc, off shoes to stop surfaces becoming slippery in the first place.

Differing types of protective footwear can also guard against things like corrosive substances, oil or heat. It is important to ensure you have those most relevant to your job.

High-visibility clothing

High-visibility clothing is especially important when loading or unloading - there could be other vehicles reversing in the area around you or forklift trucks in operation.

You should also make sure you are clearly visible during rest stops, vehicle checks or breakdowns, where you may be outside your vehicle adjacent to moving traffic.

Personal protective equipment (PPE)

Your operator should provide you with any protective equipment essential to perform your duties, but it is your responsibility to ensure that you use them properly for your own safety, even if they are only required occasionally for a specific task. In addition to a hi-vis jacket and protective footwear, other examples of important protective items might include

- hard hat or other protective headgear
- heat or corrosion-resistant gloves
- safety glasses/protective goggles
- face mask/breathing apparatus
- ear protectors/plugs.

For example, wet cement can cause skin irritation and burns. Gloves and overalls with long sleeves and trousers should be worn whilst loading and unloading it. In the event of contact the area of skin should be washed with both warm and cold, clear running water.

If you transport animals, you may also have to pass through infection control areas or decontamination procedures such as foot dips, walk-through disinfectant baths or hosing areas, for which you should have the appropriate waterproof clothing and footwear. Make sure you carefully follow any instructions or procedures provided by your operator.

Personal safety awareness

Consider your personal safety throughout any journey, especially if the load you are carrying has high commercial value, such as tobacco, alcohol, etc. There is always the possibility of an attempted theft or hi-jacking incident. Be aware of what is going on around you, especially if you have a regular known delivery route.

During breaks, walk-round checks or when locking/unlocking your vehicle, etc, proceed with caution - watch for anything unusual such as people who seem to be loitering or taking an interest in your activities. Activating the vehicle alarm could make any potential assailant back off or leave the scene. Follow any instructions given by your operator, stay aware and stay safe.

Defusing an awkward situation

Occasionally you may experience a situation where another person displays a confrontational attitude, for example following a minor road traffic incident.

If a situation does develop, stay in your vehicle if you can as it gives some physical protection. If you are already out of your vehicle when a situation develops, you can use body language to help calm things down by

- speaking in gentle, mild tones - you will seem less threatening
- keeping your hands raised and open at midriff level while talking, and not pointing

- not standing too close or making body contact, this can be misinterpreted.

Don't aggravate any situation by losing your temper or focusing on who was to blame. Most situations can be defused by using three steps, in the specific order shown below. You need to be

- **calming** - listening and encouraging them to keep talking for as long as they need
- **assuring** - repeating their main points back to them to show understanding
- **controlling** - offering a solution or a way out which is mutually acceptable.

If the situation deteriorates at any time, return to step one. Continue to show your willingness to listen until the other person has calmed sufficiently, then move on through the process gradually until resolution is reached.

Your vehicle

The law relating to vehicles is extensive. Manufacturers, operators and drivers must all obey specific regulations.

The manufacturer is responsible for ensuring that the vehicle is built to comply with the Construction and Use Regulations.

The operator is responsible for making sure that a vehicle

- continues to comply with those regulations
- meets all current requirements and new regulations as they're introduced
- is tested as required
- displays all required markings, discs and certificates
- is in a serviceable condition, including equipment, fittings and fixtures.

In addition, the operator must operate a system of reporting and recording any faults that may affect the roadworthiness of the vehicle. This reporting system should enable drivers of the vehicle to report such defects, both verbally and in writing, and have them solved effectively and rectified before the

vehicle is used. This should include problems associated with the tachograph function or speed limiter.

Operators should make drivers aware of their legal responsiblities regarding vehicle condition. It is important for all operators to ensure that company procedures for defect reporting are fully understood by their drivers. The driver shares responsibility for vehicle roadworthiness with the operator. This means a driver may be liable for prosecution if they are considered partly or wholly responsible for the existence of the found defect. It could also result in the loss of the driver's licence.

The operator shouldn't cause or permit a vehicle to be operated in any way other than the law allows. It is recommended that written records of faults and corrections to any vehicle should be kept by the operator, as a historical reference, with other documents for that vehicle. Where drivers are expected to make minor repairs themselves (eg light bulb replacement) operators should bear in mind that they may need basic training.

Daily defect checks

Daily defect checks are vital, and the results of such checks should be recorded. In addition to daily checks, the driver must monitor the roadworthiness of the vehicle when it is being driven and be alert to an indication that the vehicle is developing a fault (eg warning lights, exhaust emitting too much smoke, vibrations).

Vehicle maintenance records must be kept covering the previous 15 months. If you are an owner-driver with no-one to whom you can report defects, then you just need to record and retain defect records yourself for the prescribed 15-month period.

It is recommended that any reporting system should incorporate 'nil' reporting, when each driver makes out a report sheet confirming that the daily check has been carried out and no defects found. Nil reports are not required under the conditions of operator licensing. However they are a useful means of confirming that daily checks are being carried out.

Drivers should report any defects on the vehicle's defect report sheet and ensure faults are rectified before moving the vehicle. Details should include

- vehicle registration or identification mark
- date
- details of the defect or symptoms
- the name of the driver/reporter.

The reporting system should include a prioritising procedure, depending on the seriousness of the defect. Where road safety would be dangerously compromised, the procedure should enable urgent correction of the defect, and allow the vehicle to be taken off the road immediately. This would preferably be without disruption to business, perhaps by having the facility available to hire a similar vehicle at short notice.

Daily walk-round check

A daily walk-round check should always be carried out. As the driver, you are responsible for the condition of your vehicle when in use on the road. The driver has a legal responsibility for

- taking all reasonable precautions to ensure that legal requirements are met before driving any vehicle
- checking that the vehicle is fully roadworthy and free from significant defects before driving it
- ensuring that any equipment, fittings or fixtures required are present and serviceable
- not driving the vehicle if any fault develops that would make it illegal to be driven
- ensuring that all actions taken whilst in charge of the vehicle are lawful.

If, while on a walk-round check a defect is found such as fuel leaking out of a tanker, a supervisor should be informed immediately.

The daily walk-round check should include the items in the following list. Check

- brakes
- lights and indicators
- tyres and wheel securing nuts/markers
- windscreen wipers and washers
- horn
- mirrors
- fuel tanks/caps
- speedometer
- tachograph
- number plates
- bodywork
- reflectors and reflective plates
- exhaust system
- any coupling gear
- speed limiter
- correct plating
- current test certificate (if required)
- proper licensing with the appropriate valid disc(s) displayed
- insurance
- seat belts
- construction and use
- any load being carried.

Remember, this list is not exhaustive. There may be other checks you need to make, depending on the type of vehicle and trailer you are driving.

Any defects must be reported. Make sure you know the defect reporting procedure.

Your instructor is the best person to advise you on the necessary checks your vehicle requires.

You should consider the legal status if something is fitted to the vehicle which isn't required by law but is

- unserviceable
- in a dangerous condition
- not fitted so as to comply with the regulations.

For example, your vehicle isn't required by law to have spot or front fog lights. However, if they're fitted, they must be positioned no less than 0.6 m (2 feet) from the ground.

Roadside checks

'Red' (rebated) diesel fuel is restricted to use for authorised purposes only. Any driver whose vehicle is found to be illegally operating on this fuel will face severe penalties for attempting to evade excise duty. Roadside checks are frequently carried out by HM Revenue and Customs officers. Other checks might include the type and legality of any load being carried.

VOSA

The Vehicle and Operator Services Agency (DVA in NI) and police carry out frequent spot checks of vehicle condition. Where serious defects are found, the vehicle is prohibited from further use until the defects are rectified. Details of the prohibition are notified to the Traffic Commissioner.

DVA/VOSA officers may be accompanied by staff from other agencies or departments, for example, a local authority environmental health department, who would check the vehicle and its exhaust emissions. They have the power to prosecute the driver and/or the operator if excess emissions are found.

Staff from a trading standards department would make checks on vehicle weights, and have the power to prohibit a non-compliant vehicle and/or prosecute the driver and/or operator. Department of Works and Pensions staff would be checking for benefit fraud.

Prohibitions

A VOSA Examiner can prohibit any goods or passenger-carrying vehicle which is being used illegally in respect of Construction and Use regulations, including overloading, or if the vehicle is being used in contravention of the *Drivers' Hours and Record-Keeping Regulations*.

An Examiner issues a Prohibition in respect of the vehicle when an offence or a defect, relating either to the vehicle or to the driver, is found at an inspection. This inspection could take place either at the roadside or where the vehicle is parked.

Most prohibitions come into force immediately but some, issued in respect of less serious roadworthiness defects, are delayed so that they may come into force up to 10 days from the date of the offence being found.

The length of the delay will be decided on the road safety risk of the defect. In all cases the fault or defect has to be rectified before the prohibition is lifted. Therefore a prohibition issued in respect of a Construction and Use offence (including overloading) will only be lifted following an inspection of the vehicle. In many cases relating to more serious roadworthiness offences, that will mean a full inspection of the vehicle at a Goods Vehicle Testing Station.

In the case of overloading, the vehicle must be reweighed and found to be at or below the legal weight limits before the Prohibition is lifted. Some prohibitions issued in respect of Drivers' Hours regulations are for a specific period (eg 24 hours) after which time the driver can continue on the journey without having to be released by an examiner.

Impounding

Any laden heavy goods vehicle operating on a public road for the carriage of goods (either for hire or reward or in connection with any trade or business) without an operator's licence can be detained by a VOSA Examiner. Goods vehicles used on the road by illegal operators can be impounded and removed to a secure storage facility. (Note: an illegal operator is one who requires an operator's licence, but chooses to deliberately and knowingly operate illegally).

Cockpit drill

Make these checks for the safety of yourself, any passengers and other road users.

Every time you get into your vehicle, check that

- the driving seat is correctly adjusted so that you can sit with the correct posture, reach all controls comfortably and take effective observations
- all interior and exterior mirrors are clean and correctly adjusted
- lenses and screens of rear view video equipment are clean and clear
- gauges and warning systems are working correctly (never start a journey with a defective warning device or when a warning light is showing)
- the parking brake is applied
- the gear selector is in neutral (or in 'Park' if driving an automatic vehicle)
- you have sufficient fuel for your journey or until you can next refuel
- your mobile phone is switched off
- the doors are working correctly and are closed before moving off.

Before starting your journey, make sure you know and understand the

- controls: where they are and how they work
- vehicle size: its width, height and weight
- handling: the vehicle's characteristics
- brakes: whether ABS brakes are fitted.

Road speed limiters

Vehicles which require speed limiters

Goods vehicles requiring speed limiters are those

- with a maximum gross weight of more than 12 tonnes, first used on or after 1 January 1988, which, if a speed limiter were not fitted, would be able to achieve speeds exceeding 56 mph (90 km/h)
- with a maximum gross weight of more than 7.5 tonnes but not exceeding 12 tonnes, first used on or after 1 August 1992, which, if a speed limiter were not fitted, would be able to achieve speeds exceeding 60 mph (96 km/h)

- with a maximum gross weight of more than 3.5 tonnes but not exceeding 7.5 tonnes, first used on or after 1 January 2005.

If your vehicle is fitted with a speed limiter, lorries will be set at 56 mph (approx 90 km/h), buses at 62 mph (approx 100 km/h). Be aware that national speed limits allowed for these vehicles may also change to reflect this.

Exemptions Speed limiter requirements don't apply to a vehicle that's

- being taken to a place where a speed limiter is to be installed, calibrated, repaired or replaced
- completing a journey in the course of which the speed limiter has accidentally ceased to function
- used for police, fire or ambulance purposes
- used for naval, military or air force purposes when used by the Crown or owned by the MOD
- being used for no more than six miles on a public road in any calendar week, between land occupied by the vehicle keeper.

The legislation surrounding speed limiters is complex. For more information, contact VOSA (see page 313 for contact details).

Types

There are two main types of speed limiters. One type works by the mechanical or electrical actuator, the other works through the vehicle's engine management system.

Principles of operation

The speed limiter works by receiving a road speed signal either from the tachograph or a sensor fitted to another system on the vehicle, such as the Anti-Lock Braking System (ABS). Occasionally a specific sensor for the speed limiter system may be fitted. The vast majority of vehicles are fitted with speed limiters that take the speed signal from the tachograph.

Irrespective of the type of sensor used, the information is transmitted to the Electronic Control Unit (ECU) which, in turn, controls the equipment used to regulate the power output or revolutions of the vehicle's engine. This is normally achieved by reducing the amount of fuel supplied to the engine.

Parts

The system will consist of a road speed sensor (this may or may not be part of the tachograph system), an electronic cable, an Electronic Control Unit (this may or may not be part of the vehicle's engine management system), an actuation device (this may be a pump, relay or valve) and a plate that is fitted to the vehicle to show the set speed.

Connections

Only authorised speed limiter centres can carry out installation, repairs and calibration. These centres will seal all connections between the speed sensor, Electronic Control Unit and the actuation device to ensure the system is tamper-proof.

Maintenance

There is no day-to-day maintenance required, although any failure of the road speed limiter must be reported to the operator of the vehicle, who should arrange for the repair at the end of the journey upon which the vehicle is engaged.

Safety of loads on vehicles

The Road Traffic Act 1991 made new offences applicable to the state of vehicle loads. All loads carried should be secure whatever the journey, to protect people involved in

- loading
- unloading
- driving the vehicle

as well as all other road users and pedestrians. In the UK every year, prosecutions for unsafe loads are brought against drivers and operators for which there are stiff penalties such as possible disqualification, or even imprisonment in the most serious circumstances.

ALL equipment used for securing loads should be regularly inspected for damage or wear. Inspection arrangements should be in accordance with manufacturer's instructions.

Special attention should be paid to webbing and rope restraints to ensure that there is no visible deterioration due to constant use, such as fraying. They should also be inspected to ensure that they have not been cut or damaged in any other way, for example, through misuse or by deliberate interference. Detailed information on load types and appropriate restraints can be found in Section Two.

Anti-theft measures

Instances of theft of vehicles and trailers are unfortunately common. You're responsible for your vehicle, so you should make every effort to reduce the risk of it being stolen.

- Don't discuss details of your load with any unauthorised person.
- Never leave the keys in the cab while it's unattended, even if you're at the rear of the vehicle.
- You can't afford to give a lift to anyone, however plausible their story or innocent they look.
- Wherever possible, try to avoid using the same route and making the same drops and rest stops.
- Have all major components (plus glass) security etched with the Vehicle Identification Number (VIN).
- Only park in secure, well-lit, reputable overnight lorry parks or designated

parking areas if your rest stops can be planned this way.

- One simple but effective measure that many drivers adopt at overnight stops is to park with the rear doors of their vehicle or its trailer/container hard up against another vehicle. This works well on most occasions.

- When leaving your vehicle, eg for a statutory break, park safely. Try to park your vehicle within sight and check for signs of interference when returning to it.

- Keep your mobile telephone handset with you, if one is available.

- Avoid parking in obviously vulnerable areas if at all possible.

- Ensure that all doors are locked and the windows secure if you sleep in the cab overnight.

- Always ask to see the identity of any officer who might stop you.

- Have an alarm system and/or immobiliser fitted to the vehicle by a reputable security specialist, and approved by the insurance company.

- Avoid leaving any trailer unattended unless on approved secure premises.

- Fit a kingpin or drawbar lock to any trailer that has to be left unattended. Operators are advised to seek the advice of the local crime prevention officer, especially if engaged in the transit of high-value merchandise.

Whenever you return to your vehicle, carry out a further walk-round security check before driving away. Check that your vehicle has not been entered, or tampered with in any way, in your absence. Be aware of your own safety at all times. If you witness any suspicious behaviour around your vehicle, it's important that you call the police and inform your employer.

Large numbers of LGVs are stolen in Britain every year. Most of these vehicles are never recovered. Stay vigilant; if you see anything suspicious, ring 999 and report it.

The Association of Chief Police Officers has approved the wider use of roof markings on lorries to help police air support units to identify stolen vehicles. Fleet operators, especially those who regularly carry vulnerable/dangerous loads, are encouraged to use roof markings.

Your driving

You must drive at all times within the law and comply with

- speed limits
- weight limits
- loading/unloading restrictions
- waiting restrictions
- stopping restrictions (clearways)
- lighting regulations
- restrictions of access to
  - pedestrian precincts
  - residential areas
  - traffic calming zones
  - play streets
- all traffic signs
- road markings
- traffic signals at
  - junctions
  - level crossings
  - fire or ambulance stations
  - lifting or swing bridges
- signals given by authorised persons
  - police officers
  - traffic wardens
  - Highways Agency Traffic Officers
  - Vehicle & Operator Services Agency officers
  - local authority parking attendants
  - school crossing patrols
  - persons engaged in road repairs
- motorway regulations
- regulations governing specific locations
  - tunnels
  - bridges
  - ferries
- pedestrian crossing rules.

Driving licences

The LGV driving licence is a necessity if you wish to earn your living driving large goods vehicles. It's essential that when you drive any vehicle other than an LGV your driving continues to be up to the highest standards. If you accumulate penalty points on your category B licence, your LGV licence will be at risk.

Speed limits

Your vehicle may be fitted with a speed limiter, which will generally prevent you from exceeding motorway speed limits. However, it won't stop you exceeding lower speed limits. Observing speed limits is part of your responsibility. The speed limits that apply to different classes of vehicles on different types of roads can be found in *The Highway Code*.

Speeding offences

Police forces and local authorities are now using the most up-to-date technology in an effort to persuade drivers to comply with speed limits.

At some locations fixed cameras that photograph vehicles exceeding the speed limit have been installed. Improved detection equipment can now also lock on to individual vehicles in busy traffic flows.

In addition, new electronic systems now display the registration number and speed of any offending vehicle at selected motorway locations with a view to 'showing up' the driver concerned.

Drivers whose speed is considerably higher than the legal speed limit can expect a proportionately higher penalty if a successful prosecution results. But remember, the aim is to improve driving standards, not to increase prosecutions.

Red light cameras

Cameras have been installed at many notorious road traffic incident spots to record drivers not complying with the traffic signals. These are also intended to act as a deterrent and to improve safety for road users in general.

Whether it relates to an alleged speeding or traffic signal offence, any photograph produced as evidence and that shows the

- time
- date
- speed
- vehicle registration number
- time a red signal had already been showing

will prove difficult to dispute.

Red Routes

On many roads in London and other large towns and cities, yellow lines have been replaced with red lines. A network of priority (Red) routes for London was approved by Parliament as a means of addressing traffic congestion problems and widespread disregard of parking restrictions in the capital. Red Route measures currently apply to 580 kilometres of London's roads. Subsequently, other major towns and cities also introduced red routes.

Yellow-line exemptions don't apply on Red Routes. During the day, loading is only allowed in marked boxes. Overnight and on Sundays most controls are relaxed to allow unrestricted stopping. It's important to check signs carefully as the hours of operation for Red Routes vary from area to area.

There's a fixed fine for illegal stopping on a Red Route, with no discounts for early payment.

The police or traffic wardens are able to provide limited dispensations for the rare occasions when loading provisions are not adequate. These will be available from the local police station.

There are five main types of Red Route markings. The image below shows the layout of lines on the road. You will find all the signs more clearly laid out, along with their respective lines, in the DfT publication *Know Your Traffic Signs*.

Double red lines - These ban all stopping 24 hours a day, seven days a week. You aren't allowed to stop for

- loading
- dropping off passengers
- visiting shops.

Single red lines - These ban all stopping during the daytime, such as 7 am to 7 pm Monday to Saturday. Outside these hours unrestricted stopping is allowed.

Parking boxes allow vehicles free short term parking and can be used for loading.

- *Red* - allow parking or loading outside rush hours, eg 10 am to 4 pm, for periods of 20 minutes to one hour.
- *White* - allow parking or loading at any time, but a stay may be restricted to 20 minutes or an hour during the day.

At other times, such as 7 pm to 7 am and on Sundays, unrestricted stopping is allowed in either type of parking box.

Loading boxes mark the areas where only loading is allowed. 'Loading' is when a vehicle stops briefly to load or unload bulky or heavy goods. These goods must be heavy or bulky enough so that it isn't easy to carry them any distance and it may involve more than one trip. If this is not the case, then your vehicle should be parked legally and the goods carried to the premises. Picking up portable items, like shopping, doesn't constitute loading.

- *Red* - allow loading outside rush hours, eg 10 am to 4 pm, for a maximum of 20 minutes.
- *White* - allow loading at any time, but during the day, a stay is restricted to a maximum of 20 minutes.

At other times, such as between 7 pm and 7 am and on Sundays, unrestricted stopping is allowed in either type of loading box.

Clearways are major roads where there's no need to stop. There won't be red lines but Red Route clearway signs will indicate that stopping isn't allowed at any time.

Further red route information can be found in Section Four, and you can also contact

Transport for London Street Management
84 Eccleston Square
London SW1V 1PX

Tel: 0845 305 1234

Congestion charging

A congestion charging scheme is operational in central London to help reduce traffic and make journeys and delivery times more reliable. The congestion charge applies from 7.00 am to 6.30 pm Monday to Friday, excluding public holidays. Failure to pay the charge will lead to a fine.

Exemptions - Those who are exempt from the charge include

- disabled drivers
- alternative fuel vehicles (eg those using red diesel)
- vehicles with nine or more seats
- roadside recovery vehicles
- all two-wheeled vehicles

- London licensed taxis and minicabs.

Residents who live within the congestion charging zone pay a reduced rate.

Drivers in some categories of exemption need to register with Transport for London (see congestion charging contact details below).

Discounts - Businesses and other organisations operating a fleet of 25 or more vehicles are entitled to a discount when they register with a dedicated fleet scheme.

For more information, to register or to make a payment, ring the Congestion Charge Line, **Tel. 0870 900 1234** or visit the website **www.tfl.gov.uk/roadusers/ congestioncharging/**

Congestion charging is gradually being introduced in other towns and cities.

section **four**
DRIVER SKILLS

This section covers

- Professional driving
- Driving at night
- Motorway driving
- All weather driving
- Avoiding and dealing with congestion
- Green issues - helping the environment
- Road traffic incidents
- First aid
- Breakdowns

Professional driving

Essential skills

A professional driver should develop the skills necessary to make clear, positive decisions about situations encountered on the road. The following are the skills you'll require.

Control

You should develop the physical skills that enable you to be in control of your vehicle at all times. You should know how your vehicle and its load will handle in any situation you encounter by understanding its capabilities and limitations.

Awareness

You need to know what's happening around you so that you're always conscious of any potential hazards that might develop. This will give you the time to deal with hazards as they occur.

Planning

Proper planning means that you'll be able to act early when approaching junctions or hazards. This will prevent unnecessary braking and gear-changing, helping you to make progress in traffic. Loaded large vehicles take longer to gain speed than smaller vehicles. Other road users will appreciate your ability to avoid late signalling, constant braking and slow acceleration away from hazards.

Anticipation

By knowing the correct way of dealing with situations as they occur you'll develop anticipation of how to react in those instances. You'll also have a better insight into the way others respond to those same situations.

It's essential that you're in control of your vehicle at all times. You should drive skilfully and plan ahead so that your vehicle is travelling at the appropriate speed and in the correct position for the next manoeuvre you need to take. You should never have to rush or take action hastily. By adopting the correct techniques you'll create the time and room to complete manoeuvres safely.

Other road users

Others on the road might make mistakes. You have to accept that other road users aren't always aware of the extra room or time you need, due to the size of your vehicle.

Young children

Young children are particularly unpredictable and might run out into the road suddenly. If you're passing pedestrians who are walking on the pavement but close to the kerb, you must be aware that the size of your vehicle will cause a draught.

This could unsteady a small child or, indeed, an adult. Always check your nearside mirror as you pass pedestrians.

Older people

Some older pedestrians may have poor eyesight and/or hearing difficulties. This might make them indecisive and they may sometimes become confused. They also might take longer to cross the road. You need to understand this and allow them more time.

Older drivers might be hesitant or become confused at major junctions or gyratory systems. Don't intimidate them by driving up too close or revving the engine.

Learner drivers

Learner drivers who aren't used to all driving situations and other types of road user might be affected by a close-following LGV. They might be driving at an excessively slow speed or be hesitant. Be patient and give them room.

Cyclists

In 2005, just under a quarter of cyclist fatalities in road traffic incidents resulted from a collision with an LGV*, yet goods vehicles comprised only about 5.6% of the traffic on UK roads.

You need to allow cyclists as much room as you would a car. They might swerve unexpectedly or be blown off course by a gust of wind. If they're approaching a junction or roundabout you must be aware that they might turn right from the left-hand lane, crossing the path of traffic.

The size and shape of your vehicle makes it essential that you're aware of the presence of cyclists **all around** you. Use your nearside mirror as you pass a cyclist to ensure that you've done so safely.

* Note

These figures are taken from Road Casualties Great Britain: 2005, which is published by the Stationery Office for the Department for Transport.

Be aware when you're waiting at a junction that they might move up along either side. If they're positioned in front of your nearside mirror, between the kerb and your front nearside wheel, they'll be difficult to see. You should be aware of this situation as it develops and allow them to move away before you move off.

If you see a cyclist ahead of you glancing round to their right, they're probably about to turn right. Allow for this.

Motorcyclists

Much of what has been said about cyclists also applies to motorcyclists. They are very vulnerable because, like cyclists, they are much smaller than other vehicles, with a narrow profile, so they are difficult to see. However, they also travel much faster than cyclists so any situation develops much more quickly.

Many incidents occur because drivers fail to notice motorcyclists, so look out for them when

- emerging at junctions - the motorcyclist may be travelling along the major road and may be hidden behind other traffic. They can be completely hidden from you in the blind spots caused by the vehicle door pillars, mirrors etc. They may also be hidden by signs, trees, or street furniture
- turning into a road on your right - the motorcyclist may be following, overtaking or approaching you. Oncoming motorcyclists may be particularly difficult to see as they may be hidden behind larger vehicles
- straddling lanes, eg to turn left or to negotiate a roundabout
- changing lanes or moving out to overtake slower-moving or parked vehicles. Motorcyclists will often ride between queues of slower-moving traffic in queues to make progress (commonly known as filtering) particularly in urban areas. When you are in heavy slow-moving traffic, always ensure it's safe before you change direction.

Pay special attention to motorcycles and mopeds displaying L plates (or D plates in Wales). The riders of these machines may be riding on the road with very little experience, so are particularly vulnerable.

Horses and other animals

Horses are easily frightened by

- noise
- headlights or flashing lights
- vehicles passing too close.

If you see horse riders ahead, either on the road or on the grass verge, plan your approach carefully. Slow down safely and don't rev the engine. You should allow for the fact that some of the riders might be learners and may not have full control if the animal is startled or frightened. Novice riders may sometimes be on a leading rein and have someone walking with them. When you pass them, do so slowly and leave plenty of room.

Always check your nearside mirror to ensure that you've safely completed the manoeuvre. Don't flash your headlights unnecessarily and **DO NOT** release air brakes behind animals, particularly horses as this could cause them to shy or bolt. If someone in charge of animals signals you to stop, do so and switch off your engine.

Guide dogs

A guide dog usually has a distinctive loop type of harness. Remember the dog is trained to wait at the side of the road until it is clear before crossing.

The presence of a guide dog does not only indicate a visual impairment. When a person is both deaf and blind, they may carry a white stick with a red band and their dog may have a red and white checked harness.

Effective observation

Due to the height of the cab you may have a better view from your driving position than other road users. You can take advantage of this, for example, when approaching a blind bend, by using your added height to see over hedgerows or other obstructions; you can then scan ahead for potential hazards. However, because of its size and design an LGV will have more blind spots than many smaller vehicles.

You should use the mirrors constantly and act upon what you see in them to assess what road users around you are doing or might do next. You must check frequently down the sides of your vehicle.

Check the offside

• for overtaking traffic coming up behind or already alongside, especially cyclists or motorcyclists. Do this before signalling

• before changing lanes, overtaking, turning right or moving to the right.

Remember, just a simple glance isn't enough. You need to check carefully.

Check the nearside

• for cyclists or motorcyclists filtering up the nearside

• for traffic on your left when moving in two or more lanes

• when you've passed another road user, pedestrian(s) or parked vehicle before moving back to the left

• to verify the position of the rear wheels of your vehicle or trailer in relation to the kerb

• before changing lanes, after overtaking, turning left or moving closer to the left when leaving roundabouts.

You should ensure that you're constantly aware of what's happening around you. Because of your relatively high seating position you should check for pedestrians, cyclists or motorcyclists who may be directly in front of the vehicle but out of your normal field of vision, especially

• at pedestrian crossings

• in slow-moving congested traffic.

Some LGVs, particularly those with sleeper cabs, give very limited vision to the side. When moving away, wind down the window and lean out and look round to ensure that it's clear **before** the vehicle starts to move.

Many modern vehicles are fitted with an additional nearside mirror specifically positioned so that the driver can observe the nearside front wheel in relation to the kerb. Use it whenever you're moving off or pulling in to park alongside the kerb, and to check the vehicle's position when you have to move close to the left in normal driving.

Striking the kerb at speed or wandering onto a verge can seriously deflect the steering or damage the tyre.

Mirrors

When you're learning to drive, get into a routine of checking your mirrors. It's important to know as much about traffic conditions all around you as it is about what's going on ahead.

Remember, looking isn't enough.

Before you consider changing direction or altering speed you should assess how your actions will affect other road users. Most non-LGV traffic attempting to overtake will normally be catching up to your vehicle at noticeably higher speeds.

Check all mirrors before moving away

Regulations have changed in relation to the nearside field of vision of a large goods vehicle. A wide angle mirror covers the existing blind spot and extends the visibility outwards. Any vehicles without wide-angled mirrors will need to be retrofitted with them.

You should use the mirrors well before you signal your intention or make any manoeuvre, such as

- moving away
- changing direction
- turning left or right
- overtaking
- changing lanes
- slowing or stopping
- speeding up
- opening the cab door.

Your mirrors should be

- clean and free from dust and grime
- properly adjusted to give a clear view behind. This is particularly important when you're transporting an oversized load that projects over the normal width of the vehicle.

You must act sensibly and positively on what you see. Take note of the speed, behaviour and likely intentions of following traffic.

Remember, if you don't know, don't go.

Take care not to allow your vehicle to wander, however slightly, before changing lanes. An LGV occupies much of the available lane width already and any move away from a mid-lane position may cause

an overtaking driver or rider to assume that you're starting to pull out into their path.

Blind spots

You might not be able to see much by looking round, especially if the vehicle is fitted with a sleeper cab. This is all the more reason for being continually aware of vehicles just to the rear on either the offside or the nearside in blind spot positions. Be especially aware if your vehicle is left-hand drive, or if you are driving a right-hand drive vehicle in countries outside the UK.

A sideways glance is often helpful, especially

- before changing lanes on a motorway or dual carriageway
- where traffic is merging from the right or the left
- when approaching the main carriageway from a motorway slip road.

Sideswiping

Sideswiping is a term describing when a driver makes an unsafe lane change and collides with another road user already in that lane. An increasing number of left-hand drive vehicles have lead to sideswiping becoming more common. Despite additional kerbside mirrors there remains an area where the driver may not be fully aware of the presence of a vehicle or motorcycle. Be extra careful and signal well in advance of your manoeuvre. This allows any unseen vehicles to move into view.

Close Proximity mirrors

From the first of April 2009, most large vehicles need to be fitted with wide angle and close proximity mirrors to help the driver see into blind areas. For more information contact VOSA (see page 313 for contact details).

Observation at junctions

Despite having a higher seating position than most drivers there will still be some junctions where your view is restricted by parked vehicles.

If it's possible, look through the windows of these vehicles or, if there are shops opposite, look for reflections in the windows. If you're still unable to see any oncoming traffic you'll have to ease forward until you can see properly. Do this without encroaching too far into the path of approaching traffic.

Some road users are more difficult to see than others, particularly cyclists who will generally be approaching close to the kerb from the right. Motorcyclists are often difficult to see, can be travelling fast and may have been hidden from view by other traffic. Assess the situation. Don't emerge until you **know** that it's clear.

Pedestrians can often act unpredictably at junctions, just stepping or even running out, oblivious to your presence. Take in the whole scene before you commit yourself to moving a large (and frequently long) vehicle out across the path of oncoming traffic.

Zones of vision

As an LGV licence-holder your eyesight must be of a high standard. A skilful driver should be constantly scanning the road ahead and interpreting what's happening or likely to happen.

Always be aware of what's behind and alongside you. Use your peripheral vision to see changes 'out of the corner of your eye' before reacting to them. Look out for the possibility of

- vehicles about to emerge
- cyclists and motorcyclists
- children running out
- other pedestrians stepping out.

Safe distances

Never drive at such a speed that you can't pull up safely in the distance that you can see to be clear. This should be irrespective of

- weather
- the road surface
- any load.

Don't drive beyond the limits of your vision.

Keep a safe separation distance between you and the vehicle in front. In reasonable weather conditions leave at least 1 metre (about 3 feet) per mph of your speed, or a two-second time gap. In poor weather, on wet roads, you'll need to at least double the distance, so allow a four-second time gap.

Look well ahead

Look well ahead for stop lights. On a road with the national speed limit in force or on the motorway, watch for other vehicles' hazard warning lights. These might be flashing to indicate that traffic ahead is slowing down sharply for some reason.

The two-second rule

You can check the time gap by watching the vehicle in front pass an object such as a bridge, pole, sign, etc and then saying to yourself

'only a fool breaks the two-second rule'

You should have finished saying this by the time you reach the same spot. If you haven't finished the rhyme when you pass the spot, you're too close.

On some motorways this rule is drawn to drivers' attention by chevrons painted on the road surface. The instruction 'Keep at least two chevrons from the vehicle ahead' also appears on a sign at these locations.

In congested traffic moving at slower speeds it may not be practicable to leave as much space, but you'll still need to leave enough distance in which to pull up safely.

If you find another vehicle driving too close behind you, gradually reduce your speed to increase any gap between you and a vehicle ahead. You'll then be able to brake more gently and remove the likelihood of the close-following vehicle running into the rear of your vehicle.

If another vehicle pulls into the safe separation gap that you're leaving, ease off your speed to extend the gap again.

Traffic signals

By planning well ahead you'll ease some of the effort needed to drive an LGV.

Anticipating traffic speeds ahead and easing off the throttle means that you may be able to keep your vehicle moving. This will avoid the need to brake, to make a number of gear changes, to come to a stop, or to apply the handbrake. By driving like this you'll be able to make good progress and will keep down fuel costs.

Approaching traffic lights

Signals on green   Look well ahead and gauge how much traffic is waiting at each side of the junction you're approaching.

Ask yourself

- How long has green been showing?
- If the signals change, am I driving at such a speed that I can stop safely?
- If I have to brake hard, will following traffic be able to stop safely?
- Are there any vehicles waiting to turn across my path?
- How are the road surface and weather conditions going to affect the vehicle's braking distance?

Signals on amber   The amber signal means **STOP**. You may only continue if you

- have already crossed the stop line
- are so close to the stop line that to pull up might be unsafe or cause an incident.

Signals on red   The red traffic signal means that you **MUST** stop. You may be able to time your approach so that you're able to keep the vehicle moving as the signal changes to green. This is especially important when driving a laden vehicle uphill to traffic signals. Look well ahead.

Signals not working   If you come upon traffic signals that aren't working, or there's a sign to show that they're out of order, treat the location as you would an unmarked junction and proceed with great care.

> **Remember,** a green light means go on if the way is clear. Check the junction to make sure other traffic using the junction is stopping at their red light. Only proceed on a green light if you can clear the junction.

Don't

- accelerate to try to beat the signals
- wait until the last moment to apply the brakes – harsh braking could result in loss of control.

Harsh accelerating or braking could also cause your load to move.

Signalling

You should signal to

- warn others of your intentions, especially if this involves a manoeuvre not readily apparent to other road users
- help other road users.

Road users include

- drivers of oncoming vehicles
- drivers of following vehicles
- motorcyclists
- cyclists
- crossing supervisors
- police directing traffic
- pedestrians
- horse riders
- road repair contractors.

Give signals

- clearly and in good time
- that are illustrated in *The Highway Code.*

Your signals should be readily understood by all other road users. Try not to mislead others by giving signals that could confuse, especially when intending to pull up just after a road on the left. Another road user might misunderstand the meaning of the signal. In situations like this you should use your common sense and be ready for others' actions.

Don't use the headlights as a signal to give or claim priority. This might lead other vehicles into a hazardous situation.

Any signal that doesn't appear in *The Highway Code* is unauthorised and could be open to misinterpretation by another road user.

175

Using the horn

There are few instances when you'll need to sound the horn. Use it only if you

- assess that another road user may not be aware of your presence
- need to warn other road users of your presence – at blind bends or a humpback bridge, for example

Sounding the horn doesn't

- give you priority
- relieve you of the responsibility to drive safely.

Don't use the horn

- when stationary
- at night between 11.30 pm and 7 am in a built-up area, unless there's danger from a moving vehicle
- as a rebuke or simply to attract attention (unless to avoid an incident or collision).

Avoid long, aggressive blasts on the horn, which can alarm pedestrians. Also, remember that some pedestrians might have hearing problems and so may not hear your warning.

Driving through tunnels

On approaching and in a tunnel

- switch on your dipped headlights
- do not wear sunglasses
- observe the road signs and signals
- keep an appropriate distance from the vehicle in front
- switch on your radio and tune to the indicated frequency.

If the tunnel is congested

- switch on your hazard warning lights when stationary
- keep your distance, even if you are moving slowly or stationary
- if possible, listen to messages on the radio
- leave at least a 5 metre gap between you and the vehicle in front if you have to stop
- follow any instructions given by tunnel officials or variable message signs.

Many tunnels do have radio transmitters to give drivers information and advance warning of any incidents, congestion or roadworks. Some European tunnels can be many miles long.

When entering a tunnel in a large vehicle, you should slow down gradually, and increase the gap between you and the vehicle ahead to at least 4 seconds, to allow more time to brake if necessary. In some tunnels a legally enforceable minimum separation distance is specified. Marker lights (usually blue) may also be located in the tunnel to help drivers maintain a safe separation distance.

If you are carrying dangerous goods, remember that the height of the vehicle and the need to have an escort must be considered when approaching a tunnel.

When driving a large vehicle through a tunnel, other vehicles may become harder to see, particularly in mirrors, owing to lower light levels. This might increase drivers' response times.

Remember that larger vehicles may also block the view of following road users if they in turn do not increase their separation distances to improve their ability to see and plan ahead.

If you break down or are involved in a collision in a tunnel

- switch on your hazard warning lights

- switch off the engine
- leave your vehicle
- give first aid to any injured people, if you are able
- call for help from an emergency point.

If your vehicle is on fire and you can drive it out of the tunnel, do so. If not

- pull over to the side and switch off the engine
- leave the vehicle immediately
- DO NOT open the body panel fully
- using the vehicle's extinguisher you may be able to direct the nozzle through the small gap available when the release catch on the body panel is undone
- should the fire appear to be large, DO NOT try to tackle it, get well clear of the vehicle and leave it to the fire brigade
- DO NOT take any risks.

Driving at night

Driving an LGV at night, often over long distances, requires additional skills. It also places added responsibilities on the driver.

Problems related to driving at night include

- much less advance information
- limited lighting (street lights or vehicle lights only)
- the headlights of oncoming vehicles
- shadows created by patchy street lighting
- ineffective lighting on other vehicles, pedal cycles, etc
- dangers created by the onset of tiredness.

Many deaths have occurred because the driver of a large vehicle was either overcome by tiredness or failed to see an unlit broken-down vehicle until too late. Long night time journeys, particularly on motorway routes with little to relieve the monotony, require planning and close attention to proper rest and refreshment stops.

Tiredness

Falling asleep at the wheel can happen for only a second or two, yet may have catastrophic results.

Be on your guard.

Don't

- drive without a proper rest period
- allow the cab to become too warm
- eat a heavy meal just before setting out
- take your eyes off the road to change radio channels or a music track
- use a mobile phone or headphones when driving.

Try to

- keep plenty of cool fresh air moving through the cab
- walk around in the fresh air during a rest stop.

If you feel your concentration slipping, pull up at the next safe, convenient place and take a break.

Remember, see and be seen.

Night vision

An LGV driver's eyesight is tested at a higher standard than car drivers or motorcyclists. An optician can make sure that your night vision matches up to this higher standard. Have your eyesight checked regularly and avoid

- wearing tinted glasses at night
- using windscreen or window tinting sprays.

Lighting-up time

You should be prepared to switch on whichever vehicle lights are appropriate to the conditions, regardless of the official lighting-up times. If the weather conditions are poor or it becomes overcast early, switch on your lights. **See and be seen.**

You must drive at an appropriate speed so that you can stop in the distance which you can see to be clear. In most cases that will be within the distance illuminated by your headlights or by street lights.

Unlit vehicles

Vehicles under 1,525 kg are permitted to park in 30 mph zones without lights at night time. Look for unlit vehicles when driving in built-up areas, especially when the street lighting is patchy.

Builders' skips are required to be lit and show reflective plates to oncoming traffic. Both of these measures can be either neglected or subject to vandalism, so watch out for unlit skips.

Adjusting to darkness

When you step out from a brightly lit area into darkness, such as when leaving a motorway service area, your eyes will take a short while to adjust to the different conditions. Use this time to check and clean your vehicle's lights, reflectors, lenses and mirrors.

At dawn

Other drivers may have been driving through the night and may also be less alert. Leave your lights on until you're satisfied that other road users will see you.

It's harder to judge speed and distance correctly in the half-light at dusk and dawn. The colour of some vehicles makes them harder to see in these conditions. Switch on your lights to help others to see you.

Vehicle lighting

It's essential that all lamps are clean and bulbs and light units are operating correctly. In addition to the driver being able to see ahead properly, it's essential that other road users are able to recognise the size of your vehicle and its direction of travel.

All regulation markers and rear lights must be lit and clear of dirt and obstructions such as ropes, sheets, overhanging projections, etc.

Oversized loads at night

If you have permission to move any load at night that projects beyond the normal size of the vehicle, all additional marker lights and hazard warning lights should be on.

Oversized loads are usually parked in lay-bys, etc overnight. However, in certain circumstances the police authority responsible for that particular area may consider the load would be more safely moved when there's less traffic on the road. Look for any signals given by the escort of such vehicles.

Avoid the 'Christmas tree' effect (use of decorative lighting in or on the cab) seen on some vehicles. It can be distracting and confusing to other road users at night. Also, any red light used in the cab must not show to the front of the vehicle.

Auxiliary lighting

LGV drivers must conform to regulations governing the use and fitting of any auxiliary lamps, especially with regard to their mounting height from the road surface. It's an offence to use fog lights or spotlights whose centres are less than 0.6 metres (2 feet) from the ground, except in poor weather conditions such as mist, fog or falling snow.

Any lights showing to the front should be white (or, as allowed on some vehicles, yellow) unless they're side marker lights, required to be fitted by law to certain longer vehicles.

If your vehicle is fitted with any additional working lights to assist coupling/uncoupling, loading, etc, remember to switch them off when the vehicle is out on the road.

High-intensity rear fog lights and additional front fog lights should only be used when visibility is less than 100 metres (about 330 feet). They must be switched off when the visibility improves.

Amber hazard beacons are required, depending on the load projecting beyond specified limits or the vehicle travelling at slower speeds than normal.

Parked vehicles

Any goods vehicle exceeding 1525 kg unladen weight must have its parking lights on when parked on the road at night. A lay-by is usually within the specified distance from any carriageway, so parking lights are still required.

Unless your vehicle is in an 'off-street' parking location, such as a lorry park, it must be clearly lit to comply with the law.

Driving in built-up areas

Always use dipped headlights in built-up areas at night. It helps others to see you and assists your vision if the street lighting varies or is defective.

Be on the alert for

- pedestrians in dark clothing
- runners
- cyclists (often with poor lighting).

Take extra care when approaching pedestrian crossings. Drive at such a speed that you can stop safely if necessary.

Make sure that you still obey the speed limits, even if the roads appear to be empty.

Maintenance work

Essential maintenance work is often carried out at night time. Be on the alert for diversion signs, obstructions and coned-off sections of road when you're driving at night.

Street cleansing often takes place at night in larger cities, so be on the lookout for slow-moving vehicles.

Driving in rural areas

If there's no oncoming traffic you should use full beam headlights to see as far ahead as possible. Dip your lights as soon as you see oncoming traffic to avoid dazzling the oncoming driver or rider.

If there's no footpath, look out for pedestrians in the road. *The Highway Code* advises pedestrians to walk facing oncoming traffic in these situations, but not all pedestrians follow this advice.

Additionally, *The Highway Code* advises large groups of people on organised walks that they should walk on the left.

Fog at night

If there's any possibility of dense fog developing at night you should avoid driving.

If the fog becomes so dense that you're unable to go any further safely, your vehicle will present a serious hazard to other vehicles. Because of the difficulties of getting an LGV off the road in dense fog it's better not to start out in the first place.

If you start your journey when there's fog about and you're delayed you'll be committing an offence if you exceed the permitted hours of driving for that period, because the delay was foreseeable.

Overtaking at night

Because LGVs take some considerable time to complete an overtaking manoeuvre you must only attempt one when you can see well ahead that it's safe to do so.

This means that unless you're driving on a motorway or dual carriageway the opportunities to overtake will be limited. Without street lighting you won't be able to assess if there are bends, junctions, hills, etc, which may prevent you seeing an oncoming vehicle.

If you do decide to overtake, make sure that you can do so without cutting in on the vehicle being overtaken or causing oncoming vehicles to brake or swerve.

Never close up on the vehicle ahead prior to attempting to overtake. This will restrict your view of the road ahead.

Separation distance

Avoid driving so close to the vehicle ahead that your lights dazzle the other driver. Make sure that your lights are on dipped beam when following another vehicle.

If a vehicle overtakes you, dip your headlights as soon as the vehicle is alongside you. The beam of your headlights should fall short of the vehicle in front.

Breakdowns

If your vehicle breaks down, try to pull it as far off to the left as possible. If you can get off the main carriageway without causing danger or inconvenience to other road users, especially pedestrians, do so. But don't park on the pavement: the weight of an LGV can damage paving stones and underground services.

If you have a warning triangle, place it at least 45 metres (147 feet) behind the vehicle on normal roads. Some form of warning is vital if an electrical problem has put the rear lights out of action. However, don't attempt to place a warning triangle or any other warning device on a motorway, dual carriageway, hard shoulder or slip road.

Don't attempt to work on the offside of the vehicle unless protected by a recovery vehicle with flashing hazard lights. Even then, take great care on roads carrying fast-moving traffic. Injuries and fatalities have occurred at the scenes of initially simple breakdowns.

If your vehicle is causing an obstruction and possible danger to other road users inform the police as soon as possible. This is particularly important if your vehicle is carrying dangerous goods or other hazardous materials.

If you suspect that your vehicle has a mechanical problem, don't be tempted to continue on your journey. Small defects could become dangerous if they're left without attention. You could also end up creating traffic chaos if your vehicle eventually breaks down in a difficult location.

Recovery agencies

If you're engaged in long-distance work, especially at night, it's wise to ensure that the vehicle is covered by a reputable recovery agency. The cost of towing or repairing an LGV could be substantial without the benefit of recovery membership.

For safety reasons, vehicles that break down on the motorway are required to be removed as quickly as possible.

Motorway driving

Basic preparation

Motorways are statistically the safest roads in the UK. However, motorway incidents invariably involve a larger number of vehicles travelling at high speeds and usually result in more serious injuries and damage than incidents on normal roads.

Because of the high numbers of such vehicles using the motorway network's inter-city links, many of these incidents involve LGVs. But if everyone who used the motorway drove to the same high standard that's required of LGV drivers, it's arguable that many of these incidents could be avoided.

The higher overall speeds and the volume of traffic cause conditions to change much more rapidly than on normal roads. For this reason you need to be

- totally alert
- physically fit
- concentrating fully.

If you aren't, you may not be able to react to any sudden change taking place ahead of you.

Fitness

Don't drive if you're

- tired
- unwell
- taking flu remedies, etc

- worried
- unable to concentrate.

Any of these factors will affect your reactions, especially if you have to deal with an emergency (see pages 145-148 for information on health and safety issues).

Rest periods

You must observe mandatory rest periods in your daily driving schedule. On long journeys try to plan them to coincide with a break at a motorway service area or refreshment stop. This is especially important at night, when a long journey can cause tiredness to set in.

It's illegal to stop anywhere on the motorway hard shoulder or slip roads for a rest. If you feel tiredness coming on, open the windows, turn the heating down and get off the motorway at the next junction. When you get to a service area, have a hot drink, wash your face (to refresh you) and walk round in the fresh air, or perhaps take a short nap (15-20 minutes) before driving on.

Bear in mind that a substantial meal accompanied by the warmth in the cab, the continual resonance of the engine and long, uninterrupted stretches of road, especially at night, can produce the very conditions you need to avoid.

Regulations

Motorways are subject to specific rules and regulations that must be observed by all LGV drivers. Study those sections relating to motorways in *The Highway Code*. You also need to know, understand and obey motorway warning signs and signals.

Vehicle checks

Before driving on the motorway you should ensure that you carry out routine checks on your vehicle, especially considering the long distances and prolonged higher speeds involved. For fuller details on vehicle maintenance, see page 67-8.

Tyres

All tyres on your vehicle (and any trailer) must be in good condition. Tyres can become very hot and may disintegrate under sustained high-speed running. Check for excessive heat when you stop for a break.

Inspect both the inside and outside visible faces for signs of

- wear
- damage

- bulges
- separation
- exposed cords.

Make sure that your vehicle has the correct-sized wheels fitted. Smaller diameters will run faster and may overheat on longer journeys. Ensure that all tyres are suitable for the loads being carried.

If a tyre bursts or shreds you may be able to see this in your mirrors. If you see smoke from the tyres you should stop as soon as it's safe to do so.

Also make a habit of checking the tyre pressures regularly when the tyres are cold.

Mirrors

Ensure that all mirrors are properly adjusted to give the best possible view to the rear. They should also be clean. The simple device of tying a piece of cloth to the mirror bracket cleans them effectively as the air flow causes it to continually wipe the surface. Make sure that you tie it on tightly so that it doesn't work free and fly off.

Windscreen

All glass must be

- clean
- clear
- free from defects.

Keep all windscreen washer reservoirs topped up and the jets clear. Make sure that all wiper blades are in good condition.

Spray-suppression equipment

It's essential that you check all spray-suppression equipment fitted to the vehicle and any trailer. Make sure it is serviceable before setting out, especially if bad weather is expected.

Instruments

Check all gauges and warning lights such as

- anti-lock brakes (ABS)
- air pressure
- oil pressure
- coolant
- temperature
- lights.

Lights and indicators

To comply with the law all lights must be in working order even in daylight. Make sure that all bulbs, headlight units, lenses and reflectors are fitted, clean and function as intended.

High-intensity rear fog lights and marker lights (if fitted) must operate correctly. Indicator lights must operate and 'flash' within the specified frequency range. Reversing lights must either automatically operate by the selection of reverse gear or be switched on from the cab with a warning light to show when they're lit.

Fuel

Make sure that you either have enough fuel on board to complete the journey or have the facility (cash, agency card, etc) to refuel at a service area.

Oil

The engine operates at sustained high speeds on a motorway, so it's vital to check all oil levels before setting out.

Running low can result in costly damage to the engine and could cause a breakdown at a dangerous location.

Coolant

The engine will be running for sustained periods so it's essential to check the levels of coolant in the system.

Joining a motorway

There are three alternative ways in which traffic can join a motorway. All these access routes will be clearly signed.

At a roundabout

The exit from a roundabout will be signposted. Signs are displayed prominently to prevent non-motorway traffic accidentally entering the system.

Main trunk road becomes a motorway

There will be prominent advance warning signs so that prohibited traffic can leave the main route before the motorway regulations apply.

Via a slip road

Slip roads leading directly onto the motorway will be clearly signed to prevent prohibited traffic entering the motorway.

Effective observation Before joining the motorway from a slip road try to assess traffic conditions on the motorway itself. You may be able to do this as you approach from a distance or if you need to reach the entry point by means of an over-bridge.

Get as much advance information as you can to help plan your speed on the slip road. You'll need to build up your speed and emerge safely onto the main carriageway.

Plan your approach and try to avoid having to stop at the end of the slip road. But if the motorway is extremely busy you may **have to** stop and filter into the traffic. Don't use the size of your vehicle to force your way onto the motorway. Use your mirror and signal as you pull out onto the main carriageway, if it's safe to do so. Watch out particularly for motorcyclists, they can be difficult to see due to their narrow profile and they can approach quickly. They may also be hidden behind slower-moving traffic which they are overtaking.

A quick sideways glance may be necessary to ensure that you correctly assess the speed of any traffic approaching in the nearside lane. If your vehicle is left-hand drive, be particularly aware of your blind spots and check them carefully.

Don't

- pull out into the path of traffic in the nearside lane if this will cause it to slow down or swerve
- drive along the hard shoulder to filter into the left-hand lane.

There are a small number of locations where traffic merges onto the motorway from the right. Take extra care in these situations.

Making progress approaching access points

After passing a motorway exit there will often be an entrance or access point onto the motorway. Look well ahead and if there are vehicles joining the motorway

- don't try to race them while they're on the slip road
- be prepared to adjust your speed
- move to the next lane, if it's safe to do so, to allow joining traffic to merge.

Lane discipline

Keep to the left-hand lane unless overtaking slower vehicles.

Goods vehicles which are required to be fitted with a speed limiter aren't allowed in the right-hand lane on a three-lane or multi-lane motorway, unless there are roadworks or signs that indicate otherwise. Details of which vehicles are required to be fitted with speed limiters and are therefore prohibited

are shown on page 144. On two-lane motorways these vehicles are permitted to use the right-hand lane for overtaking.

Use the MSM/PSL routine well before signalling to move out. Don't start to pull out and then signal.

On a three- or four-lane motorway make sure that you check for any vehicle in the right-hand lane(s) that might be about to move back to the left. Most of the traffic coming up behind will be travelling at a much higher speed, and motorcyclists may be particularly difficult to see.

Look well ahead to plan any overtaking manoeuvre, especially given the effect a speed limiter will have on the power available to you.

Observe signs showing a crawler/climber lane for LGVs. This will suggest a long, gradual climb ahead.

If a slow-moving oversized load is being escorted, look for any signal the escort might give. They may permit you to move into the right-hand lane to pass the obstruction.

If a motorway lane merges from the right (in a few cases only) you should move over to the left as soon as it's safe to do so. At these specific locations no offence is committed if an LGV is initially travelling in the extreme right-hand lane. Move over to the left as soon as it's safe to do so.

Separation distance

On motorways you should allow

- greater safety margins than on normal roads
- a safe separation distance.

In good conditions you'll need at least

- a stopping distance of one metre (about 3 feet 3 inches) for every mph
- a two-second separation gap from the vehicle in front.

In poor conditions you'll need at least

- double the stopping distance
- a four-second separation gap from the vehicle in front.

In snow or icy conditions the stopping distances can be **ten times** those needed in normal dry conditions.

Seeing and being seen

Make sure that you start out with a clean windscreen, mirrors and windows. Use the washers, wipers and demisters to keep the screen clear. In poor conditions use dipped headlights.

Keep reassessing traffic conditions around you. Watch out for brake lights or hazard warning lights that show the traffic ahead is either stationary or slowing down.

High-intensity rear fog lights should only be used when visibility falls below 100 metres (about 330 feet). They should be switched off when visibility improves, unless fog is patchy and danger still exists.

Motorway signs and signals

Motorway signs are larger than normal road signs. They can be read from greater distances and can help you to plan ahead.

Know your intended route. Be ready for the exit that you need to use and prepare for it in good time, well before you reach it.

Where there are major roadworks there may be diversions for LGVs in operation. Look for the yellow

- square
- diamond
- circle
- triangle

symbols combined with capital route letters. Follow the symbol on the route signs.

Signals

Warning lights show when there are dangers ahead such as

- incidents
- fog
- icy roads.

Look out for variable message warning signs advising

- lane closures
- speed limits
- hazards
- standing traffic ahead.

You need to comply with advisory speed limit signs shown on the motorway hazard warning lights matrix.

Red light signals If the red X signals show above your lane don't go beyond the red light

- be ready to comply with any signs that tell you to change lanes
- be ready to leave the motorway
- observe brake lights or flashing hazard warning lights, which show that there's stationary or very slow-moving traffic ahead.

Weather conditions

Because of the higher speeds on motorways it's important to take into account any effects the weather may have on driving conditions. Listen to weather forecasts on the radio.

Rain

Visibility can be reduced by the spray thrown up by numbers of LGVs travelling at speed. You should

* use headlights so that other drivers can see you

* reduce speed when the road surface is wet. You need to be able to pull up in the distance that you can see to be clear

* leave a greater separation gap. Use the four-second rule as a minimum

* make sure that all spray-suppression equipment fitted to your vehicle is effective

* take extra care when the road surface is wet after rain. The roads may still be slippery even if the sun is out.

Crosswinds

Be aware of the effects strong crosswinds can have on other road users. Watch out especially

* after passing motorway bridges
* on elevated exposed sections
* when passing motorcyclists
* when passing vehicles towing caravans, horse boxes, etc.

If you're driving a high-sided vehicle such as a

* furniture removal van
* box van carrying comparatively light merchandise
* curtain-sided vehicle

take special notice of warnings for drivers of such vehicles. Avoid known problem areas such as viaducts, high suspension bridges, etc.

Motorcyclists are especially vulnerable to severe crosswinds on motorways, so allow room when overtaking them. Check the nearside mirror to observe them after you've overtaken.

Ice or frost

In cold weather, especially at night when temperatures can drop suddenly, be on the alert for any feeling of lightness in the steering. This may suggest frost or ice on the road. Watch for signs of frost along the hard shoulder as well. A warm cab can isolate you from the real conditions outside.

Motorways that appear wet may in fact be frozen. There are devices that fix onto the exterior mirror to show when the outside temperature drops below freezing.

Allow up to **ten times** the normal distance for braking in icy conditions. Remember, all braking should be carried out gently to reduce the risk of losing control.

Fog

If there's fog on the motorway you must reduce speed so that you can pull up in the distance that you can see to be clear. You should

- slow down
- use dipped headlights
- use rear high-intensity fog lights if visibility is less than 100 metres (about 330 feet)
- keep a safe separation gap from the vehicle in front
- check your speedometer.

Don't

- speed up again if the fog is patchy. You could run into dense fog again within a short distance
- hang onto the rear lights of the vehicle in front.

Fog affects your judgement of speed and distance. You may be travelling faster than you realise. Multiple pile-ups on motorways don't just happen – they're caused by drivers who

- travel too fast
- drive too close
- assume there's nothing stopped ahead
- ignore signals.

If you see fog warning signs but visibility is clear, there may be foggy conditions ahead. Be prepared and reduce speed in good time. Also, remember that motorcyclists can be much more difficult to see in fog.

Remember, you can't see well ahead in fog, slow down.

When driving in fog, watch out for any signals that tell you to leave the motorway. Also, look for incidents ahead and for emergency vehicles coming up behind (possibly on the hard shoulder). Police cars may be parked on the hard shoulder with their lights flashing. This might mean that traffic has stopped on the carriageway ahead.

'Motorway madness' is the term used to describe the behaviour of those reckless drivers who drive too fast for the conditions. The police prosecute drivers after serious multiple incidents. This is to get the message across to all drivers that they must **slow down in fog.**

section four **driver skills**

Contraflows and roadworks

Essential roadworks involving opposite streams of traffic sharing one carriageway are known as contraflow systems. The object is to permit traffic to continue moving while repairs or resurfacing take place on the other carriageway or lanes.

Red and white marker posts are used to separate opposite streams of traffic. The normal white lane-marking reflective studs are replaced by temporary yellow/green fluorescent studs.

A 50 mph (80 km/h) mandatory speed limit is usually imposed over the stretch affected. This means a closing speed of 100 mph (160 km/h) in the event of a collision. When you are driving in roadworks or contraflow areas, you should

- concentrate on what's going on ahead
- keep a safe separation distance from the vehicle in front
- look well ahead to avoid the need to brake sharply
- comply with advance warning signs, which indicate lanes that must not be used by LGVs (this applies to vehicles over 7.5 tonnes MAM)
- avoid sudden steering movements
- be aware that lanes may be narrower than normal. You must take care not to let your vehicle 'wander' out of such lanes.

You should not

- let the activity on the closed section distract you
- exceed the speed limit
- change lanes if signs tell you to stay in your lane
- speed up until you reach the end of the roadworks and normal motorway speed limits apply again.

Road traffic incidents

Serious incidents can often occur when vehicles cross into the path of the other traffic stream in a contraflow. You must

- keep your speed down
- keep your distance
- stay alert.

Signs

Take notice of advance warning signs (often starting five miles before the roadworks). Get into the correct lane in good time and don't force your way in at the last moment.

Drivers of LGVs carrying oversized loads MUST comply with the advance warning notices. These will tell you either to leave the motorway or to stop and telephone the police and wait for an escort through the roadworks.

Breakdowns

If your vehicle breaks down in a roadworks section, remain with the vehicle. These sections of motorway are usually under TV monitoring. A recovery vehicle, which is provided free of charge in the roadworks section, will be with you as soon as possible.

Be on the lookout for broken-down vehicles causing an obstruction ahead.

Breakdowns on the motorway

If your vehicle develops a problem, leave the motorway at the next exit or pull into a service area. If you can't do this, pull onto the hard shoulder and stop as far to the left as possible

- don't attempt even minor repairs on the motorway
- switch on the hazard warning lights
- make sure that the vehicle lights are on at night time, unless an electrical fault prevents this.

You must not place a warning triangle or any other warning device on the motorway carriageway, hard shoulder or slip road.

Emergency telephones

Motorway emergency telephones are free and easily located. You'll be connected directly to the motorway police or Highways Agency regional control centre, who will then get in touch with a recovery company for you.

In most cases the emergency telephones are 1.6 km (about 1 mile) apart. The direction of the nearest phone will be shown by the arrow on the marker posts along the edge of the hard shoulder. Don't cross the carriageway or any slip road to get to a telephone. Face the oncoming traffic while using the telephone.

If your vehicle has its own telephone, or you use a mobile phone to contact the police, identify your location from the marker posts on the hard shoulder before you phone.

If anything falls from either your vehicle or another vehicle

- use the nearest emergency telephone
- don't attempt to recover it yourself
- don't stand on the carriageway to warn oncoming traffic.

Leaving the motorway

Progressive signs will show upcoming exits. At one mile you'll see

- the junction number
- the road number
- the one-mile indicator.

Half a mile from the exit you'll see signs for

- the main town or city served by the exit
- the junction number
- the road number
- the half-mile exit.

Finally, 300 yards (270 metres) before the exit there will be countdown markers every 100 yards.

A lorry travelling at 56 mph (90 km/h) has only just over 60 seconds from the one-mile sign to the exit. So even at a speed of 50 mph (80 km/h) there's still only 80 seconds from the one-mile sign to the actual exit.

Plan well in advance in order to be in the left-hand lane in good time. Large vehicles in the left-hand lane may prevent a driver in the second lane from seeing the one-mile sign, leaving very little time to move to the left safely.

You must use the MSM/PSL routine in good time before changing lanes or signalling. Assess the speed of traffic ahead in good time in order to avoid overtaking and then having to pull back in and reduce speed to leave at the next exit.

Watch out for motorcyclists filtering between other vehicles or coming up quickly behind you.

Don't

- pull across at the last moment
- drive over the white chevrons that divide the slip road from the main carriageway.

Occasionally there are several exits close together, or a service area close to an exit. Look well ahead and plan your exit in good time. Watch out for other drivers' mistakes, especially those leaving it too late to exit safely.

Traffic queuing

At some locations traffic can be held up on the slip road. Look well ahead and be prepared for this. **Don't queue on the hard shoulder.**

Illuminated signs have been introduced at a number of such locations to give advance warning messages of traffic queuing on the slip road or in the first lane. Watch out for indicators and hazard warning flashers when traffic is held up ahead.

Use the MSM/PSL routine in good time and move to the second lane if you aren't leaving by such an exit.

End of the motorway

There are 'End of Motorway' regulation signs

- at the end of slip roads
- where the road becomes a normal main road.

These remind you that different rules apply to the road that you're joining. Watch out for signs advising you of

- speed limits
- dual carriageways
- two-way traffic
- clearways
- motorway link roads
- part-time traffic signals.

Reduce speed

After driving on the motorway for some time it's easy to become accustomed to the speed. When you first leave the motorway, 40 or 45 mph can seem more like 20 mph. You should

- adjust your driving to the new conditions as soon as possible
- check the speedometer to see the real speed.

Start reducing speed when you're clear of the main carriageway. Motorway slip or link roads often have sharp curves that need to be taken at lower speeds.

Be prepared for the change in traffic at the end of the motorway. Look well ahead for traffic queuing at a roundabout or traffic signals. Look out for more vulnerable road users such as

- pedestrians
- cyclists
- motorcyclists
- horses and riders.

All-weather driving

Goods need to be delivered 24 hours a day all year round. With that in mind, you should employ safe driving techniques to ensure that you, your vehicle and the goods in your care always arrive safely at their destination with the minimum of delay. You'll need all your skills to achieve this objective during periods of bad weather.

It's essential that you take notice of warnings of severe weather such as

- snow or blizzard conditions
- floods
- fog
- high winds.

If an LGV becomes stranded the road may well be blocked for essential rescue and medical services. In the case of fog it could result in other vehicles behind colliding with the stranded vehicle.

Training and preparation are vital. Don't venture out in severe weather conditions without being properly prepared.

Your vehicle

Your vehicle must be in a fit and proper condition at all times. This means regular safety checks and strict observance of maintenance schedules. For fuller details on vehicle maintenance, see page 67-8.

Tyres

Check the tread depth and pattern. LGVs must have a tread depth of at least 1mm across three quarters of the breadth of the tread and in a continuous band around the entire circumference. Examine tyres for cuts, damage and signs of cord visible at the side walls. Also check between double wheels for any debris which may have become trapped. If double-wheel tyres are touching or rubbing, this may be an indication of either under-inflation or overloading of your vehicle.

Brakes

It's essential that the brakes are operating correctly at all times. Any imbalance could cause a skid if the brakes are applied on a slippery surface.

Oil and fuel

Use the correct grades of fuel and oil for any extreme conditions.

Prolonged hot weather will place additional demands on the lubricating oil in engines and turbochargers. In extremes of cold it will be necessary to use diesel fuel with anti-waxing additives to prevent fuel lines freezing up.

Before making a journey in very cold weather, you should ensure you have sufficient fuel in case of extra delays. It is a good idea to make an extra check of the fuel tank and mountings to be sure their condition is good and that fuel lines are not damaged or frozen.

In excessively dusty conditions, which can be encountered on construction sites, quarries, etc, you should strictly follow schedules relating to filter changes.

Icy weather

Ensure the whole of the windscreen is cleared before attempting to move off in frosty conditions. You may be able to avoid having to use a scraper or canned de-icer if you

• park under cover overnight
• use the cab night heater.

If you're driving at night, be alert for any drop in temperature that could cause untreated roads to become icy. If the steering feels light you're probably driving on a frozen road surface, so ease your speed as soon as it's safe to do so. All braking must be gentle and over much longer distances, especially when driving articulated vehicles or those with a trailer.

You'll have to allow more time for the journey because overall speeds will need to be lower. Also, keep a safe separation distance from any vehicle ahead. Allow **ten times** the normal stopping distance.

Drive sensibly and allow for the fact that other road users might get into difficulties. Remember that motorcyclists and cyclists are especially vulnerable on slippery roads. Avoid any sudden

- braking
- steering
- acceleration.

Heavy rain

Ensure that the wipers are clearing the windscreen properly – you'll need to be able to see clearly ahead. Make sure that the screen is also demisted efficiently and that the washer containers are filled with suitable fluid, especially in winter conditions.

Allow at least twice as much separation distance as you would in dry conditions. If you must brake, do it while the vehicle is stable and preferably travelling in a straight line. Avoid sudden or harsh braking.

Obey advisory speed limit signs on motorways. Other road users will have more difficulty seeing when there's heavy rain and spray. Make sure that all spray-suppression equipment on your vehicle is secure and operating.

Construction sites

Heavy rain can turn construction sites into quagmires. Take care when driving on off-road gradients, or when getting down from the cab. If the vehicle is fitted with a switch for locking up the differential mechanism on the drive axle (the 'diff-lock'),

engage it. This will ensure that the power is transmitted to all driven wheels and will assist traction. Remember to disengage the diff-lock as soon as you return to normal road surfaces again. Neglecting to do this can

- seriously affect handling and stability
- cause severe and expensive damage to the differential and axle
- cause excessive tyre wear.

It's an offence to deposit mud on the roadway to the extent that it could endanger other road users. This may involve hosing down the wheels and undergear of your vehicle before it leaves such a site. You should also check between double wheels before leaving the site for any large stones or building bricks wedged between the tyres. Such objects can fly out at speed, with serious consequences for following traffic.

Snow

Falling snow can reduce visibility dramatically. Use dipped headlights and reduce your speed. Allow a much greater stopping and separation distance – up to **ten times** the stopping distance on dry roads.

Road markings and traffic signs can become obscured by snow. Take extra care at junctions.

Deep snow as a result of drifting in high winds can often lead to the closure of high-level roads. Don't attempt to use such roads if

- broadcasts tell LGV drivers to avoid those routes
- warning signs indicate that the road is closed to LGVs or other traffic
- severe weather conditions are forecast.

Some rural roads in exposed places have marker posts at the side of the road that will give a guide to the depth of the snow.

In prolonged periods of snow the fixing of snow chains to driven wheels will often prove to be of value. Remember, a stranded LGV could

- prevent snow ploughs clearing the route
- delay emergency vehicles
- block the road for other road users.

Ploughs and vehicles spreading salt or other de-icers

Don't attempt to overtake a snow plough or a vehicle spreading salt or other de-icers.

You may find yourself running into deep snow or skidding on an untreated section of roadway which these maintenance vehicles could have cleared or treated had you followed on behind them. Keep well back from vehicles spreading salt or other de-icers. If they're on the road there could be bad weather on the way.

Deep snow

If your vehicle becomes stuck in deep snow, engage the diff-lock (if one is fitted) to regain forward traction. Switch it off as soon as the vehicle is moving and before attempting a turn.

Another technique for freeing a vehicle stuck in the snow is to use the highest gear you can to improve traction. Then try alternating between reverse and the forward gear until forward motion is possible. Avoid continual revving in a low gear. This will only result in the drive wheels digging an even deeper rut.

It's often helpful to keep a couple of strong sacks in the cab to put under the drive wheels if the vehicle becomes stuck. A shovel is also handy if the journey is likely to involve crossing areas where snow is known to be a hazard during the winter.

When operating independent retarders care must be taken on the descent of snow-covered gradients. The retarders could cause the rear wheels to lock. Some retarders are managed by the ABS to help avoid this problem.

Fog

Don't drive in dense fog if you can postpone your journey and avoid driving at all at night if there is fog. Don't start a journey that might need to be abandoned because it becomes too dangerous to proceed any further.

The options for finding a safe place to park an LGV off the road in dense fog are limited. You must not leave an LGV on public roads where it would be a danger to other road users. Never leave any LGV or trailer without lights where it would endanger others.

Lights

Use dipped headlights in any reduced visibility. You need to see and be seen.

Use rear high-intensity fog lights and front fog lights when visibility is less than 100 metres (330 feet). Rear fog lights must only be capable of operating with dipped headlights or front fog lights. Switch off front and rear fog lights when visibility improves above 100 metres (330 feet), but beware of patchy fog.

Keep all lenses and reflectors clean. You may need to check more often in poor weather conditions. Ensure that all lights are working correctly.

In fog, don't

- drive too close to the centre of the road
- confuse centre lines and lane markings

- drive without using headlights
- speed up because the fog appears to thin out
- use full beam when following another vehicle – the shadows will make it difficult for the driver ahead to see.

A large vehicle travelling ahead of you may temporarily displace some of the fog, making it appear clearer than it really is. Then again, in a larger vehicle you may be able to see ahead over low-lying fog. Don't speed up in case there are smaller vehicles, cyclists or motorcyclists in front that may be hidden from view.

Slow down.

- Don't speed up if the fog appears thinner. It could be patchy and you could run into it again.
- Keep checking the speedometer to see your true speed. Fog can make it difficult to judge speed and distance.

Stay back.

- Keep a safe separation distance from any vehicle ahead.
- Don't speed up if a vehicle appears to be close behind.
- Only overtake if you can be *sure* the road ahead is clear.

Remember, don't use high intensity rear fog lights unless visibility is less than 100 metres (330 feet).

Reflective studs and markings

Reflective studs are provided on dual carriageways to help drivers in poor visibility. The colours of reflective studs are

- **red** on the left-hand edge of carriageways
- **white** to indicate lane markings
- **green** at slip roads and lay-bys
- **amber** on the right-hand edge of carriageways and the centre reservation
- **fluorescent yellow/green** at roadwork contraflow systems.

On some rural roads there are black and white marker posts, with red reflectors on the left-hand side and white reflectors on the right-hand side of the road. The continuous white line between the left-hand lane and the hard shoulder, and at the left-hand edge of some trunk roads, incorporates a rumble strip. This produces a vibration designed to warn drivers when their vehicle crosses the line.

High winds

In severe weather conditions you should plan your journey well in advance (24 hours ahead, if possible). Listen to, watch or read the weather forecast especially if you're the driver of

- a high-sided vehicle (removal vans, long wheelbase box vans, etc)
- a vehicle with a curtain-side body or trailer
- a vehicle transporting portable buildings, etc with large flat surfaces susceptible to wind pressures
- a vehicle towing a trailer box
- an unladen van of any description.

Take notice if your route includes any locations that are frequently subjected to high winds such as

- high-level bridges or roads
- exposed viaducts
- exposed stretches of motorway.

Watch out for signs indicating high winds. Also, beware of fallen trees or damaged branches that could fall on your vehicle.

Take notice of advance warnings and always remember that

- the route may be closed to certain LGVs
- there may be additional delays due to lane closures. This is done on high-level bridges to create empty buffer lanes, which cope with vehicles that are blown off course into the next lane
- you may need to use an alternative route
- if you ignore the warnings, your vehicle and its load could be affected by the strong winds and could place you and other road users in danger.

Bear in mind that ferry sailings are likely to be affected by gale force winds, resulting in delays or cancellation.

Other road users

In windy conditions other road users are likely to be affected when

- overtaking your vehicle
- you overtake them.

Motorcyclists and cyclists are particularly vulnerable to the effects of wind pressure produced by a passing vehicle. Check the nearside mirror(s) as you overtake to ensure that they still have control of their vehicle. In addition, be on the alert for vehicles or motorcyclists wandering into your lane.

Don't ignore warnings of severe winds. If your vehicle is blown over you could delay the emergency services from reaching an even more serious incident.

Avoiding and dealing with congestion

The increasing level of vehicles on the roads has caused a level of congestion which can lead to frustration and increases in journey times. This affects urban areas, higher speed roads and motorways. However, there is an opportunity for all drivers to help alleviate this problem to some extent by changing their driving habits. Detailed below are ways to do this.

Journey Planning

Time of day

If possible, try to plan journeys to avoid the busy times of day. Much congestion is generated by work/school related travel, causing delays in the early morning and late afternoon/early evening. If you don't have to travel at these times try to avoid them. This will both ease the congestion caused by traffic governed by work/school schedules, and allow you an easier, more pleasant journey less likely to experience delays.

Route planning

Make sure you know where you're going by planning beforehand. If possible, include alternatives in your plan in case you find your original route blocked especially if the route is unknown to you. You could

- use a map - you may need to use different scale maps depending on how far and where you're travelling

- refer to a satellite navigation system (but don't rely on it exclusively)

- consult a motoring organisation or use one of the route planners available on the internet

- print out or write down the route, using place names and road numbers to avoid problems if a certain place is not adequately signed.

Be aware of the size of your vehicle in relation to the width of certain accesses or narrow town roads - it can be very difficult or impossible to manoeuvre a large vehicle if, for example, a one way street or sharp turn is found to be too narrow; or where weight or height restrictions apply.

Satellite navigation systems are a useful tool when in transit. They encourage efficiency thereby improving fuel consumption and reducing emissions. However, you should never rely upon them exclusively. Most are designed only for cars and smaller vehicles. These will not filter out inappropriate items such as narrow lanes, weight-restricted areas or low bridges, all of which physically restrict or prohibit the passage of larger vehicles.

Only those systems specifically designed for use in large goods vehicles, coaches and mobile homes will have the facility to identify and filter out areas through which it would be difficult, unsafe or impossible for such a vehicle to manoeuvre. Even those designed

A satellite navigation system will identify your route for you.

for large vehicles may not have been updated with the latest information at any given time.

Be aware also that, because situations can change very quickly on roads, it's possible there may be sudden delays or diversions which a satellite navigation system cannot detect. It's best to identify narrow roads, height restrictions, tight turnings or overhanging buildings (eg in town areas) for yourself, by manually planning your route before starting your journey.

Remember that any in-vehicle navigation system can reduce your concentration on the road and your level of control of the vehicle. It's advisable to restrict any visual or manual interaction with a system to an absolute minimum (see Rule 150 in *The Highway Code*). In the interests of safety, you should find a safe and legal place to stop before making adjustments.

When in transit, your vehicle radio may pick up and broadcast local warnings of any sudden emergencies, delays or diversions in your vicinity. This extra warning

information will help you make any urgent or necessary adjustments to your route plan.

Your journey

Leave plenty of time, especially if you're connecting with other forms of transport. Concern about reaching your destination in time can lead to frustration and the increased tendency to take risks which in turn could lead to a collision. Delivery schedules need to allow for this so the driver isn't forced into taking unnecessary risks to stay on time. Carry your map or directions with you so you can check positions or identify alternative routes if you're delayed or diverted, but **don't** attempt to look at a map or read directions whilst driving.

Mobile phones

A mobile phone can be useful in case of delays or breakdowns. However, remember that it is illegal to use a hand-held mobile phone whilst driving - including while you are waiting in a queue of traffic. Find a safe place to stop before making a call. If you are driving alone on a motorway, you must leave the motorway before using the phone.

Hazard perception

Looking well ahead to see what other road users in front of you are doing will enable you to plan your driving. If you see any changes that could cause you to slow down or alter course, ease off the accelerator and gradually slow down rather than leaving it late and having to brake harshly. Slow down early - the traffic situation ahead will often have cleared by the time you get there.

Constant speed

When you can see well ahead and the road conditions are good, you should try to drive at a constant speed - this is the time to use cruise control if it is fitted to your vehicle.

Whether or not you have cruise control, choose a speed which is within the speed limit and one which you and your vehicle can handle safely. Make sure you also keep a safe distance from the vehicle in front. Remember to increase the gap on wet or icy roads. Also remember that, in foggy conditions, you will have to slow down so you can stop in the distance you can see to be clear.

At busy times there are some stretches of motorway which have variable speed limits shown above the lanes. The maximum speed limits shown on these signals are mandatory and appear on the gantries above the lanes to which they apply.

These speed limits are in place to make traffic proceed at a constant speed as this has been shown to reduce bunching and consequently, over a longer distance, congestion has been shown to ease. Your overall journey time normally improves by keeping to the constant speed, even if, at times, it may appear that you could have travelled faster for shorter periods.

Lane discipline

You should drive in the left-hand lane of a dual carriageway or motorway if the road ahead is clear.

If you are overtaking a number of slower-moving vehicles it may be safer to remain in the centre lane until the manoeuvre is completed rather than continually changing lanes. Return to the left-hand lane once you have overtaken all the vehicles or if you are delaying traffic behind you. Don't stay in the middle lane after overtaking.

If you are overtaking another large vehicle, and the speed differential between the two is slight, this causes a slow overtake situation. This can delay other faster vehicles, and cause frustration which can lead to dangerous situations. It also means that you are effectively turning a three-lane motorway into a two-lane motorway.

You must not normally drive on the hard shoulder, but at roadworks and certain places where signs direct, the hard shoulder may become the left-hand lane.

Using sign information

Look well ahead for signals or signs, especially on a motorway. Signals situated on the central reservation apply to all lanes.

On very busy stretches, there may be overhead gantries with messages about congestion ahead and a separate signal for each lane. The messages may also give an alternative route which you should use if at all possible.

If you're not sure whether to use the alternative route (for example, can you reach your destination if you use the route suggested), take the next exit, pull over at the first available safe area (lay-by or service area) and look at a map. You can always rejoin the motorway if you feel that is the best course of action once you have had time to consider the options.

Remember, on a motorway, once you have passed an exit and encounter congestion, there may not be another opportunity to leave and you could be stuck in slow-moving or stationary traffic for some time.

If you need to change lanes to leave the motorway, do so in good time. At some junctions a lane may lead directly off the motorway. Only get in that lane if you wish to go in the direction indicated on the overhead signs.

Motorway signals can be used to warn you of danger ahead. For example, there may be an incident, fog, or a spillage, which you may not immediately be able to see.

Amber flashing lights warn of a hazard ahead. The signal may show a temporary maximum speed limit, lanes that are closed or a message such as 'Fog' or 'Q'. Adjust your speed and look out for the danger. Don't increase your speed until you pass a signal which is not flashing or one that gives the 'All clear' sign and you are sure it is safe to increase your speed.

Active Traffic Management

Active Traffic Management (ATM) is a project to try to reduce congestion and make journey times more reliable.

ATM features benefits including

- close circuit television monitoring every section
- high-visibility driver information panels
- new lighting to improve visibility at night and in poor light
- new emergency roadside telephones for use in an emergency or breakdown
- emergency refuge areas for vehicles to use in an emergency or breakdown
- use of the hard shoulder as an additional running lane under controlled conditions to manage traffic in peak congestion or during an incident
- Highways Agency traffic officer patrols monitoring the motorway (see page 210).

Gantries

The new gantries have been built about 500 metres apart. They feature a large message sign board and signal boxes above each of the lanes and the hard shoulder.

Emergency refuge areas

These are 100 metres long, wider than the hard shoulder and are located about every 500 metres. They are designed to be used in cases of emergency or breakdown.

Features include

- sensors to alert the control centre that a vehicle has entered
- CCTV enabling the control centre to monitor the vehicles and send assistance as necessary
- new generation emergency roadside telephones containing additional multilingual and hard of hearing support, and the ability to pinpoint your location
- additional distance from the main carriageway.

Driving in actively managed areas

As with driving on any motorway, you must obey the signals displayed on the overhead gantries. In addition to the normal signals which are used on any motorway, there will also be a single red X without flashing beacons which is applicable to the hard shoulder only. When you see this sign don't use this lane, except in an emergency or breakdown. There are three driving scenarios

* normal motorway driving conditions
* actively managed mode
* hard shoulder running mode

Normal motorway conditions

* no congestion or incident
* no speed limits shown on signals
* National speed limits apply
* hard shoulder for emergency and breakdown use only
* use emergency refuge areas in an emergency for added safety and increased distance from the carriageway
* use emergency roadside telephone for assistance.

Actively managed mode

* there may be an incident or congestion ahead
* all speed limit signals are set and must be obeyed
* driver information panels will provide information for road users
* red cross over hard shoulder means do not use this lane, except in an emergency or breakdown
* use emergency refuge areas in an emergency or breakdown for added safety and increased distance from the carriageway
* use emergency roadside telephone for assistance.

Hard shoulder running mode

This is similar to the actively managed mode, except that the hard shoulder may be used as a running lane between junctions. In this case the red cross above the hard shoulder will be replaced by the appropriate speed limit.

Highways Agency traffic officers

Working in partnership with the police, Highways Agency traffic officers are extra eyes and ears on the motorways. They are a highly trained and highly visible service patrolling the motorway to help keep traffic moving and make your journey as safe and reliable as possible.

Traffic officers wear a full uniform, including a high-visibility orange and yellow jacket, and drive a high-visibility vehicle with yellow and black chequered markings.

Every traffic officer will also have a unique identification number and photographic identity card. They will normally patrol in pairs.

The vehicles contain a variety of equipment for use on the motorway, including temporary road signs, lights, cones, debris removal tools and a first aid kit.

Role of a traffic officer

They will

- help broken down motorists to arrange recovery
- offer safety advice to motorists
- clear debris from the carriageway
- undertake high-visibility patrols
- support the police and emergency services during incidents
- provide mobile/temporary road closures
- manage diversion routes caused by a road traffic incident.

If you have an emergency or breakdown on the motorway, the best action to take is to use an emergency roadside telephone.

In some areas, emergency roadside telephones are answered by Highways Agency control centre operators located in a regional control centre.

Control centre operators are able to monitor any stranded motorists on close circuit television screens and despatch the nearest available traffic officer patrol to assist.

Powers of traffic officers

Unlike the police, traffic officers will not have any enforcement powers. However they are able to stop and direct anyone travelling on the motorway.

It is an offence not to comply with the directions given by a traffic officer. Refer to *The Highway Code*, Rules 107 and 108.

Extent of scheme

There are seven regional control centres in England, managed by the Highways Agency, able to despatch traffic officers to any motorway in England.

Urban congestion

Congestion in urban areas leads to

- longer journey times
- frustration
- pollution through standing and slow-moving traffic.

London suffers the worst traffic congestion in the UK and amongst the worst in Europe. It has been estimated that

- drivers in central London used to spend 50% of their time in queues
- London lost between £2-4 million every week in terms of lost time caused by congestion.

Various measures have been introduced to try to reduce and alleviate the congestion and make traffic flow more freely. Red routes and congestion charging are two of the schemes initiated in the London area. These have also been introduced into other congested towns and cities.

Red Routes

Red routes keep traffic moving and reduce the pollution that comes from vehicle emissions. Stopping and parking is allowed only within marked boxes at certain times.

There is a fixed penalty for an offence and illegally parked vehicles may be towed away.

There are five main types of Red Route markings, as detailed below.

Double red lines - stopping is not allowed at any time, for any reason. They are normally placed at road junctions or where parking or loading would be dangerous or cause serious congestion.

Single red lines - parking, loading or picking up passengers is not allowed during the day (generally 7am to 7pm). Stopping is allowed outside these hours and on Sunday.

Red boxes - indicate parking or loading is permitted during the day at off-peak times, normally 10am to 4pm. Some allow loading and some allow parking, the rules in each case are clearly shown on a sign beside the box.

White boxes - indicate that parking or loading may be allowed at any time, restrictions being clearly shown on the sign beside the box.

Red route clearway - there are no road markings but clearway signs indicate that stopping isn't allowed at any time apart from in marked lay-bys.

Green issues - helping the environment

The effects of pollution

If you follow the principles of Ecosafe driving set out in the following pages, you will become a more environmentally friendly driver. Your journeys will be more comfortable and you could considerably reduce both your fuel bills and those emissions that cause damage to the atmosphere.

As a professional driver, you can set an example to other road users in helping to keep the environment green. Fossil fuels are a finite resource which must be used wisely. Use the advice contained in this book to become an ecosafe driver.

Developing your planning, perception and anticipation skills will obviously help to make you a safer driver. However, although it's beneficial to save fuel, you mustn't compromise the safety of yourself and other road users when attempting to do so. Road safety is more important. At all times you should be prepared to adapt to changing conditions and it may be that you'll have to sacrifice fuel saving for safety.

It's vital that professional operators monitor and manage the fuel used by their vehicles. This can be done by implementing a fuel management programme, which can help reduce fuel consumption across the fleet by at least 5%, as well as providing cost savings. As part of this management process, use of safe and fuel-efficient driving techniques will contribute to this fuel saving.

Reducing fuel consumption by 1000 litres per year will

- save 2.6 tonnes of carbon dioxide emissions per year
- save £1000 per year for the operator (assuming a price of £1.00 per litre, excluding VAT).

Using fuel more efficiently means

- improved profit margins
- lower emissions
- lower costs
- improved environmental performance.

What you can do to help

Driving in a more fuel-efficient way is known to save on costs. It is better for the environment and can also improve the image of a company and the transport industry as a whole, by showing that they are making an effort to reduce their carbon footprint.

It is still possible to drive a large goods vehicle in a manner more beneficial to the environment by applying a little care and thought to how, and when, you drive. You will find some suggestions on the next page about what you can do.

Becoming an ecosafe driver

Ecosafe driving is a recognised and proven style of driving that contributes to road safety, whilst reducing fuel consumption and emissions.

One of the main factors in increasing road safety is the emphasis on planning ahead so that you are prepared in advance for potential hazards. By increasing your hazard perception and planning skills you can make maximum use of your vehicle's momentum and engine braking. By doing this, you can help reduce damage to the environment.

Momentum allows the engine to run more efficiently, with less strain on components. Keeping your vehicle moving at a slow walking pace, instead of moving it from a standstill, will use less fuel.

Descending a hill without using the accelerator uses little or no fuel as the engine management system regulates the fuel supply.

Hazard awareness and planning

You should be constantly scanning all around as you drive. Check into the far distance, midground and foreground, also check behind and to the sides by frequent use of all mirrors. The higher seating within your vehicle gives you the advantage of seeing further ahead. This in turn gives you the opportunity to act earlier and so improve overall road safety.

Early recognition of potential hazards is important, but just looking isn't enough, you need to act correctly on what you have seen. This will mean you are able to

- anticipate problems
- take appropriate action in good time to ensure you are travelling at the correct speed when dealing with a hazard.

By doing this you will avoid late braking and harsh acceleration, both of which lead to higher fuel consumption. Whenever you drop down a gear, fuel consumption increases.

Forward planning helps to eliminate excessive gear changes, eg, when approaching junctions or roundabouts.

It is not always necessary to use every gear. Reducing the number of gear changes not only improves fuel consumption but also means you save time and physical energy, which in turn can mean less fatigue. This is known as 'block' gear changing.

Keep a safe distance from the vehicle in front as this will help you to plan your driving. Try to leave yourself sufficient room so you don't always have to brake immediately or harshly when traffic in front of you slows down. By simply taking your foot off the accelerator, your vehicle will slow down and fuel consumption will be reduced. However, you may wish to use your brakes to advise vehicles behind that you're slowing down.

If you plan early for hazards you will avoid causing bunching of other road users, traffic will flow more smoothly and you will use less fuel. When in non-moving traffic, you could save fuel by switching off the engine when stationary.

Height and positioning of a load can also influence fuel consumption and aerodynamic drag. Minimising load height reduces the drag coefficient of the vehicle, especially when using a flat-bodied vehicle. The position of the load should be calculated to reduce drag whilst also avoiding any overload to the axles (see Section Two on loading).

In cold weather, fuel-efficient ways of avoiding ice on the windows include

- pre-setting the night heater to warm up the cab
- parking the vehicle under cover at the end of the previous shift.

Driving away

Avoid over-revving your engine when you start your vehicle and try to pull away smoothly.

Choosing your speed

Always drive sensibly and keep within the speed limit. Exceeding a speed limit by only a few miles per hour will mean that you use more fuel but, more importantly, you are breaking the law and increasing the risk of serious injury if you're involved in a collision.

Cruise Control

Cruise control will help to optimise the electronic control system's ability to deliver the appropriate amount of fuel for any given situation, thus improving fuel efficiency. If it's fitted, it should be used whenever safe and appropriate, to maximise fuel economy.

Use of cruise control, combined with effective route planning and keeping the rev counter in the green band, can all help to minimise the amount of fuel used.

Using cruise control keeps a steady setting on the accelerator so not varying the intake of fuel. Use of constant speeds on motorways and dual carriageways enables full use of cruise control, which helps to optimise the engine management system's ability to precisely measure and deliver the appropriate amount of fuel for any given situation. This not only gives more economic fuel use but also reduces engine and driveline wear and maintenance costs.

Remember cruise control should not be used as a substitute for concentration - you must exercise proper control of your vehicle at all times. It is not advisable to use cruise control in stop/go traffic or in hilly terrain. In these conditions it may not help fuel economy and it could also be dangerous.

If your vehicle has a fuel consumption readout display on the instrument panel, use it to monitor the fuel used during the journey. It can also help to maintain your speed within the speed limit.

The accelerator

Try to use the accelerator smoothly and progressively. When appropriate, take your foot off the pedal and allow the momentum of the vehicle to take you forward. Taking your foot off the accelerator when going downhill can save a considerable amount of fuel without any loss of vehicle control. Rather than use your brakes for a long period with the risk of brake fade, you should control downhill speed by use of lower gears.

Whenever possible, avoid rapid acceleration or heavy braking as this leads to greater fuel consumption and more pollution. Driving smoothly can reduce fuel

consumption by about 15% as well as reducing wear and tear on your vehicle.

Selecting gears

It is not always necessary to change up or down through each gear - it is possible to miss out intermediate gears ('block' gear changing). This helps to reduce the amount of time you spend accelerating, and as this is when fuel consumption is at its highest, you can save fuel by missing out some gears. Accelerate smoothly up to an appropriate speed and, as soon as conditions allow, use the highest gear possible without making the engine struggle.

Fuel consumption

Check your fuel consumption regularly. To make sure you are getting the most from your vehicle, simply record the amount of fuel you put in against miles travelled. This will help you check whether you're using fuel efficiently. See page 325 for more details. Keeping the engine revs in the green band without labouring the engine will help maximise fuel economy.

If you haven't changed your driving method, or the conditions in which you're driving, an increase in the average fuel consumption can mean the vehicle needs servicing. An eco-friendly driver is constantly aware of how much fuel their vehicle uses. If a trip computer is fitted, this can help you check fuel consumption.

Overfull fuel tanks can cause fuel to leak through the breather vent. Fuel expands when hot, so leaks can happen once expansion occurs if the tank is filled to the brim. This can waste fuel and make the road surface dangerous for other road users. Always leave a little room for expansion in the interests of safety.

Using the lift axle when applicable will also help to save fuel by reducing rolling resistance. However, when doing this, you must make sure that the weight limits on the remaining axles are not exceeded. See Section 2 for information about axle loads and weight limits.

Braking

Smooth and progressive braking will save fuel and reduce stress on vehicle, driver and passengers (eg co-driver, assistant). When using the footbrake, the lost road speed has to be made up by accelerating which burns fuel. If it is necessary to change down a gear or half gear, even more fuel is used.

Harsh braking uses more fuel and increases the number of gear changes required to regain speed. It is possible that the safety and comfort of any co-workers being carried is more likely to be compromised under heavy or sharp braking.

By using smooth, progressive braking, the amount of road speed lost can be minimised. Also, use of retarders can contribute to fuel efficiency as well as increasing the life of the brake lining - both with significant cost savings to operators.

Engine power

Modern vehicles are designed to deliver power even when engine revs are quite low. You'll find that you can make use of the higher gears at low speeds.

Engine braking

With your foot fully off the accelerator the engine uses little or no fuel, so take advantage of engine braking wherever possible. Use lower gears rather than extended brake use to avoid brake fade.

Route planning

• Plan your route to avoid known hold ups and roadworks.

• Refer to a satellite navigation system but don't rely on it exclusively as it may have out-of-date or incomplete information at any given time, even if the system you're using is specifically designed for large vehicles.

• Always know where you're going - you'll use lots of fuel by getting lost.

• If you're likely to be making a prolonged stop, say for more than two minutes at a level crossing or road works, you may consider it best to stop the engine.

- Make sure you know of any narrow roads or areas where it may be difficult to pass through or manoeuvre a very large vehicle, or where there may be weight, width or height restrictions.
- Try to plan for the easiest way to access your destination.
- Try to use uncongested routes.

Continuous research has resulted in new methods of helping the environment by easing traffic flow (see page 204-5 for advice on avoiding congestion).

Minimising drag

Aerodynamic styling, eg a curved trailer roof, side skirts or wind deflectors, help minimise drag. Spoiler drag/wind resistance can increase fuel consumption by more than 15%, so a correctly adjusted air deflector will save fuel. Roof spoilers should be adjusted to guide airflow over the highest point at the front of the trailer or load. As a guide, for every 10 cm of trailer

front exposed to airflow, fuel consumption will worsen by 0.1 mile per gallon.

To improve aerodynamics, retrofitted parts can assist vehicle stability in windy conditions and also help prevent build-up of road film and dirt.

If it's fitted, use air conditioning only when you need to - running it continuously may increase fuel consumption by about 15%. The alternative to air conditioning may be to open your windows but this will increase drag, and consequently fuel consumption, when you're driving.

Select for economy and low emissions

There are advantages and disadvantages in all types of fuel. However most large goods vehicles are now diesel-powered. These engines are very fuel efficient and produce less carbon dioxide (a global warming gas) than any other road transport fuel. They

also emit less carbon monoxide and hydrocarbons than petrol engined vehicles but do produce more emissions of oxides of nitrogen (NOx) and particulates, which are bad for local air quality.

Fitting a particulate trap to a vehicle can help to reduce harmful emissions by filtering hydrocarbons, carbon monoxide and particulate matter.

Newer vehicles have to meet strict new emissions standards aimed at reducing these pollutants, and all diesel vehicles can now use ultra-low sulphur diesel fuel to reduce exhaust pollution. When obtaining a new vehicle, the vehicle's handbook will be helpful in advising how to drive it in the most fuel-efficient way. Some advantages of driving in a fuel-efficient way are

* reduced emissions
* improved operating costs.

Diesel Emissions Fluid (DEF)

Some manufacturers reduce emissions of oxides of nitrogen by pumping a mixture of urea and water into the exhaust. This converts oxides of nitrogen to nitrogen gas and water.

Low emission zones (LEZ)

The Low Emission Zone (LEZ) is a specified area in Greater London within which the most polluting diesel-engined vehicles are required to meet specific emissions standards. If they do not, they will need to pay a daily charge.

The zone applies to all lorries over 3.5 tonnes as well as to all buses and coaches. From October 2010, minibuses and large vans will also be covered.

Further information on this subject can be found at **www.tfl.gov.uk/roadusers/lez**

Keep your vehicle well-maintained

You should make sure that your vehicle is serviced and maintained regularly. Some suggestions are listed below.

* Make sure the engine is tuned correctly. Badly tuned vehicles use more fuel and emit more exhaust fumes. MOT tests include a strict exhaust emission test to ensure correct tuning so vehicles run more efficiently, causing less air pollution.

* Have your vehicle suitably serviced as recommended by the manufacturer. The cost of a service may well be less than the cost of running a badly maintained vehicle - for example, even slight brake drag can increase fuel consumption.

- If you do your own maintenance, make sure that you send oil, old batteries and used tyres to a garage or local authority site for recycling or safe disposal. Don't pour oil down a drain; it's illegal, harmful to the environment and could lead to prosecution.
- Rips or tears to curtain sides will affect fuel consumption so make sure they are repaired immediately (see page 103).
- Use good quality engine oil - if you use synthetic engine oils rather than the cheaper mineral oil, you can save fuel.
- Make sure your tyres are properly inflated. Incorrect tyre pressure results in shorter tyre life and may create a danger as it can affect stability and braking capacity. In addition, under-inflation can increase fuel consumption and emissions.

When refuelling your vehicle, you should aim to fill to the bottom of the filler neck and no further. As previously stated, if you fill the tank to the brim, once the fuel becomes hot it expands and its only way of escape is via the breather vent. If, at any time, you notice that your fuel filler cap is missing you MUST get it replaced before continuing.

Also, knowing your particular vehicle's average miles or kilometres per gallon (mpg or km/g) can help early identification of problems. If the ratio drops, this may indicate a problem with the vehicle.

Drivers are usually the first to notice problems, for example dragging brakes. Here's a checklist of tell-tale signs which may indicate that a commercial vehicle needs workshop attention to stop it wasting fuel.

Make this list part of your regular vehicle examination - check for

- any fuel or oil leaks including missing or broken fuel caps
- missing seals in fuel tank cap or signs of fuel spills around filler neck
- low tyre pressure
- tyre wear suggesting faulty steering or axle alignment
- missing tyre valve caps
- traces of black smoke in exhaust
- tears in body curtains/any body damage
- missing/damaged air management equipment
- excessive engine oil consumption (no leaks) suggestive of internal wear
- maintenance records showing rapid wear of clutch or brake friction material.

Road traffic incidents

You should drive at all times with anticipation and awareness. By acting in this way you lessen the risk of being involved in a road traffic incident.

It's important to recognise the effects your vehicle can have on more vulnerable road users such as cyclists, pedestrians and motorcyclists. An LGV can create a vacuum effect when travelling at speed. Cyclists, and pedestrians near the edge of the kerb, are especially vulnerable to the danger of being drawn under the wheels of your vehicle or any trailer. You should anticipate at all times the actions of other road users around you.

You should

- concentrate
- stay alert
- be fully fit
- observe the changes in traffic conditions
- plan well ahead
- drive at a safe speed to suit the road and traffic conditions
- keep your vehicle in good mechanical condition
- ensure that the load is securely stowed
- drive safely and sensibly
- avoid the need to rush
- not act hastily.

Reporting your incident

You must

- produce your insurance documents and driving licence, give your name and address and the name and address of the vehicle owner to any police officer who may require it
- give your details to any other road user involved in the incident if they have reasonable grounds to request them

If you're unable to produce your documents at the time, you must report the incident to the police as soon as possible or in any case within 24 hours. (In Northern Ireland you must report it to the police immediately).

Give your details to any other road user involved in the incident

You must inform the police as soon as possible, and in any case within 24 hours (you must do this immediately in Northern Ireland), if

- there's injury to any person not in your vehicle
- damage is caused to another vehicle or property and the owner is either not present or can't be found easily
- the incident involves any of the animals specified by law.

The police may require you to produce your documents within seven days at a police station of your choice. If you're on a journey that takes you out of the country at the time and you can't produce the documents within the seven days specified, they may allow you to do so as soon as is reasonably possible.

At the incident scene you **MUST**

- exchange particulars with any other driver or road user involved in the incident. These details should include
  - your name and address
  - the name and address of the vehicle's owner
  - the registration number of the vehicle you are driving

Also try to obtain the names and addresses of any witnesses who **saw** the incident.

You should make a note of

- the time and date
- the location
- street names
- vehicle registration numbers
- weather conditions
- lighting (if applicable)
- any road signs or road markings
- road conditions
- damage to vehicles or property
- traffic lights (colour at the time)
- any indicator signals or audible warning given
- any statements made by the other party or parties
- any skid marks, debris, etc.

Company documentation

If you are involved in an incident or near-miss at work, a superior must be informed as soon as possible because it is their legal duty to report it.

It is likely that, regardless of the operator or insurer, the information required when completing any incident report form will be very similar, with only slight variations.

It is a good idea, therefore, to familiarise yourself with your operator's particular reporting requirements, to make sure you collect all the necessary details at the time of the incident.

Your operator may have a company procedure for completing incident reports and there may already be some forms available in your vehicle, which you should use when collecting the required details. A company incident report should be completed immediately after the event.

Many operators have standardised the procedure for reporting incidents and crashes. Drivers carry a 'bumpcard' which they use to record details at the scene then transfer to an official form held at base. Some operators have set up call centres so that drivers can instantly call in if they are involved in an incident. You should record the details shown in the bulleted list above and should also include

• purpose of journey

• starting time

• sketch or photograph of scene

• account of what happened

• any injuries sustained

• cause of incident.

Drivers are often supplied with incident packs which include bumpcard, disposable camera, a guide to reporting incidents, pen and torch.

In most cases a senior manager will interview the driver about what happened. Blame may be laid on the driver if they are found to be

• driving too fast for the conditions

• applying the brakes too fiercely (skids are blameworthy unless due to certain exceptions, ie oil that could not be seen on the road)

• failing to anticipate possible difficulties and danger

• failing to give proper signals of intentions

• failing to comply with *The Highway Code*.

Reaction in the event of aggression

Be aware that others involved in an incident may initially behave in an agitated or aggressive manner. This can often be a symptom of shock, so try to be as reasonable and softly-spoken as possible when asking for personal details or insurance information. The fact that you appear calm and in control may be all that is needed to diffuse a situation.

At an incident scene

If you're the first, or among one of the first, to arrive at the scene of an incident, your actions could be vital. Find a safe place to stop, so you do not endanger yourself, any passengers or other road users.

It's essential to

- warn other traffic approaching the scene by means of hazard warning flashers, beacons, cones, advance warning triangles, etc
- reduce the risk of fire by making sure that all naked lights – cigarettes, etc – are extinguished
- **make sure that someone phones 999**, giving details of any injury or danger to other road users
- protect injured persons from any danger from traffic, hazardous materials, etc. It may well be best to keep them still until the emergency services arrive
- be especially careful about moving any casualties – incorrect handling could cause more injury or even prove fatal
- move any apparently uninjured persons away from the vehicle(s) to a place of safety
- give first aid if anyone is unconscious. For advice on first aid, see pages 228-230.
- check for the effects of shock. A person may appear to have no injuries but may be suffering from shock
- keep casualties warm but give them nothing to drink
- give the **facts** (not assumptions, etc) to the ambulance crew when they arrive.

Do not remove a motorcyclist's helmet unless it is essential to do so, eg if they aren't breathing normally.

Incidents on the motorway

Because of the higher speeds on motorways and the increased danger of a collision becoming a serious incident, it's essential to inform the motorway police and emergency services as quickly as possible.

You should

- use the nearest emergency telephone – it is free and connects directly to the Highways Agency regional control centre or the police. If you use a mobile telephone, first make sure you have identified your location
- not cross the carriageway to get to an emergency telephone
- try to warn traffic behind if possible, without placing yourself in danger
- move any uninjured people well away from the main carriageway and onto an embankment, etc
- be on the alert for emergency vehicles approaching the incident along the hard shoulder.

Emergency vehicles

Be aware that emergency vehicles may approach at any time while you are on the road. You should look and listen for flashing blue, red or green lights, headlights or sirens being used by ambulances, fire engines, police or other emergency vehicles.

When one approaches do not panic; consider the route it is taking and take appropriate action to let it pass. If necessary, pull to the side of the road and stop. Make sure you are aware of other road users and that you do not endanger them in any way.

If you see or hear emergency vehicles in the distance, be aware that there may be an incident ahead and that other emergency vehicles may be approaching.

Remember, if your vehicle is involved in a road traffic incident, you must stop. It's an offence not to do so.

Dangerous goods

If a road traffic incident involves a vehicle displaying either a hazard warning information plate or a plain orange rectangle

- give the emergency services as much information as possible about the labels and any other markings
- contact the emergency telephone number on the plate of a vehicle involved in any spillage, if a number is given
- do not use a mobile telephone close to a vehicle carrying flammable loads
- keep well away from such a vehicle unless you have to save a life
- beware of any dangerous liquids, dusts or vapours – no matter how small the concentration may appear to be. People have received extremely serious injuries as a result of a fine spray of corrosive fluid leaking from a pinhole puncture in a tank vessel.

Examples of various hazard labels are shown on page 326.

Fire

Fire can occur on LGVs in a number of locations, for example

- engine
- load
- transmission
- tyres
- fuel system
- electrical circuits.

It's vital that any fire is tackled without delay. A vehicle and its load can be destroyed by fire within an alarmingly short period of time.

If fire is suspected or discovered, in order to avoid danger to others it's essential to

- stop as quickly and safely as possible
- get all individuals out of the vehicle
- either dial 999 or get someone else to do it immediately.

Carrying a suitable fire extinguisher in your vehicle may help you to put out a small fire. If you suspect a fire in the engine compartment, take the actions shown in the previous three bullet points. In addition

- DO NOT open the body panel. You may be able to direct any available fire extinguisher nozzle through the small gap available when the release catch is operated.
- If the fire appears to be large DO NOT try to tackle it, get well clear of the vehicle and leave it to the fire brigade.
- DO NOT take any risks.

If the fire involves a vehicle carrying dangerous goods

- the driver must have received training in dealing with such an emergency
- specialist fire-fighting equipment must be available on the vehicle.

You should

- keep all members of the public and other traffic well away from the incident
- isolate the vehicle to reduce danger to the surrounding area
- ensure that someone contacts, without delay, the emergency telephone number given on either the hazard warning plate or the load documents
- warn approaching traffic.

Remember, stay calm and react promptly.

Fire extinguishers

You should be able to recognise the various types of fire extinguisher and know which fires they're intended to tackle. For example, it's dangerous to tackle a fuel fire with a water or carbon dioxide fire extinguisher, since this may only spread the fire further.

Most extinguishers are intended to smother the source of the fire by either the action of an inert gas or a dry powder. Try to isolate the source of the fire. If at all possible

- disconnect electrical leads
- cut off the fuel supply.

Don't open an engine housing wide if you can direct the extinguisher through a small gap. Also, avoid operating a fire extinguisher in a confined space.

Vehicles carrying dangerous goods and other materials which may pose a hazard are subject to detailed emergency procedures which must be followed. Never put yourself in danger when tackling a fire. Always call the fire service as quickly as possible because they are the experts. Make sure any passengers leave the vehicle and go to a place of safety.

Note

Halon fire extinguishers may still be used. However, **halon is no longer manufactured in the EU for environmental reasons**. Once used, a halon extinguisher cannot be refilled and should be replaced with a suitable alternative such as a dry powder extinguisher.

First aid

Regulations require many LGVs carrying chemicals, etc, to carry first aid equipment. Even if you don't have to carry a kit by law, it's sensible for every LGV driver to have a first aid kit available.

You should really consider undertaking first aid training. One day it could save a life. There are courses available from the

- St John Ambulance Association and Brigade
- St Andrew's Ambulance Association
- British Red Cross Society.

The following information may be of some assistance, but it is no substitute for proper training.

First aid on the road

Any first aid given at the scene of an incident should only be looked on as a temporary measure until the emergency services arrive. If you haven't any training the following points could be helpful.

Incident victims (adults and children)

It is essential that the following are given immediate priority if the casualty is unconscious and permanent injury is to be avoided.

D – Danger - check that you are not in danger

R – Response - try to get a response by asking questions and gently shaking their shoulders

A – Airway - the airway must be cleared and kept open

B – Breathing - normal breathing must be established. If normal breathing is absent:

C – Compressions - compressions should be administered to maintain circulation as described below.

Airway Place one hand on the forehead and two fingers under the chin, then gently tilt the head back.

Breathing Once the airway is open, check breathing by placing your cheek over their mouth and nose, listen for breath, look to see if the chest rises and feel for breath; do this for up to 10 seconds.

Compressions If they are not breathing normally, place two hands in the centre of the chest and press down 4-5 cms at a rate of 100/minute. You may only need one hand and less pressure for a child. Give 30 chest compressions.

Then tilt the head back gently, pinch the casualty's nostrils together and place your mouth over theirs. Give two breaths, each lasting 1-second (use gentle breaths for a small child). Continue with cycles of 30 chest compressions and 2 breaths until medical help arrives.

Incident victims (Infants under 1 year)

Use the same procedures as for the adult and children, except:

- use two fingers in the middle of the chest when delivering compressions
- to deliver breaths, make a seal over the infant's mouth AND nose with your mouth and breathe **gently.**

Unconscious and breathing

Do not move a casualty unless there's further danger. Movement could add to spinal/neck injury.

If breathing is not normal, or stops, treat as recommended in the breathing section.

Don't attempt to remove a motorcyclist's safety helmet unless it's essential (casualty not breathing normally) otherwise serious injury could result.

The recovery position

If an adult or child is unconscious and breathing, place them on their side in the recovery position as described below until help arrives.

- Place the arm nearest you in a right angle, move the other arm, palm upwards, against the casualty's cheek.
- With your other hand, grasp the far leg just above the knee and pull it up, keeping the foot flat on the ground.
- Pull the knee towards you, keeping their hand pressed against their cheek, and position the leg at a right angle.

Make sure their airway remains open and that you monitor the casualty's condition until medical help arrives.

Bleeding

First check for anything that may be in the wound, such as glass. Then, taking care not to press on the object, build up padding on either side of the object. If there is nothing embedded, apply firm pressure over the wound to stem the flow of blood.

As soon as practical, fasten a pad to the wound with a bandage or length of cloth. Use the cleanest material available.

If a limb is bleeding but not broken, raise it above the level of the heart to reduce the flow of blood. Any restriction of blood circulation for more than a short time could cause long-term injuries. It's vital to obtain skilled medical help as soon as possible. **Make sure that someone dials 999.**

Burns

Check the casualty for shock, and if possible, try to cool the burn. Try to find a liquid that is clean, cold and non-toxic with which to douse it.

Do not try to remove anything which is stuck to the burn.

Dealing with shock

The effects of shock may not be immediately obvious.

Warning signs to look for include

- rapid pulse
- pale grey skin
- sweating
- rapid, shallow breathing.

Prompt treatment can help to minimise the effects of shock. You should

- reassure the victim confidently and keep checking them
- keep any casualties warm and make them as comfortable as possible
- try to calm a hysterical person by talking to them in firm, quiet tones
- make sure that shock victims don't run into further danger from traffic
- avoid leaving the casualty alone
- avoid unnecessary movement of a casualty
- if a casualty does need to be moved for their own safety, take care to avoid making their injuries worse.

You should not give victims anything to drink until medical advice is available.

Electric shock

A vehicle can come into contact with overhead cables or electrical supplies to traffic bollards, traffic lights or street lighting standards as a result of a collision. Make a quick check before attempting to pull someone from a vehicle in such cases.

Don't touch any person who is obviously in contact with a live electric cable unless you can use some non-conducting item, such as a length of **dry** wood, plastic or similar - nothing wet should be used. Use it to push away any electrical equipment or loose cables if you can and separate any contact the casualty has with the electricity supply. You **must not** try to give first aid until contact has been broken.

A person can also be electrocuted by simply being too close to a high voltage overhead cable. Contact the provider (a number may be shown on a nearby pole) then follow their advice.

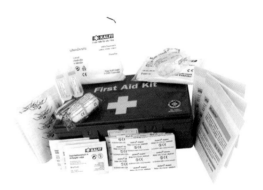

Breakdowns

Tyre failures

Many LGV breakdowns involve tyre failures or blow-outs. Not only are these dangerous in themselves, causing loss of control, but the resulting debris also presents a hazard to other road users.

Front wheel blow-outs

A sudden deflation of the front tyre on an LGV can result in a loss of steering control. You should

- keep firm hold of the steering wheel
- always be aware of anything on your nearside
- signal to move to the left
- try to steer a steady course to the nearside (or hard shoulder on the motorway)
- reduce speed gradually and avoid any harsh braking
- try to bring the vehicle to rest under control and as far to the left as possible
- use a warning triangle, if you have one. Place it behind the vehicle and operate the hazard flashers if the vehicle is causing an obstruction. Don't try to place or retrieve a triangle on a motorway
- avoid sharp braking and excessive steering movements. You should be able to bring the vehicle to rest safely by reducing the risk of skidding.

Rear wheel blow-outs

If a rear tyre on either the vehicle or a trailer deflates the effects may not be quite so severe. On a large vehicle this may not be immediately obvious to you, especially if it's a multi-axle trailer. Keep the trailer under observation at all times during a journey.

Lost wheels

Regular maintenance is essential to help prevent wheels becoming detached during use. When the wheels have been removed and replaced for any reason, it's important to re-check the wheel nuts shortly after their initial tightening. Check the wheel fixings regularly during use, preferably as part of your inspection routine prior to starting any journey.

It's essential that wheel fixings are tightened to the torque specified by the vehicle manufacturer. You should also use a torque wrench that's frequently calibrated.

Further information is given in the British Standard Code of Practice for the selection and care of tyres and wheels for commercial vehicles. This has been developed with the support and involvement of the major transport operators' associations.

The relevant reference number is **BS AU 50: Part 2: Section 7a: 1995,** and it's available from

British Standards Institution
389 Chiswick High Road London W4 4AL.
Tel: 0208 996 9000
Website: www.bsi-global.com

section **five**
PREPARING FOR THE DRIVING TEST

This section covers

- About the driving test
- The theory test
- How to apply for your tes
- Before attending your tes
- Legal requirements
- At the test centre
- The official syllabus

About the driving test

When taking the LGV practical driving test you should aim for a professional standard. You'll pass if your examiner sees that you can

- drive safely to a high standard
- show expert handling of the controls
- carry out the set exercises accurately and under control
- demonstrate through your driving that you have a thorough knowledge of *The Highway Code* and other matters concerning vehicle safety.

Does the standard of the test vary?

No. All examiners are trained to carry out the test to the same standard.

Test routes are as uniform as possible and include a wide range of typical road and traffic conditions.

You should have the same results from different examiners or at different LGV driving test centres.

How your driving test is assessed

Your examiner will assess any errors you make. They will be assessed and recorded depending on their degree of seriousness and marked on the *Driving Test Report form (DL25)*.

You will fail your test if you commit a serious or dangerous fault. You will also fail if you accumulate too many driving faults.

The criteria the examiner will use are as follows

Driving fault – less serious but has been assessed as such because of circumstances at that particular time.

Serious fault – recorded when a potentially dangerous incident has occurred or a habitual driving fault indicates a serious weakness in a candidate's driving.

Dangerous fault – recorded when a fault is assessed as having caused actual danger during the test.

At the end of the test you will be offered some general guidance to explain your driving test report.

Are examiners supervised?

Yes, they're closely supervised. A senior officer may sit in on your test if there are two or more passenger seats in your vehicle.

Don't worry about this. The supervising officer won't be examining you, but will be checking that the examiner is carrying out the test properly. Just carry on as if she or he wasn't there.

Can anyone accompany me on the test?

Due to lack of seats this isn't always possible. If there are three or more seats in the cab of your vehicle, and provided a DSA supervisor isn't intending to observe the test, your instructor is allowed to be present but can't take any part in the test.

How should I drive during the test?

Drive in the way that your instructor has taught you. If you make a mistake, try not to worry. It might be minor and may not affect the result of the test. Your examiner will be looking for a high overall standard. Don't worry about one or two minor mistakes.

What will my examiner want from me?

Your examiner will want you to drive safely to a high standard under various road and traffic conditions.

You'll be

* given directions clearly and in good time
* asked to carry out set exercises.

Due to the higher level of engine noise in the cab your examiner will make sure that you're able to hear the directions clearly.

Your examiner will be understanding and sympathetic. They will try to put you at your ease to help you to do your best.

What will the test consist of?

Apart from general driving, the test will include

* reversing within a marked area into a restricted opening
* a braking exercise
* moving off on the level, at an angle, uphill and downhill
* demonstrating the uncoupling and recoupling procedure (if you're taking your test with a trailer).

You will also need to satisfy the examiner that you're capable of preparing to drive safely by carrying out simple safety checks on the vehicle you're using on the test.

Some of these exercises are always carried out at the test centre. These are the

* safety check questions
* reversing exercise
* braking exercise
* uncoupling and recoupling exercise.

The rest of the exercises will take place during the road section of the test.

During the reversing exercise your examiner will remain outside the vehicle.

Your examiner will join you in the cab before explaining the braking exercise to you. They will watch your handling of the controls as you carry out the exercise.

This exercise will be carried out before you leave the test centre. If your vehicle doesn't pull up satisfactorily, your examiner may decide not to continue the test in the interest of safety.

What if I don't understand?

Your examiner will be as helpful as possible and will explain what's required. Before the exercises you'll be shown a diagram. This will make it easier to understand what's required. You'll then be asked to carry out the exercise. If you aren't sure, ask. Your examiner won't mind explaining again.

How long will the test last?

About 90 minutes.

When will I be ready for my test?

When you've reached the standards set in this book – not before. You should ensure that you receive good instruction, together with as much practice as you can.

How will I know when I'm ready?

You're ready for your practical test when you're driving

* consistently well
* with confidence
* in complete control
* without assistance and guidance from your instructor.

Most people fail because they haven't had enough instruction and practice. Make sure that all aspects of the syllabus for learning to drive an LGV are covered (see pages 243-255).

Special circumstances

You'll have had to pass a medical in order to obtain your provisional licence. Your doctor will have had to declare if there's any reason why you wouldn't have full control of a large vehicle. There may be circumstances when adaptations to a vehicle may overcome a particular disability.

To make sure that enough time is allowed for your test it would help DSA to know

* if you're restricted in any way in your movements
* if you have any disability that might affect your driving.

Please include this information when you apply for your test.

Your examiner may wish to talk to you about your disability and any adaptations you may have fitted to your vehicle.

Language difficulties

If you have difficulty speaking or understanding English, you can bring an interpreter with you. Remember, the vehicle must have enough seats. The interpreter must be 16 years or over and must not be your instructor.

The theory test

Before you take your practical LGV driving test you'll have to pass an LGV theory test. You must satisfy your examiner that you've **fully understood** everything that you learned for the theory test.

The various aspects include knowledge of

- the height, weight, width and length of your vehicle. This enables you to drive on roads with a full knowledge of any restrictions that might apply to your vehicle
- rules on drivers' hours and rest periods, so that you can obey the legal requirements and are fit to drive safely
- braking systems and speed limiters. You should be fully aware of how your brakes work and the importance of using them effectively
- the restricted view you have around your vehicle due to its size and dimensions. This size will also affect other road users' view – you must be aware of this
- faults on your vehicle and being able to recognise and report any defects
- the factors relating to loading a vehicle safely and securely
- the effect of wind on your vehicle and on other road users around you
- the dangers of splashing spray or mud on other road users when overtaking them
- the course you have to take when turning, in order to allow for the length or overhang of your vehicle

- the correct actions to take if you're involved in or arrive at an incident
- reducing the risks when overtaking other road users
- the dangers of leaving the cab of your vehicle on the offside.

As well as the multiple choice questions, the theory test now includes a hazard perception part. To prepare for this DSA strongly recommends that you study and work through the hazard perception training material. The DVD is entitled *The Official DSA Guide to Hazard Perception* which will assist you.

If you've passed your LGV theory test you'll have shown that you've taken the time to learn the basic aspects of becoming an LGV driver.

At the start of the drive in your practical test your examiner will ask you to follow the road ahead, unless asked to turn or traffic signs direct you otherwise. From this point you should be able to demonstrate your understanding of the topics covered in the theory test.

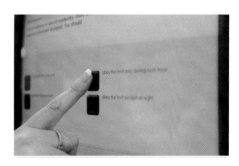

How to apply for your test

You must have a provisional licence for the category of vehicle that you're going to drive.

Booking online or by phone

You can book your theory and practical tests online or by telephone using a credit or debit card. Most major credit and debit cards are accepted. You must be the card holder; if you aren't then the card holder must be present.

You can book online at
www.businesslink.gov.uk/transport

To book by telephone, refer to the information given on page 308.

You will need to provide

- your driver number, shown on your licence
- the type of test you wish to book
- your personal details (name, address, day/evening telephone numbers)
- any special circumstances, such as being accompanied by an interpreter
- your credit card number and expiry date (and the issue number when using Switch).

If you're booking your practical test you'll need to provide your theory test certificate number.

If you use either of these services, you'll be offered a date and time for your test immediately. You'll be given a booking number and sent an appointment within a few days.

More information and guidance on all aspects of booking and taking a driving test, including information about fees, can also be obtained from the website or booking number given above.

Booking by post

If you prefer to book by post, you can obtain an application form (DL26) from a DSA LGV/PCV driving test centre. Look at the guidance notes carefully, especially those that refer to vehicle categories.

Make sure that you give all the particulars asked for on the application form. If you miss anything out it could delay the date of your test.

Don't forget to send your fee. You may do this by sending a cheque or postal order. Make sure that it's crossed and made payable to the Driving Standards Agency. If you send a postal order keep the counterfoil.

Send your application form to

DSA
PO Box 280
Newcastle-Upon-Tyne
NE99 1FP

Remember, please don't send cash.

Trainer booking

If you're learning to drive with a training organisation they'll normally book your test for you. An arrangement with the Area Office allows them to book and pay for test appointments in advance. This enables them to arrange courses to culminate with a test appointment.

If you're a trainer and are interested in this scheme contact DSA's booking section (refer to the information on page 308).

Visit the website

More information and guidance on all aspects of booking or taking a driving test can be found at www.businesslink.gov.uk/transport

Saturday and evening tests

Saturday and weekday evening tests are available at some driving test centres. The fees for these are higher than for a driving test during the normal working hours on weekdays.

Evening tests are available during the summer months only.

You can get details from

- the DSA national booking number (refer to the information on page 308).
- driving test centres
- your instructor.

Your test appointment

The DSA will send you a notification of your appointment, which is the receipt of your fee. Take this with you when you attend your test. The notification will include

- the time and place of your test
- the address of the driving test centre
- other important information.

If you haven't received notification after two weeks contact the national booking number (refer to the information on page 308).

To change or cancel your test

If you need to change or cancel the appointment, you should notify DSA as soon as possible. You may even be able to switch to an earlier date.

You can do this online at **www.businesslink.gov.uk/transport** or by phone (refer to the information on page 308).

You must give at least three clear working days notice. That means three whole working days, counting Saturday as a working day, but not counting the day DSA received your notification nor the day of your test. If you don't give enough notice you'll forfeit your fee and will have to re-apply with another fee.

Before attending your test

Documents

You must have applied for and received a provisional licence for the category in which you wish to take your test. Make sure that you have your provisional driving licence and your theory test pass certificate with you. Photocopies are not acceptable. Your test might be cancelled if you haven't done this.

If you have a photo licence you must bring both parts of the licence (photocard and paper counterpart) to the test.

Remember, no photo, no licence, no test!

If your licence does not show your photograph you must also bring your valid passport with you (your passport doesn't have to be British). No other form of identification is acceptable. Other forms of identification may be acceptable in Northern Ireland. For the list of items which qualify as confirming personal identity, go to **www.dvani.gov.uk**

If you don't bring these documents with you on the day you won't be able to take your test and you will lose your fee.

Your supervising driver

After April 2010 anyone training or supervising (accompanying) must

- hold a full (ie NOT implied rights*) entitlement for the category of vehicle you are driving, and
- have held that entitlement for the relevant period of time - usually three years.

*Implied rights means those drivers who passed their car driving test before January 1997. They were granted implied rights to drive small lorries (C1 and C1+E), subject to certain restrictions. Those people will still be able to drive a small lorry, but cannot supervise a learner C1 or C1+E driver after April 2010.

Legal requirements

Your test vehicle

Make sure that the vehicle you intend to drive

- is legally roadworthy and has a current certificate issued by the Vehicle Inspectorate
- is fully covered by insurance for its present use and for you to drive
- is unladen and doesn't have any large advertising boards fixed to the flat bed of the vehicle
- is in the category in which you want to hold a licence
- has ordinary L plates visible to the front and rear (or D plates if you wish when driving in Wales)
- has a seat in the cab for the examiner, which must be fitted with a seat belt
- has enough fuel, not only for the test (at least 20 miles) but also for you to return to base
- isn't being used on a trade licence.

Test vehicles in all categories must be fitted with an anti-lock braking system and a tachograph.

Vehicle-trailer combinations must be fitted with nearside and offside externally mounted mirrors for use by the examiner. You should also check the vehicle's

- stop lamps
- headlights and rear lights
- direction indicators
- lenses and reflectors
- mirrors
- brakes
- tyres
- exhaust system (for excessive noise)
- windscreen and washers
- wipers.

Make sure that the cab is clean and free from any loose equipment.

Change of vehicle

Please let the Area Office know if you want to bring a different vehicle from the one described on your application form. This will avoid unnecessary delay when you arrive for your test.

Minimum Test Vehicles (MTVs)

For full details of minimum test vehicle requirements, see pages 315-317.

Other legal requirements

You must show that you're competent to drive the vehicle in which the test is being conducted without danger to, and with due consideration for, other persons on the road. The legal requirements state that you must be able to

- start the engine
- move off straight and at an angle
- maintain a proper position in relation to other vehicles
- overtake and take an appropriate course in relation to other vehicles
- turn left and right
- stop within a limited distance, under full control
- stop normally and bring the vehicle to a rest on an appropriate part of the road
- drive the vehicle forward and backward, and whilst driving the vehicle backward steer it along a permitted course so that it enters a restricted opening and then bring it to rest in a predetermined position

- indicate your intended actions by appropriate signals at appropriate times
- act correctly and promptly in response to all signals given by any traffic sign, any person lawfully directing traffic or any other person using the road
- uncouple and recouple your trailer (if appropriate).

Your examiner won't carry out an eyesight test at the beginning of the practical test. You should already have met the requirements before your provisional licence was issued.

At the test centre

Before the drive

Make sure that you arrive in good time. The test will take about 90 minutes, so you need to ensure that you won't exceed the number of hours that you're allowed to drive by law.

Your examiner will ask to see your licence and photo ID and, if appropriate, your theory test pass certificate.

You will be asked to sign a declaration that

- your vehicle is insured
- you meet the residency requirement
- your health has not changed in a way that might affect your driving since your last licence application.

The test won't be conducted if you're unable to do so. When you've done this you'll be asked to lead the way to your vehicle.

The official syllabus

As the driver of a large vehicle you must make safety your first priority – not just your own safety, but also that of other road users. The information in this book describes and encourages the safe driving techniques you should put into practice.

Driving in itself is a life skill, but when considering driving an LGV it's also the means by which you earn your living. It may take many years to gain the skills set out here, but you'll need to aim for professional standards right from the very start.

Whether you learn with an instructor or as work experience with a colleague, you must be satisfied that you've fully covered all aspects of the officially recommended syllabus. You may find it helpful to check your progress against the actual syllabus requirements, so they're given here in full.

This syllabus lists the skills that you must have in order to reach the high standards required to pass the LGV driving test and to become a professional lorry driver. It's impossible to give details of all the rules and regulations that apply to both the driver and their vehicle in a book of this size. However, you'll need to know and keep up-to-date with current requirements.

You must have a thorough knowledge of

- the latest edition of *The Highway Code,* especially those sections that concern lorries
- regulations governing drivers' permitted hours
- regulations relating to the carriage of hazardous and other specialised goods.

You must also have a thorough understanding of general motoring regulations, especially

- road traffic offences
- licences, relating to both drivers and operators, where applicable
- insurance requirements
- vehicle road tax relating to LGVs (and any trailer) in your charge
- plating of LGVs and their trailers
- annual testing of LGVs.

Legal requirements

To learn to drive an LGV you must

1. Normally be at least 21 years old.

2. Meet the stringent eyesight requirements.

3. Be medically fit to drive lorries.

4. Hold a full car licence (category B).

5. Hold and comply with the conditions for holding a provisional licence in the category of LGV being driven.

6. Hold a full licence in category C and a provisional licence for C + E if driving a vehicle in that category.

7. Ensure that the vehicle being driven

   - is legally roadworthy
   - is correctly plated
   - has a current test certificate (MOT)
   - is properly licensed with the correct tax disc displayed.

8. Make sure that the vehicle being driven is properly insured for its use, especially if it's on contract hire.

9. Display L plates to the front and rear of the vehicle (D plates, if you wish, when driving in Wales).

10. Be accompanied by a supervisor who has held a valid full licence for the category of vehicle being driven for over three years and is over the age of 21.

11. Wear a seat belt, if fitted, unless you're exempt. Ensure that all seat belts in the vehicle, and their anchorages and fittings, are secure and free from obvious defects.

   Children shouldn't normally be carried in LGVs. However, if a child is carried in the vehicle with permission, you must comply with all regulations relating to the wearing of seat belts by children or the use of child restraints.

12. Be aware that it's a legal requirement to notify the DVLA of any medical condition that could affect safe driving, if the period for which you are affected is likely to be three months or more.

13. Ensure that any adaptations are suitable to control the vehicle safely if the vehicle has been adapted for any disability.

Vehicle controls, equipment and components

You must

1. Understand the function of the
   - accelerator
   - clutch
   - gears
   - footbrake
   - handbrake
   - secondary brake
   - steering

   and be able to use these competently.

2. Know the function of all other controls and switches on the vehicle and be able to use them competently.

3. Understand the meanings of
   - gauges
   - warning lights
   - warning buzzers
   - other displays on the instrument panel.

4. Be familiar with the operation of tachographs and their charts, or the operation of a digital tachograph if fitted.

5. Know the legal requirements that apply to the vehicle's
   - speed limits
   - weight limits
   - braking system (ABS)
   - number of fire extinguishers to be carried.

6. Know how to carry out routine safety checks and identify defects, especially on the
   - power steering
   - brakes (tractor unit + semi-trailer on articulated, or rigid vehicle + trailer on combinations
   - air pressure in the air tanks
   - suspension
   - wheels, wheelnuts and mudguards
   - tyres on all wheels
   - seat belts
   - lights
   - reflectors/reflective plates
   - direction indicators
   - marker lights
   - windscreen, wipers and washers
   - horn
   - rear view mirrors
   - speedometer
   - instruments, including tachograph
   - exhaust system
   - brake line and electrical connections on rigid vehicles + trailers, or articulated vehicles
   - coupling gear
   - hydraulic and lubricating systems
   - self-loading or tailgate equipment
   - drop-side hinges and tailgate fastenings
   - curtain-side fittings/fastenings
   - winches or auxiliary gear, where these items are fitted.

7. Know the safety factors relating to
   - stowage
   - loading
   - stability
   - restraint of any load carried on the vehicle.

8. Know the effects speed limiters will have on the control of your vehicle, especially when you intend to overtake.

9. Know the principles of the various systems of retarders that may be fitted to LGVs including

   – electric

   – engine-driven

   – exhaust brakes

   and when they should be brought into operation.

Road user behaviour

You must

1. Know the most common causes of road traffic incidents.

2. Know which road users are more vulnerable and how to reduce the risks to them.

3. Know the rules, risks and effects of drinking and driving.

4. Know the effects that

   – illness (even minor ones)

   – drugs or cold remedies

   – tiredness

   can have on driving performance.

5. Recognise the importance of complying with rest period regulations.

6. Be aware of the age-dependent problems among other road users including

   – children

   – young cyclists

   – young drivers

   – older drivers

   – older or infirm pedestrians.

7. Concentrate and plan ahead in order to anticipate the likely actions of other road users and be able to select the safest course of action.

Vehicle characteristics

You must

1. Know the most important principles concerning braking distances under various

   – road

   – weather

   – loading

   conditions.

2. Know the different handling characteristics of other vehicles with regard to

   – speed

   – stability

   – braking

   – manoeuvrability.

3. Know that some other vehicles, such as bicycles and motorcycles, are less easily seen than others.

4. Be aware of the difficulties caused by the characteristics of both your own and other vehicles, and be able to take the appropriate action to reduce any risks that might arise.

Examples are

– LGVs and buses moving to the right before making a sharp left turn

– drivers of articulated vehicles having to take what appears to be an incorrect line before negotiating corners, roundabouts or entrances

– blind spots that occur on many large vehicles

– bicycles, motorcycles and high-sided vehicles being buffeted in strong winds especially on exposed sections of road

– turbulence created by LGVs travelling at speed, affecting pedestrians, cyclists, motorcyclists, vehicles towing caravans, and drivers of smaller motor vehicles.

At all times remember that other road users may not understand the techniques required to manoeuvre an LGV safely.

Road and weather conditions

You must

1. Know the various hazards that can arise when driving
   – in strong sunlight
   – at dusk or dawn
   – during the hours of darkness
   – on various types of road such as
      – country lanes in rural areas
      – one-way streets
      – two-way roads in built-up areas
      – three-lane roads
      – dual carriageways with various speed limits
      – trunk roads with two-way traffic
      – motorways.

2. Gain experience in driving on urban roads with 20 or 30 mph speed limits, and also on roads carrying dense traffic volumes at higher speed limits in both daylight and during the hours of darkness.

3. Gain experience in driving on both urban and rural motorways.

4. Know which road surfaces will provide better or poorer grip when braking.

5. Know all the associated hazards caused by bad weather such as
   – rain
   – snow
   – ice
   – fog.

6. Be able to assess the difficulties caused by
   – road
   – traffic
   – weather
   conditions.

7. Drive professionally and anticipate how the prevailing conditions may affect the standard of driving shown by other road users.

Traffic signs, rules and regulations

You must

1. Have a thorough knowledge and understanding of the meanings of traffic signs and road markings.

2. Be able to recognise and comply with traffic signs that indicate
   – weight limits
   – height limits
   – when LGVs are prohibited
   – loading/unloading restrictions
   – traffic calming measures
   – 20 mph zones
   – road width restrictions
   – speed reduction humps
   – roads designated Red Routes
   – night time and weekend lorry bans, such as those used in the London boroughs.

Vehicle control and road procedure

You must have the knowledge and skill to carry out safely and expertly the following list of tasks (when appropriate) in daylight and, if necessary, during the hours of darkness. Where the tasks involve other road users you must

- make proper use of the mirrors
- take effective observation
- give signals where necessary.

1. Take the following necessary precautions, where they're applicable, before getting into the vehicle

  - ensure that number plates are correct and securely fitted
  - check all round for obstructions
  - ensure that any load is secure
  - check that air lines are correctly fitted and free from leaks
  - check all couplings to the drawing vehicle and trailer
  - check that the landing gear is raised
  - check that the trailer brake is released
  - check that all bulbs, lenses and reflectors are fitted.
  - make sure that all lights, indicators and stop lights are working
  - ensure that all reflective plates are visible, clean and secure
  - examine tyres for defects

  - examine all load restraints for tension, etc
  - ensure that any unused ropes are safely stowed.

2. Before leaving the vehicle cab make sure that

  - the vehicle is stopped in a safe, legal and secure place
  - the handbrake is on
  - the engine is stopped
  - the electrical system is switched off
  - the gear lever/selector is in neutral
  - all windows are closed
  - the passenger door is secure
  - the keys have been removed from the starter switch
  - you won't endanger anyone when you open the door.

3. Before starting the engine carry out the following safety checks

  - handbrake is applied
  - gear lever is in neutral
  - doors are properly closed
  - your seat is adjusted for
      - height
      - distance from the controls
      - back rest support and comfort
  - the mirrors are correctly adjusted
  - your seat belt is fastened and adjusted.

4. Start the engine, but before moving off check that

   - the vehicle (and any trailer) lights are on, if required
   - gauges indicate correct pressures for the braking system
   - no warning lights are showing
   - no warning buzzer is operating
   - no ABS fault indicator is lit (where fitted)
   - all fuel and temperature gauges are operating normally
   - it's safe to move off by looking all round, especially in the blind spots.

5. Move off

   - straight ahead
   - at an angle
   - on the level
   - uphill
   - downhill.

6. Select the correct road position for normal driving.

7. Practise effective observation in all traffic conditions.

8. Drive at a speed appropriate to the road, traffic and weather conditions.

9. Anticipate changes in traffic conditions, adopt the correct action at all times and exercise vehicle sympathy.

10. Move into the appropriate traffic lane correctly and in good time.

11. Pass stationary vehicles safely.

12. Meet, overtake and cross the path of other vehicles safely.

13. Turn right or left at
    - junctions
    - crossroads
    - roundabouts.

14. Drive ahead at crossroads and roundabouts.

15. Keep a safe separation gap when following other vehicles.

16. Act correctly at all types of pedestrian crossing.

17. Show proper regard for the safety of all other road users, with particular respect for those most vulnerable.

18. Drive on
    - urban roads
    - rural roads
    - dual carriageways

keeping up with the traffic flow (but still observing speed limits) where it's safe and appropriate to do so.

19. Comply with
    - traffic regulations
    - traffic signs
    - signals given by authorised persons
    - signs given by police officers.

20. Take the correct action on signals given by other road users.

21. Stop the vehicle safely at all times.

22. Select safe and suitable places to stop the vehicle when requested, reasonably close to the nearside kerb
    - on the level
    - facing uphill
    - facing downhill
    - before reaching a parked vehicle, but leaving sufficient room to move away again.

23. Stop the vehicle on the braking exercise manoeuvring area
    - safely
    - as quickly as possible
    - under full control
    - within a reasonable distance from a designated point.

24. Reverse the vehicle on the manoeuvring area
    - under control
    - with effective observation
    - on a predetermined course
    - to enter a restricted opening
    - to stop with the extreme rear of the vehicle within a clearly defined area.

25. Cross all types of level crossings
    - railway
    - rapid transit systems (trams)
    where appropriate.

26. Uncouple and recouple the tractor unit and trailer. When uncoupling you must
    - select a place with safe and level ground
    - apply the brakes on both the vehicle and trailer
    - lower the landing gear
    - stow the handle away safely
    - turn off any taps fitted to the air lines
    - disconnect the air lines and stow them away safely
    - disconnect the electric lines and stow them away safely

- remove any dog clip securing the kingpin release handle
- release the fifth wheel coupling locking bar, if fitted
- drive the tractor unit away slowly, checking the trailer either directly or in the mirrors
- take any anti-theft precautions (kingpin lock, etc)
- remove the number plate.

With a rigid vehicle and trailer you might have to support the trailer drawbar before you pull away.

For drivers of articulated vehicles with close-coupled trailers, the uncoupling sequence is as follows

- ensure that the brakes are applied on both the tractive unit and the trailer
- lower the landing gear and stow the handle away safely
- disconnect the dog clip (if fitted) and release the fifth wheel coupling
- drive the tractive unit far enough forward so that you can stand on the catwalk
- turn off any taps fitted to the air lines
- disconnect the air lines (or 'suzies') and electrical connections and stow safely
- drive the tractive unit away slowly, checking the trailer either directly or in the mirrors.

When recoupling you must

- ensure the trailer brake is applied
- check that the height of the trailer is correct so that it will receive the unit safely
- reverse slowly up to the trailer ensuring that the kingpin locking mechanism is in place
- do two pull tests to ensure that the locking mechanism is secure by selecting a low gear and attempting to move forward
- apply the parking brake before leaving the cab
- connect any dog clip to secure the kingpin release handle
- connect the air and electric lines
- turn on taps, if fitted
- raise the landing gear and stow away the handle
- ensure that the trailer brake is released before moving off
- check that all electrics are working
- start up the engine and ensure that the gauges register correct pressures in air storage tanks and that no warning buzzer/light is operating
- obtain assistance to check for air line leaks and operation of all rear, marker or reversing lights, indicators, stop lights and fog light(s)

- secure the correct number plate and check that all reflectors are present and clean
- examine all tyres, wheel nuts, fastenings, ropes, sheets, drop-side locking clips, rear doors, hydraulic rams, tail-lift gear, etc to ensure that the trailer and any load won't present a danger to other road users
- check the function of any ABS warning lights, etc
- make sure that your mirrors are properly adjusted to give the best view down each side of the trailer before driving off
- test the operation of the brakes at a safe place, ideally before moving out onto a public road.

When recoupling a rigid vehicle and trailer combination the sequence is similar, but the trailer drawbar will need to be adjusted to the correct height before the towing vehicle reverses to recouple the trailer. When necessary a suitable and safe method of height adjustment should be used. Be on the alert for the safety of anyone at the rear of your vehicle who is assisting you to recouple the trailer.

For drivers of articulated vehicles with close-coupled trailers, the recoupling sequence is as follows

- ensure that the trailer brake is applied
- make sure nobody is either standing at, or working near, the rear of the trailer
- reverse slowly up to the trailer, stop just short and apply the tractive unit parking brake
- check that the height of the trailer is correct so that it will receive the unit safely
- reverse far enough under the trailer so that you can stand on the catwalk
- apply the tractive unit parking brake
- connect the air and electric lines. Turn on taps, if fitted
- reverse under the trailer and connect the fifth wheel
- select a low gear and try to move forward in order to test that the locking mechanism is secure. Do this twice to make sure

- apply the tractive unit parking brake
- connect any dog clip to secure the kingpin release handle
- raise the landing gear and stow away the handle
- release the trailer parking brake
- start up the engine
- check that air is building up in the storage tanks
- check all the lights and indicators.

section **six**

THE LGV DRIVING TEST

This section covers

- Safety check questions
- The reversing exercise
- The braking exercise
- The vehicle controls
- Other controls
- Moving off
- Using the mirrors
- Giving signals
- Acting on signs and signa
- Awareness and anticipatic
- Making progress
- Controlling your speed
- Separation distance
- Hazards
- Selecting a safe place to stop
- Uncoupling and recouplin
- Your test result

Safety check questions

What the test requires

The examiner will ask you to demonstrate, or explain, how to carry out safety checks on your vehicle before driving. If you are taking a test in a rigid vehicle you will be asked to demonstrate, or explain, how to carry out five separate checks. The questions will be based on the skill list shown below.

Here are two examples of the type of question you might be asked.

- Show me how you would check the wheel nuts are secure on this vehicle.
- Tell me the main safety factors involved in loading this vehicle.

If you are taking a test in a vehicle towing a trailer, you will be asked to demonstrate or explain how to carry out two separate checks.

Skills you should show

You will be expected to know how to check that

- your tyres are correctly inflated, have a safe tread depth and are generally safe to use on the road
- your brakes are working effectively and the pedal does not have excessive travel
- your vehicle has sufficient oil, coolant and hydraulic fluid
- you have sufficient windscreen washer fluid
- the power-assisted steering is working and that excessive free play is not apparent
- your headlights, tail lights and reflectors are working and clean

- your brake lights are working and clean
- your horn is working
- the wheel nuts and mud guards are secure
- the vehicle has sufficient air pressure
- all cargo doors are secure.

You will also be expected to know how to

- check for air leaks
- replace the tachograph disc (analogue units)
- operate a digital tachograph
- check the windscreen wipers for wear and that the windscreen is clean
- check the suspension for defects
- load a vehicle safely
- check for signs of overloading
- ensure the load is secure.

For more information about vehicle safety checks see pages 67-8, and 152-4.

Faults to avoid

You should avoid

- being unfamiliar with the vehicle you are using on test
- being unable to explain or carry out safety checks on the vehicle you are using on test.

Your vehicle will have been left unattended so walk around it and make a visual check of

- lights
- tyres
- number plates
- couplings (if appropriate)
- cab locking mechanism (if fitted).

Before you start the engine you must always check that

- all doors are properly closed
- your seat is properly adjusted and comfortable so that you can reach all the controls easily
- you have good all round vision
- your driving mirrors are properly adjusted
- if fitted, your seat belt is fastened, correctly adjusted and comfortable
- the handbrake is on
- the gear lever is in neutral.

Develop this routine while you're learning.

Once you've started the engine, if your vehicle is fitted with air brakes, wait until the gauges show the correct pressure or until any device (a buzzer sounding or a light flashing) has stopped operating.

The reversing exercise

The exercise is started from a position with the front of the vehicle in line with cones A and A1. You should reverse your vehicle into the bay, keeping marker B on the offside. You should stop with the extreme rear of your vehicle within the stopping area.

The stopping area will have both a solid yellow line and a yellow and black hatched section, and a barrier will be situated at the end of the reversing bay. You should stop with the extreme rear of your vehicle in the 75 cm wide yellow and black stopping area.

The distances

A to A1 = 11/2 times the width of the vehicle

A to B = twice the length of the vehicle

B to line Z = 3 times the length of the vehicle.

What the test requires

You should be able to reverse your vehicle and trailer in a restricted space. You must be able to do this

- under control and in reasonable time
- with good observation
- with reasonable accuracy
- starting with the front of the vehicle at a fixed point (cones A and A1)
- inside a clearly defined boundary (yellow lines)
- by reversing so that you pass cone B on the offside of your vehicle
- so that the extreme rear of your vehicle or trailer is stopped within the 75 cm yellow and black stopping area and in a position to load or unload safely at the simulated loading platform. You may touch the barrier gently.

Your examiner will show you a diagram of the manoeuvring area and explain what's required.

Z

Bay

92.5 metres

Cone B

A1

18.5 metres

259

When you are in the bay you may leave the cab once to check where the back of the vehicle is in relation to the barrier. Make sure the vehicle is safe before leaving the cab.

Skills you should show

You should complete the exercise

- reversing under complete control
- using good, effective, all round observation
- ensuring accurate judgement of the size of your vehicle and trailer from the cab
- driving with careful co-ordination of the clutch, accelerator and footbrake until the exercise is completed.

Faults to avoid

You should avoid the following

- approaching the starting point too fast
- not driving in a straight line as you approach cones A and A1
- stopping beyond the first marker cones A and A1
- turning the steering wheel incorrectly when starting to reverse
- oversteering so that any wheel goes over the yellow boundary
- not practising effective observation or misjudging the position of your vehicle so that it comes in contact with any cone or pole

- incorrect judgement so that the rear of your vehicle and trailer is either short of or beyond the yellow and black area
- hitting the barrier hard
- using excessive steering movements or shunts to complete the manoeuvre
- driving down the area ahead of a position level with cones A and A1, when taking a forward shunt
- carrying out the manoeuvre at a very slow pace.

The braking exercise

There's no emergency stop exercise in the LGV driving test but there is a braking exercise. For safety reasons the braking exercise takes place at a special area and not on the public roads.

What the test requires

Your examiner will be with you in the vehicle for this exercise.

The examiner will point out two marker cones about 61 metres (200 feet) ahead. You should build up a speed of about 20 mph. When the front of the vehicle passes between the two markers you should apply the brakes. You must stop your vehicle and trailer with safety and under full control.

Skills you should show

You should stop the vehicle

- as quickly as possible
- under full control
- as safely as possible
- in a straight line.

Faults to avoid

You should avoid

- driving too slowly (less than 20 mph)
- braking too soon (anticipating the marker points)
- braking too harshly, causing loss of control
- depressing the clutch well before the brake
- depressing the clutch too late, stalling the engine
- taking too long to stop.

(Note: For vehicles fitted with ABS, please refer to the vehicle handbook)

The vehicle controls

What the test requires

You must show your examiner that you understand the functions of all the controls. You should use them

- smoothly
- correctly
- safely
- at the right time.

The main controls are

- accelerator
- clutch
- footbrake
- handbrake
- steering
- gears.

You must

- understand what these controls do
- be able to use them competently.

How your examiner will test you

For this aspect of driving there isn't a special exercise. Your examiner will watch you carefully to see how you use these controls.

Skills you should show

Accelerator and clutch

The accelerator controls the rate at which the mixture of fuel and air is supplied to the engine. The more you press the accelerator, the more fuel goes to the engine and the greater the power generated. Use the accelerator smoothly; harsh or uncontrolled use wastes fuel and produces more harmful emissions.

The clutch is the connection between the engine and gearbox. It's a connection over which the driver has control, but which requires practice in its use.

You should

- balance the accelerator and clutch to pull away smoothly
- accelerate gradually to gain speed
- when stopping the vehicle, press the clutch in just before it stops.

If your vehicle has automatic transmission ensure that your foot is on the footbrake when you engage 'drive' (D).

Gears

The gears are designed to assist the engine to deliver power under a variety of conditions. The lowest gears may only be necessary if the vehicle is loaded or when climbing steep gradients. However, please be guided by the manufacturer's specification for your vehicle.

The gearbox may have one or more crawler gear positions. Using the highest gear possible, matched to the speed of your vehicle and road/traffic conditions, aids fuel economy.

You should

- move off in the most suitable gear
- change gear in good time before a junction or hazard
- show an understanding of the type of gearbox you're using by demonstrating its abilities
- plan well ahead, whether climbing or before starting to descend a long hill.

If you leave it until you're either losing or gaining too much speed you may have difficulty selecting gears and maintaining control.

Modern vehicles may be fitted with sophisticated systems controlled by computer. These systems can sense the load, speed or gradient and select the correct gear for the conditions. With these systems the driver may only have to ease the accelerator, or depress the clutch pedal, to allow the system to engage the gear required.

If you're driving a vehicle with a range change gearbox you should ensure that you've selected the correct range before changing gear.

Faults to avoid

Accelerator

You should avoid

- loud over-revving, causing excessive engine noise and exhaust fumes, and also alarming or distracting other road users.

Clutch

You should avoid

- jerky and uncontrolled use of the clutch when moving off or changing gear.

Gears

You should avoid

- taking your eyes off the road when you change gear
- coasting with the clutch pedal depressed or leaving the gear lever in neutral. This is highly dangerous if you're driving a vehicle with air brakes. The engine-driven compressor won't be able to replace the air being used by the brakes due to the engine running only at idle speed
- holding onto the gear lever unnecessarily
- forgetting to move the range selector switch.

Skills you should show

Brake

You should brake

- in good time
- lightly, in most situations
- progressively.

Most large vehicles are equipped with air brake systems. There's no direct relationship between the pressure applied to the pedal and the braking force exerted on the wheels. This means that good control is needed at all times. Plan ahead whilst driving, use engine braking when safe to do so and always be aware of the traffic situation behind.

Faults to avoid

You should avoid

- braking harshly
- excessive and prolonged use of the footbrake
- braking and steering at the same time, unless already travelling at a low speed.

Skills you should show

Handbrake

You should know how and when to apply the handbrake effectively. Some modern vehicles will apply a parking brake when the vehicle is brought to a stop by the footbrake.

Steering

You should

- place your hands on the steering wheel in a position that's comfortable and which gives you full control
- keep your movements steady and smooth
- turn the steering wheel to turn a corner at the correct time.

Power-assisted steering

Most modern vehicles are fitted with power assisted steering. The power assistance is often incorporated within the steering box or uses an engine-driven pump to supply hydraulic fluid under pressure, which operates rams attached to the steering arms. Power assistance relieves the driver of steering effort, especially at slow speeds.

When the engine is running, hydraulic pressure is built up in the system to make the steering easier. If the steering becomes heavy, check for leaks in the system.

Do not attempt to turn the steering whilst stationary (known as dry steering), as this will cause wear to the mechanism.

If a fault develops whilst travelling, stop as soon as you can safely do so and seek expert advice.

Faults to avoid

Handbrake

You should avoid

- applying the handbrake before the vehicle has stopped
- trying to move off with the handbrake on
- allowing the vehicle to roll back as you move off.

Steering

Don't steer too early when turning a corner. If you do, you risk

- cutting the corner when turning right, causing the rear wheels to cut across the path of traffic waiting to emerge
- striking the kerb when turning left.

Don't turn too late. You could put other road users at risk by

- swinging wide at left turns
- overshooting right turns.

Avoid

- crossing your hands on the steering wheel whenever possible
- allowing the wheel to spin back after turning
- resting your arm on the door.

Other controls

You should understand

The functions of all controls and switches on your vehicle that have a bearing on road safety, such as

- indicators
- lights
- windscreen wipers
- demisters.

You should know the meaning of all gauges and switches on the instrument panel, such as

- air pressure gauges
- speedometer
- various warning lights and buzzers
- on-board computer displays
- ABS failure warnings
- bulb failure warnings
- gear-selection indicators.

Safety checks and fault recognition

You should be able to carry out routine checks, such as on

- steering
- brakes
- tyres
- seat belts
- lights
- reflectors
- horn
- rear view mirrors
- speedometer
- exhaust system
- direction indicators
- windscreen, wipers and washers
- wheel nut security.

You should be able to understand the effect any fault may have on your vehicle.

Moving off

Balance your use of the accelerator when moving away. How much you depress it will depend on the weight of your vehicle and the circumstances, such as moving off uphill. However, remember that accelerating fiercely wastes fuel.

What the test requires

You should be able to move off safely and under control

- on the level
- from behind a parked vehicle
- uphill
- downhill.

How your examiner will test you

Your examiner will watch your use of the controls as you move off.

Skills you should show

Before you move off

- use your mirrors
- look all around your vehicle.

You should be aware of

- other vehicles
- cyclists and motorcyclists
- pedestrians outside the range of your mirrors.

You should move off under control, making balanced and safe use of the

- accelerator
- clutch
- brakes
- steering
- correct gear.

Uphill

You should

- practise effective observation before moving off, checking all blind spots
- give a signal, if required, at the correct time
- use sufficient acceleration, depending on the gradient
- move off smoothly
- change up as soon as it's safe to do so.

Downhill

You should

- move off only when it's safe to do so
- practise effective observation before moving off, checking all blind spots
- give a signal, if required, at the correct time.

When you move off you should

- engage the correct gear for the gradient
- hold the vehicle on the footbrake and release the handbrake until it's safe to move away
- co-ordinate the clutch and accelerator
- build up speed when it's safe to do so.

Faults to avoid

Uphill

You should avoid moving off without

- using both nearside and offside mirrors
- looking around to check all blind spots
- giving a correct signal if it's required
- using enough revs for the gradient.

You should avoid moving off without good control of the accelerator, clutch and handbrake. Don't

- stall
- roll backwards
- surge away.

Downhill

You should avoid moving off without

- using both nearside and offside mirrors
- looking around to check all the blind spots
- giving a correct signal, if it's required
- co-ordinating the accelerator, clutch and handbrake so that the vehicle stalls or surges.

How your examiner will test you

At an angle

Your examiner will ask you to pull up on the left just before you reach a parked vehicle. You'll be asked to move away to show your ability to move off at an angle.

Skills you should show

When moving out from behind a parked vehicle you should

- practise effective all-round observation
- check any blind spots
- give a signal, if it's necessary
- move out only when it's safe to do so
- move out well clear of the parked vehicle
- check your mirrors, especially the nearside, to confirm that you're clear of the parked vehicle.

Faults to avoid

You should avoid

- pulling out unsafely
- causing other road users to stop or alter their course
- excessive acceleration
- moving off in too high a gear
- failing to co-ordinate the controls correctly and stalling the engine
- swinging excessively wide into the path of oncoming traffic.

Using the mirrors

What the test requires

You must always use your mirrors effectively

- before any manoeuvre
- to keep up-to-date on what's happening behind you.

Use them before

- moving off
- signalling
- changing direction
- turning left or right
- overtaking or changing lanes
- increasing speed
- slowing down or stopping
- opening your cab door.

Check again in your nearside mirror after passing

- parked vehicles
- horse riders, motorcyclists or cyclists
- any pedestrians standing close to the kerb
- any vehicle that you've just overtaken

before moving back into the left.

How your examiner will test you

For this aspect of driving there isn't a special exercise. Your examiner will watch you use your mirrors as you drive.

Skills you should show

Use the Mirrors – Signal – Manoeuvre (MSM) routine and also the Position – Speed – Look (PSL) routine. You should

- look before you signal
- signal before you act
- act sensibly on what you see in the mirrors
- be aware that the mirrors won't show everything behind you.

You should check your nearside mirror every time you pass

- parked vehicles
- vulnerable road users
- vehicles you've just overtaken
- pedestrians near the kerb.

Always have as good an idea of what's happening behind you as what's going on in front. You should also be aware of the effect your large vehicle has on other road users around you.

Giving signals

What the test requires

You must give clear signals in good time so that other road users know what you're about to do. This is particularly important with LGVs because other road users may not understand the position you need to move into

- before turning left
- before turning right
- at roundabouts
- to move off at an angle.

You should only give signals that are in *The Highway Code.*

Correct signals should help other road users to

- understand what you intend to do next
- take appropriate action.

Always check that you've cancelled an indicator as soon as it's safe to do so.

How your examiner will test you

For this aspect of driving there isn't a special exercise. Your examiner will watch you carefully to see how you use your signals as you drive.

Skills you should show

You should give signals

- clearly
- at the appropriate time
- by indicator
- by arm, if necessary.

Faults to avoid

You should avoid

- giving misleading or incorrect signals
- omitting to cancel signals
- waving on pedestrians to cross in front of your vehicle
- giving signals other than those shown in *The Highway Code.*

Acting on signs and signals

What the test requires

You should have a thorough knowledge of traffic signs, signals and road markings. You should be able to

- recognise them in good time
- take appropriate action on them.

At the start of the drive your examiner will ask you to follow the road ahead, unless traffic signs indicate otherwise or you're asked to turn. From this point your examiner will expect you to understand and act correctly on road signs or signals that occur.

Skills you should show

Traffic lights and signals

You should

- comply with traffic lights and signals
- approach at a speed that allows you to stop, if necessary, under full control
- only move forward at a green traffic light if it's clear for you to do so and you won't block the junction.

Authorised persons

You must comply with the signals given by

- police officers
- traffic wardens
- school crossing patrols
- Highways Agency Traffic Officers
- an authorised person controlling the traffic, eg, at road repairs.
- Vehicle & Operator Services Agency Officers.

Other road users

You should look out for signals given by other road users and

- react safely
- take appropriate action
- anticipate their action
- use your brakes and/or give arm signals, if necessary, to any traffic following your vehicle.

You need to be aware that, due to the size of your vehicle, road users behind you may not be able to see signals given by a vehicle ahead of you, for example if they are stopping or turning. Therefore, special care should be taken if you need to alter your speed or course as a result of a vehicle ahead of you carrying out such a manoeuvre.

Awareness and anticipation

Try to plan further ahead when driving. Using the rolling momentum of the vehicle to prevent stopping and moving off again in first gear saves fuel. At roundabouts, look well ahead on approach to assess the traffic situation. Fit in safely with the flow of traffic to prevent unnecessary stops.

What the test requires

You must be aware of other road users at all times. You should also always plan ahead and

- judge what other road users are going to do
- predict how their actions would affect you
- react safely and in good time.

Skills you should show

You should show

- awareness of and consideration for all other road users
- anticipation of possible danger and concern for safety.

Pedestrians

You should

- give way to pedestrians when turning from one road into another
- take particular care with the very young, the disabled and the elderly. They may not have seen you and might not be able to react quickly to danger.

Cyclists

Take special care

- when crossing bus or cycle lanes
- with cyclists passing on your left
- with child cyclists.

Moped riders and motorcyclists

Look out for mopeds and motorcyclists

- in slow-moving traffic
- coming up on your left
- at junctions.

Horse riders and animals

Take special care with people in charge of animals, especially horse riders.

Faults to avoid

You should avoid

- reacting suddenly to road or traffic conditions rather than anticipating them
- showing irritation with other road users
- sounding the horn aggressively
- revving your engine or edging forward when waiting for pedestrians to cross.

Making progress

Your examiner will be looking for a high standard of driving from an experienced driver. You'll need to display safe, confident, positive driving techniques.

How your examiner will test you

For this aspect of driving there isn't a special exercise. As an experienced driver you'll be expected to drive accordingly. Your examiner will watch your driving and expect you to make good progress safely.

Skills you should show

You should

- make reasonable progress where conditions allow
- keep up with the traffic flow when it's safe to do so
- make positive, safe decisions as you make progress.

You should be able to drive at the appropriate speed depending on the

- type of road
- weather conditions and visibility
- traffic conditions.

Approach all hazards at a safe speed without

- being unduly cautious
- holding up following traffic unnecessarily.

Faults to avoid

You should avoid

- driving so slowly that you hinder other traffic
- being over-cautious or hesitant
- stopping when you can see it's obviously clear and safe to go on.

Controlling your speed

What the test requires

You should make good progress along the road, taking into consideration

- the type of road
- the volume of traffic
- the weather conditions and the state of the road surface
- the braking characteristics of your vehicle
- speed limits that apply to your vehicle
- any hazards associated with the time of day (schools, etc).

How your examiner will test you

For this aspect of driving there isn't a special exercise. Your examiner will watch you control your speed as you drive.

Skills you should show

You should

- take great care in the use of speed
- drive at the correct speed for the traffic conditions
- be sure that you can stop safely in the distance that you can see to be clear
- leave an appropriate separation distance between your vehicle and the traffic ahead according to the road and traffic conditions

- observe the speed limit that applies to your vehicle
- anticipate any hazards that could arise
- allow for the mistakes of others.

Faults to avoid

You should avoid

- driving too fast for the road traffic conditions
- exceeding speed limits
- varying your speed erratically
- having to brake hard to avoid a situation ahead
- approaching bends, traffic signals and any other hazards too fast.

Remember, always keep a safe separation distance between you and the traffic in front.

Separation distance

What the test requires

You should always drive so that you can stop safely in the distance you can see to be clear.

In good weather conditions, leave a gap of at least 1 metre (about 3 feet) for each mph of your speed, or a two-second time gap.

In bad conditions, leave at least double that distance, or a four-second time gap.

In slow-moving congested traffic it may not be practical to leave as much space.

How your examiner will test you

For this aspect of driving there isn't a special exercise. Your examiner will watch you as you drive and take account of your

- use of the MSM/PSL routine
- anticipation
- reaction to changing road and traffic conditions
- handling of the controls.

Skills you should show

You should

- judge a safe separation distance from the traffic in front
- show correct use of the MSM/PSL routine, especially before reducing speed
- avoid the need to brake sharply if the vehicle in front slows down or stops
- take extra care when your view ahead is limited by large vehicles
- keep a good separation distance from traffic queues in front.

Look out for

- brake lights ahead
- direction indicators
- vehicles ahead braking without warning.

Faults to avoid

You should avoid

- following too closely or tailgating
- braking suddenly
- swerving to avoid the vehicle in front, which may be slowing down or stopping.

Hazards

What is a hazard?

A hazard may present itself when you're either stationary or on the move. Hazards may be included in any situation that involves you adjusting your speed or altering your course. In addition, hazards can be created by the actions of other road users around you. Look well ahead for

- road junctions or roundabouts
- parked vehicles
- cyclists or horse riders
- pedestrian crossings
- pedestrians on or near the kerbside
- cyclists or motorcyclists moving up alongside
- drivers edging up on the nearside before you make a turn
- vehicles pulling up close behind when you want to reverse.

Traffic situations are constantly changing. These changes might depend on the

- time of day
- location
- density of traffic.

You should be aware of and anticipate potential hazards when you drive.

Skills you should show

Your higher seat position in an LGV may mean that you're able to see more clearly some of the hazards around you. As a professional driver you must be able to anticipate what might happen. You should be driving with a sense of awareness and anticipation. Know

- what's happening ahead
- what other road users are about to do
- when to take action.

Scan the road ahead and be alert in case you have to

- speed up
- slow down
- prepare to stop
- change direction.

Hazards - other road users

Skills you should show

Pedestrians

Give way to pedestrians when turning from one road into another or when entering premises such as supermarkets, shops, warehouses, etc. Take extra care with

- the young
- older people

and people who appear to have a disability.

Look out for pedestrians at all times but especially in shopping areas, where there might be a number of people waiting to cross the road, often at junctions.

Drive slowly and considerately when you need to enter pedestrianised areas to deliver to premises during times when unloading or loading is permitted.

Cyclists

Take extra care when

- crossing cycle lanes
- you're about to turn left and you can see a cyclist near the rear of your vehicle or moving up along the nearside
- approaching any children on cycles
- there are gusty wind conditions.

Motorcyclists

Look out for motorcyclists who are

- filtering in slow traffic streams
- moving up alongside your vehicle, especially the nearside.

They can be difficult to see. Be especially aware when you're waiting to move out from a junction.

> **Think once**
> **Think twice**
> **Think bike.**

Horse riders and animals

The size and noise of your vehicle can easily unsettle a horse. You should

- give riders as much room as is safe
- slow down even if the horse and rider are on the grass verge rather than the road
- avoid revving the engine/releasing air brakes
- look out for young riders who are learning and might not be able to control their horses. (They may be on a leading rein with someone walking beside them)
- react in good time to anyone who is herding animals
- look out for warning signs, eg cattle.

Faults to avoid

You should avoid

- sounding the horn aggressively
- revving the engine and causing the air brakes to hiss
- edging forward when pedestrians are crossing in front
- showing any sign of irritation.

Hazards - positioning and lane discipline

What the test requires

You should

- normally keep well to the left
- keep clear of parked vehicles
- avoid weaving in and out between parked vehicles
- position your vehicle correctly for the direction you intend to take.

You should obey all lane markings, especially

- left- or right-turn arrows at junctions
- when approaching roundabouts
- in one-way streets
- for bus lanes
- road markings for LGVs approaching arches or narrow bridges with restricted headroom.

How your examiner will test you

For this aspect of driving there isn't a special exercise. Your examiner will watch carefully to see that you

- use the MSM/PSL routine
- select the correct lane in good time.

Skills you should show

You should

- plan ahead and choose the correct lane in good time
- use the MSM/PSL routine correctly
- position your vehicle sensibly, even if there aren't any road markings
- be aware that other road users might not understand your actions, so signal in good time.

Faults to avoid

You should avoid

- driving too close to the kerb
- driving too close to the centre of the road
- changing lanes at the last moment or without good reason
- hindering other road users by being badly positioned or in the wrong lane
- straddling lanes or lane markings
- cutting across the path of other traffic in another lane at roundabouts.

There may be occasions, due to the length of your vehicle, when you have to straddle lane markings to avoid mounting the kerb or colliding with lamp posts, traffic signs, etc. Use your own skill and judgement in making these decisions.

Hazards - junctions

What the test requires

The size of your vehicle means that it's essential to make the correct decisions at junctions. Look well ahead and assess the situation as you approach.

Judge carefully when it's safe to emerge. Road users such as motorcyclists, cyclists and pedestrians may be completely obscured by the pillar between your windscreen and side window. Motorcyclists will be moving quickly and may be obscured by other traffic or parked vehicles. Act on what you see. Wait until you can see that it's clear, then move away safely.

If you don't know, don't go

Skills you should show

You should

- use the MSM/PSL routine in good time when you approach a junction or roundabout
- assess the situation correctly so that you can position your vehicle to negotiate the junction safely
- take as much room as you need as you approach a junction if you're driving a long rigid vehicle or a vehicle and trailer combination
- be aware of any lane markings and the fact that your vehicle may have to occupy part of the lane alongside

- get into position as early as it's practicable to do so in one-way streets
- make sure that you take **effective** observation before emerging from any junction.

Left or right turns

Extra care should be taken if you're driving a long or an articulated vehicle, or a vehicle and trailer combination.

When turning left or right, position your vehicle so that you can

- see into the road
- turn without the rear/trailer wheels mounting the kerb
- turn without any part of the vehicle colliding with bollards or guard rails.

If you're crossing a dual carriageway or turning right onto one, don't move forward unless you can clear the central reservation safely. If your vehicle is too long for the gap, wait until it's clear from both sides and there's a safe opportunity to go.

Always

- watch for motorcyclists coming up from behind as you approach the junction
- use your mirrors to check the rear wheels of your vehicle or trailer as you turn into or out of a junction
- assess the speed of oncoming traffic correctly before crossing or entering roads with fast-moving traffic
- allow for the fact that you'll need more time to build up speed on the new road.

Observe, assess, then judge before you act.

Hazards - roundabouts

What the test requires

Roundabouts can vary in size and complexity, but the object of them all is to allow traffic to flow wherever possible.

Some roundabouts are so complex or busy that they require traffic lights to control the volume of traffic. The lights may be used at peak times when the traffic becomes very heavy.

At the majority of roundabouts, the approaching traffic is required to give way to traffic approaching from the right. There are some locations where a Give Way sign and markings apply to traffic already on the roundabout. You must be aware of these differences.

Skills you should show

It's essential that you plan your approach well in advance and use the MSM/PSL routine in good time. It's most important that you get into the correct lane as you approach, bearing in mind that you may have to straddle the lanes. You should know the exit you wish to take and choose the most appropriate route into and through the roundabout, taking into consideration the size of your vehicle.

On approach

You should adjust the speed of your vehicle in good time on the approach to roundabouts. Check your speed and select the correct gear to negotiate the roundabout safely. Get into the most appropriate lane (you may have to straddle the lanes). You should

- plan well ahead
- look out for traffic signs as you approach
- have a clear picture of the exit you intend to take
- look out for the number of exits before yours
- either follow the lane markings, as far as possible, or select the lane most suitable for the size of your vehicle
- use the MSM/PSL routine in good time
- signal your intentions in good time
- avoid driving into the roundabout too close to the right-hand kerb. If you're driving a long or articulated vehicle you may have to steer to the left to avoid the kerb as you turn.

Whenever you enter a roundabout watch the vehicle in front of you. Make sure that it hasn't stopped while you were looking to the right. The driver ahead might be hesitant, so don't drive into the rear of it.

Turning left

You should

- check your mirrors - nearside and offside
- give a left-turn signal in good time as you approach
- approach in the left-hand lane. If you're driving a long vehicle you might need to take up some of the lane on your right
- adopt a path that ensures that the rear/trailer wheels don't mount the kerb
- give way to traffic approaching from the right
- use the nearside mirrors to be sure that no cyclists or motorcyclists are trapped along the nearside
- continue to signal through the turn
- keep checking your mirrors as you turn
- look well ahead for traffic islands or bollards in the centre of your exit road. These could restrict the width available to you.

Going ahead

You should

- approach in the left-hand lane unless blocked or clearly marked for 'left turn' only
- check your mirrors
- not give a signal on approach (other than brake lights, if you need to reduce speed)

- try to stay in the lane although this will depend on the size of your vehicle. If you have to straddle the lanes, do so in good time
- keep checking the mirrors - both nearside and offside
- give way to traffic from the right, if necessary
- keep checking your mirrors
- indicate left as you pass the exit just before the one that you intend to take
- look well ahead for traffic islands or bollards in the centre of your exit road
- make sure that the rear/trailer wheels don't mount the kerb as you leave the roundabout.

Turning right or full circle

You should

- look well ahead and use the MSM/PSL routine
- signal right in good time before moving over to the right on approach. Watch for any vehicles, especially motorcycles, accelerating up on the offside of your vehicle
- take up the most appropriate position with a long or wide vehicle, if there's a choice of two lanes for turning right. This may mean you have to straddle the lanes. If only one lane is marked for right turns you might have to occupy part of the lane on your left, not only on approach but also through the roundabout

- keep checking your mirrors as you circle the roundabout
- signal left as you pass the exit before the one you want and move over to the left
- look out for any traffic attempting to accelerate up on the offside of your vehicle.

Mini-roundabouts

You might have restricted room, so keep a constant check in the mirrors. You should

- give way to traffic from the right
- be aware that the rear of a long vehicle can easily clip a car waiting to enter a mini-roundabout
- be aware that it is unlikely that LGVs will be able to turn at a mini-roundabout without driving over the marked centre area
- position your vehicle correctly on approach so that you don't mount any kerbs
- understand that other road users might not be aware of the room you need to complete a turn.

Double mini-roundabouts

These require even more care and planning, since traffic will often back up from one to the other at busy times. Make sure that there's room for you to move forward and that, by doing so, your vehicle won't block the whole system.

Although traffic is advised not to carry out U-turn manoeuvres at a mini-roundabout, be alert for any oncoming traffic doing so.

Avoid giving signals that might confuse. Because of the limited space and the comparatively short time it takes to negotiate a mini-roundabout, it's important to give only signals that will help other road users.

If you have to drive over a raised mini-roundabout, do so slowly and carefully so as not to damage your vehicle or its load.

At any roundabout, cancel your signal as soon as you've completed the manoeuvre.

Multiple roundabouts

Plan your approach early. You should

- be extra vigilant in your use of mirrors
- ensure that your eventual exit is clear so that you don't block the roundabout
- give clear signals
- look out for road users carrying out U-turns.

In a number of locations, complex roundabout systems have been designed which incorporate a mini-roundabout at each exit. The main thing to remember at such places is that traffic will be travelling in all directions. You must give way to traffic on the right.

Road surfaces

At the entrances to roundabouts there will have been a great deal of braking and accelerating. This will often make the road surface slippery, especially when it's wet.

You should

- brake in good time
- enter the roundabout ensuring that other road users don't have to brake suddenly or swerve.

Cyclists and horse riders

These road users might be in the left-hand lane on approach, but may intend to turn right. Be aware of this and give them plenty of room.

Hazards - overtaking

What the test requires

Before overtaking you should look well ahead for any hazards, such as

- oncoming traffic
- bends
- junctions
- the vehicle in front about to overtake
- any gradient
- those pointed out by road markings or traffic signs.

You should assess the

- speed of the vehicle that you intend to overtake
- speed differential of the two vehicles, to judge how long the manoeuvre could take
- time you have to complete overtaking safely.

Avoid the need to cut in on the vehicle that you've just overtaken.

How your examiner will test you

For this aspect of driving there isn't a special exercise. Your examiner will watch you and take account of your

- use of the MSM/PSL routine
- reaction to road and traffic conditions
- handling of the controls
- choice of a safe opportunity to overtake.

Skills you should show

You should be able to assess all the factors that will decide if you can or can't overtake safely, such as

- oncoming traffic
- the type of road
- the speed of the vehicle ahead
- continuous white line markings on your side of the road
- how far ahead the road is clear
- whether the road will remain clear
- whether traffic behind is about to overtake your vehicle.

Only overtake where you can do so safely, legally and without causing other road users to slow down or alter course. Be aware of motorcyclists who may be coming up behind you. They are more difficult to see and may be obscured by other vehicles.

Faults to avoid

Don't overtake when

- your view of the road ahead isn't clear
- you would have to exceed the speed limit
- to do so would cause other road users to slow down or stop
- there are signs or road markings that prohibit overtaking.

Hazards - meeting and passing other vehicles

What the test requires

You should be able to meet and deal with oncoming traffic safely and confidently

- on narrow roads
- where there are obstructions such as parked cars
- where you have to move into the path of oncoming traffic.

How your examiner will test you

For this aspect of driving there isn't a special exercise. Your examiner will watch you and take account of your

- use of the MSM/PSL routine
- reactions to road and traffic conditions
- handling of the controls.

Skills you should show

You should

- show good judgement when meeting other traffic
- be decisive when stopping and moving off
- stop in a position that allows you to move out smoothly when the way is clear
- allow adequate clearance when passing stationary vehicles. Slow right down if you have to pass close to them.

Be aware that the wind pressure created by your vehicle may have an effect on vulnerable road users. Look out for

- doors opening
- children running out
- pedestrians stepping out from between parked cars or from buses
- vehicles pulling out without warning.

Faults to avoid

Avoid causing other vehicles to

- slow down
- swerve
- stop.

Avoid

- passing too close to parked vehicles
- using the size of your vehicle to force other traffic to give way.

Hazards - crossing the path of other vehicles

What the test requires

You should be able to cross the path of oncoming traffic safely and with confidence. You'll need to do this when you

- turn right at a road junction
- enter premises on the right-hand side of the road.

You should

- use the MSM/PSL routine
- position the vehicle as correctly as possible, depending on the size of your vehicle
- assess accurately the speed of any approaching traffic
- wait if necessary
- look into the road entrance into which you're about to turn
- look out for any pedestrians.

How your examiner will test you

For this aspect of driving there isn't a special exercise. Your examiner will watch you and take account of your judgement of oncoming traffic.

Skills you should show

You should

- make safe and confident decisions about when to turn across the path of vehicles approaching from the opposite direction
- ensure that the road or entrance is clear for you to enter
- be confident that your vehicle won't endanger any road user waiting to emerge from the right
- assess whether it's safe to enter the road entrance
- show courtesy and consideration to other road users, especially pedestrians.

Faults to avoid

You should avoid

- cutting the corner
- overshooting the turn so that the front wheels mount the kerb
- turning across the path of any oncoming traffic, causing it to
  - slow down
  - swerve
  - stop.

Hazards - pedestrian crossings

What the test requires

You should

- recognise the different types of pedestrian crossing
- show courtesy and consideration towards pedestrians
- stop safely when necessary.

How your examiner will test you

For this aspect of the test there isn't a special exercise. Your examiner will watch you carefully to see that you

- recognise the pedestrian crossing in good time
- use the MSM/PSL routine
- stop when necessary.

Skills you should show

Controlled crossings

These crossings may be controlled by traffic signals at junctions or by

- police officers
- traffic wardens
- school crossing patrols.

Slow down in good time and stop if you're asked to do so.

Zebra crossings

These crossings are recognised by

- black and white stripes across the road
- flashing amber beacons on both sides of the road
- tactile paving on both sides of the crossing
- zigzag road markings on both sides of the crossing.

You should

- slow down and stop if there's anyone on the crossing
- slow down and be prepared to stop if there's anyone waiting to cross.

Pelican crossings

These crossings have traffic signals that are activated by pedestrians pressing a button on the panel at either side of the crossing. There's a flashing amber phase that allows pedestrians who are already on the crossing to continue to cross safely.

There are also zigzag lines on each side of the crossing and a stop line at the crossing.

You must

- stop if the lights are red or steady amber
- give way to any pedestrians crossing if the amber lights are flashing

- approach all crossings at a controlled speed
- stop safely when necessary
- only move off when it's safe to do so
- be especially alert
  - near schools
  - at shopping areas
  - when turning at junctions.

Puffin crossings

This type of crossing has been installed at a number of selected sites. They have infra-red detectors sited so that the red traffic signal phase may be held until pedestrians have cleared the crossing. No flashing amber is then necessary. The lights operate in the normal traffic light sequence.

Toucan crossings

There are a few of these crossings installed throughout the country. They're usually found where there are large numbers of cyclists.

The cyclists share the crossing with pedestrians without having to dismount. They're shown a green cycle light when it's safe to cross.

Equestrian crossings

These are especially for horses and riders and have higher controls, a fence along the kerb and a wider crossing area. Be especially aware of the danger that excess or sudden vehicle noise, air brake release or flashing lights could cause.

Faults to avoid

You should avoid

- approaching any type of crossing at too high a speed
- driving on without stopping or showing awareness of pedestrians waiting to cross
- driving onto or blocking a crossing
- overtaking within the zigzag lines
- waving pedestrians, cyclists or horseriders across
- revving the engine
- causing unnecessary air brake noise
- sounding the horn.

Selecting a safe place to stop

What the test requires

When you make a normal stop you must be able to select a safe place where you won't

- cause an obstruction
- create a hazard
- be illegally parked.

You should stop reasonably close to the kerb.

How your examiner will test you

At some stage during the test your examiner will ask you to pull up on the left at a convenient place.

Skills you should show

When selecting a safe place to stop

- identify it in good time
- make proper use of the MSM/PSL routine
- only stop where you're allowed to do so
- don't cause an obstruction
- recognise, in good time, road markings or signs indicating any restriction
- pull up close to, and parallel with, the kerb
- apply the parking brake while the vehicle is stationary
- stop at the correct place when asked.

Faults to avoid

You should avoid

- pulling up with late warning to other road users
- causing danger or inconvenience to other road users
- stopping at or outside
  - school entrances
  - fire or ambulance stations
  - bus stops
  - pedestrian crossings.

You must comply with

- 'No Waiting' signs or markings
- 'No Parking' signs or markings
- other 'No Stopping' restrictions.

Uncoupling and recoupling

What the test requires

You should know and be able to demonstrate how to uncouple and recouple your vehicle and trailer safely. Stopping the engine of your vehicle at the correct time during the exercise is not only safe but saves fuel and reduces air and noise pollution.

Uncoupling

When uncoupling you should

- ensure that the brakes are applied on both the vehicle and trailer
- lower the landing gear and stow the handle away safely
- turn off any taps fitted to the air lines
- disconnect the air lines (sometimes referred to as 'suzies') and stow the lines away safely
- disconnect the electric line and stow it away safely
- remove any dog clip securing the kingpin release handle
- release the fifth wheel coupling locking bar, if fitted
- drive the tractive unit away slowly, checking the trailer either directly or in the mirrors.

If you're driving a drawbar outfit, you might have to support the trailer drawbar before you pull away. The 'suzies' on a draw-bar trailer are left with the trailer and should be left in a safe position, for example laid over the draw-bar.

For drivers of articulated vehicles with close-coupled trailers, the uncoupling sequence is as follows

- ensure that the brakes are applied on both the tractive unit and the trailer
- lower the landing gear and stow the handle away safely
- disconnect the dog clip (if fitted) and release the fifth wheel coupling
- drive the tractive unit far enough forward so that you can stand on the catwalk
- apply the tractive unit parking brake
- turn off any taps fitted to the air lines
- disconnect the air lines (or 'suzies') and electrical connections and stow safely
- drive the tractive unit away slowly, checking the trailer either directly or in the mirrors.

Recoupling

When recoupling, treat the trailer as you would a new trailer that you haven't seen before. You should

- ensure that the trailer brake is applied
- check that the height of the trailer is correct so that it will receive the unit safely
- reverse slowly up to the trailer until you hear the kingpin mechanism locking into place. Carry out a visual inspection to check that the fifth wheel jaws have correctly engaged, that the release handle is in the locked position and that the king pin is located correctly in the jaws
- connect any dog clip to secure the kingpin release handle. If the dog clip does not fully engage, pull the release handle to disengage the jaws, slowly move the tractive unit away from the trailer, then repeat the fifth wheel coupling procedure
- select a low gear and try to move forward in order to test that the locking mechanism is secure. Do this twice to make sure
- ensure that the vehicle parking brake is applied
- connect the air and electric lines. Turn on taps, if fitted
- raise the landing gear and stow away the handle
- release the trailer parking brake
- start up the engine

- check that the air is building up in the storage tanks
- check the trailer lights and indicators.

For drivers of articulated vehicles with close-coupled trailers, the recoupling sequence is as follows

- ensure that the trailer brake is applied
- reverse slowly up to the trailer, stop just short and apply the tractive unit parking brake
- check that the height of the trailer is correct so that it will receive the unit safely
- reverse far enough under the trailer so that you can stand on the catwalk
- apply the tractive unit parking brake
- connect the air and electric lines. Turn on taps, if fitted
- reverse under the trailer and connect the fifth wheel
- select a low gear and try to move forward in order to test that the locking mechanism is secure. Do this twice to make sure
- apply the tractive unit parking brake
- connect any dog clip to secure the kingpin release handle
- raise the landing gear and stow away the handle
- release the trailer parking brake
- start up the engine
- check that air is building up in the storage tanks
- check all the lights and indicators.

How your examiner will test you

You'll normally be asked to uncouple and recouple your vehicle and trailer at the end of the test. Your examiner will ask you to do this where there's safe and level ground.

You'll be asked to

- demonstrate the uncoupling of your vehicle and trailer
- pull forward and park the vehicle alongside the trailer
- realign the vehicle with the trailer before recoupling the trailer
- recouple the vehicle and trailer.

Your examiner will expect you to make sure that the

- coupling is secure
- lights and indicators are working
- trailer brake is released.

Skills you should show

You should be able to uncouple and recouple your vehicle and trailer

- safely
- confidently and in good time
- showing concern for your own and others' health and safety.

Faults to avoid

When uncoupling

You should avoid

- uncoupling without applying the brakes on the towing vehicle
- releasing the trailer coupling without the legs being lowered
- moving forward before the entire correct procedure has been completed.

When recoupling

You should avoid

- not checking the brakes are applied on the trailer
- not using good, effective observation around your trailer as you reverse up to it
- recoupling at speed
- leaving the cab without applying the vehicle's parking brake.

Don't attempt to move away without checking the

- lights
- indicators
- trailer brake function.

Note: During the practical test you won't be asked to move your vehicle away after recoupling. You should, however, be aware of the safety precautions for this given in the official syllabus (see pages 243-255).

Your test result

If you pass

Well done. You've demonstrated that you can drive an unladen LGV to the high standard required to obtain a vocational licence.

Your examiner will ask you for your provisional licence so that an upgraded licence can automatically be sent to you through the post.

They will take your provisional licence and, once the details have been taken, shred it. You will be given a pass certificate as proof of success, until you receive your new licence.

If you don't want to surrender your licence you don't have to, and there will be certain circumstances when this isn't possible, if you have

- a foreign licence (CLH or NI)
- changed your name.

In these cases you'll have to send your provisional licence together with your pass certificate and the appropriate fee to DVLA (DVA in Northern Ireland), and they'll send you your full licence. You have to do this within two years or you'll have to take your test again.

You'll also be offered a brief explanation of any driving faults marked. This is to help you overcome any weaknesses in your driving as you gain experience.

After you've passed

You should always aim to improve your driving standards. Experience will present situations that you may not have encountered before. Learn from these and this will increase your ability to become a safe and reliable professional driver. Speak to your trainer about learning to drive laden vehicles.

If you don't pass

Your driving hasn't reached the high standard required to obtain the vocational licence. You've made mistakes that either caused - or could have caused - danger on the road.

Your examiner will give you

- a copy of the driving test report which will show all the faults marked during the test
- an explanation of why you failed.

You should study the driving test report carefully and refer to the relevant sections in this book.

Show the report to your instructor, who will help you to correct the points of failure. Listen to the advice your instructor gives and try to get as much practice as you can before you retake your test.

Right of appeal

Although your examiner's decision can't be altered, you have the right to appeal if you consider that your driving test wasn't conducted according to the regulations.

If you live in England or Wales you have six months after the issue of the statement of failure in which to appeal (Magistrates' Courts Act 1952, Ch. 55 part VII, Section 104). If you live in Scotland you have 21 days in which to appeal (Sheriff Court, Scotland Act of Sederunt (Statutory Appeals) 1981).

See also the DSA complaints guide for test candidates on page 307.

Department for Transport

Less
REV REV REV
REV REV
means less
CO2

REVVING HARD ISN'T GOOD FOR YOUR ENGINE. BY ANTICIPATING THE ROAD AHEAD AND SHIFTING UP A GEAR A LITTLE EARLIER YOU CAN KEEP YOUR REVS DOWN. THIS REDUCES YOUR ENGINE'S WORKLOAD, BURNS LESS FUEL AND COULD CUT YOUR CO2 EMISSIONS BY AROUND 8%. FOR MORE TIPS VISIT dft.gov.uk/ActOnCO2

ACT ON CO2

section seven
ADDITIONAL INFORMATION

This section covers

- Disqualified drivers
- DSA service standards
- Contact details
- LGV test centres
- Traffic commissioners and traffic area offices
- Other useful addresses
- Categories of LGV licence
- Minimum test vehicles (MTVs) requirements
- Cone positions
- Glossary
- Hazard labels
- Tying a dolly knot

Disqualified drivers

Retesting once disqualified

Tougher penalties now exist for anyone convicted of certain dangerous driving offences. If a driver is convicted of a dangerous driving offence they'll lose all LGV entitlement.

The decision as to whether they'll be required to undergo an extended car driving test before they're allowed to drive an LGV again rests with the courts.

An LGV driving licence can't stand on its own. You must also possess a valid full driving licence for category B (that is, a car licence). If you lose your category B licence entitlement you also lose your LGV licence.

Applying for a retest

A person subject to a category B retest can apply for a provisional licence at the end of the period of disqualification.

The normal rules for provisional licence holders apply

- the driver must be supervised by a person who's at least 21 years old and has held (and still holds) a full licence for at least three years for the category of vehicle being driven
- L plates (or D plates, if you wish, in Wales) must be displayed to the front and rear of the vehicle
- driving on motorways isn't allowed
- LGVs may not be driven on a provisional car licence (category B).

Having passed a category B extended test, an LGV driver has to apply to the Traffic Commissioner for their LGV licence. The return of the licence is at the discretion of the Traffic Commissioner, who can order a retest if he considers that it is necessary.

A further retest is not ordered in all cases.

DSA Service Standards

The Driving Standards Agency (DSA) is committed to providing a high quality service for all its customers. If you would like information about our standards of service please contact

Customer Service Unit
PO Box 280
Newcastle-Upon-Tyne
NE1 6PB

Email: **customer.services@dsa.gsi.gov.uk**

For telephone enquiries, there are two sets of numbers as follows

DSA North (covering Scotland, the North and the Midlands)

Tel: **0191 201 8161**
Fax: **0191 201 8056**

DSA South (covering London, the South East, Wales and the West)

Tel: **0292 058 1218**
Fax: **0292 058 1050**

Refund of out-of-pocket expenses

DSA will normally refund the fee, or rebook your test at no further charge, where

- an appointment is cancelled by DSA – for any reason

- an appointment is cancelled by the candidate, who gives at least three clear working days notice (Saturday is counted as a working day)

- the candidate keeps the test appointment, but the test doesn't take place or isn't completed for reasons not attributable to him or her nor to any vehicle provided for the test by the candidate.

In addition, DSA will normally consider reasonable claims from the candidate for financial loss or expenditure unavoidably and directly incurred by him or her as a result of DSA cancelling the test at short notice (other than for reasons of bad weather). For example, a claim for the commercial hire of a vehicle for the test will normally be considered. Applications should be made to the Area Office where the test was booked.

This compensation code doesn't affect your existing legal rights.

Complaints guide

DSA aims to give its customers the best possible service. Please tell us

- when we've done well
- when you aren't satisfied.

Your comments can help us to improve the service we have to offer.

If you have any questions about how your test was conducted please contact the local Sector Manager, whose address is displayed at your local driving test centre. If you're dissatisfied with the reply or you wish to comment on other matters you can write to the Operational Delivery Manager.

Finally, you can write to

The Chief Executive
Driving Standards Agency
The Axis Building
112 Upper Parliament Street
Nottingham
NG1 6LP

If you remain dissatisfied, you can ask the Chief Executive to refer your complaint to the Independent Complaints Assessor. None of this removes your right to take your complaint to

- your Member of Parliament, who may decide to raise your case personally with the DSA Chief Executive, the Minister, or the Parliamentary Commissioner for Administration (the Ombudsman)

  Ann Abraham
  Millbank Tower
  Millbank
  London SW1P 4QP

  Tel: **0845 015 4033**

- a magistrates' court (in Scotland to the Sheriff of your area) if you believe that your test wasn't carried out according to the regulations.

Before doing this you should seek legal advice.

DSA contact details

Head Office

The Axis Building
112 Upper Parliament Street
Nottingham NG1 6LP

Tel: **0115 936 6666**

National Telephone Numbers

Practical & Theory Tests
Enquiries & Bookings **0300 200 1122**
Welsh speakers **0300 200 1133**

Practical Tests
Minicom **0300 200 1144**
Fax **0300 200 1155**

Theory Tests
Minicom **0300 200 1166**
Fax **0300 200 1177**
Customer Enquiry Unit **0300 200 1188**

DVA (Northern Ireland)
Theory test **0845 600 6700**
Practical test **0845 247 2471**

Postal applications

All postal applications should be sent to

DSA
PO Box 280
Newcastle-upon-Tyne
NE99 1FP

LGV test centres

You'll find LGV driving test centres in the following places. Some test centres aren't open full-time. Contact the national telephone numbers for details of the full office address and telephone number.

Scotland

Aberdeen
Benbecula*
Bishopbriggs (Glasgow)
Dumfries
Elgin
Galashiels
Inverness
Kilmarnock
Kirkwall
Lerwick
Livingstone (Edinburgh)
Machrihanish (Kintyre)*
Perth
Port Ellen*
Portree*
Stornoway
Wick

Tests are only conducted occasionally at these centres

Midlands and Eastern

Alvaston (Derby)
Chelmsford
Culham
Featherstone (Wolverhampton)
Garretts Green (Birmingham)
Harlescott (Shrewsbury)
Ipswich
Leicester
Leighton Buzzard
Norwich
Peterborough
Swynnerton (Stoke-on-Trent)
Watnall (Nottingham)
Weedon (Northampton)

Northern

Berwick-on-Tweed
Beverley
Bredbury (Manchester)
Carlisle
Darlington
Gosforth (Newcastle)
Grimsby
Kirkham (Preston)
Patrick Green (Leeds)
Sheffield
Simonswood
Steeton (Keighley)
Walton (York)

Wales and Western

Bristol
Caernarfon
Camborne
Chiseldon (Swindon)
Exeter
Gloucester
Haverfordwest (Withybush)
Llantrisant
Neath
Plymouth
Pontypool
Poole
Reading
Rookley (Isle of Wight)
Southampton
Taunton
Wrexham

London and the South East

Canterbury
Croydon
Enfield
Gillingham
Guildford
Hastings
Lancing
Purfleet
Yeading

309

Traffic commissioners and Traffic area offices

Scotland

J Floor
Argyll House
3 Lady Lawson Street
Edinburgh EH3 9SE

Tel: **0131 200 4955**
Fax: **0131 529 8501**

Area covered:
All Scotland and the Islands.

North Eastern and North Western traffic area

Hillcrest House
386 Harehills Lane
Leeds LS9 6NF

Tel: **0113 254 3290/1**
Fax: **0113 248 9607**

Area covered:
Blackburn with Darwen
Blackpool
Cheshire
Cumbria
Darlington
Derby City
Derbyshire
Durham
East Riding of Yorkshire
Greater Manchester
Halton
Hartlepool
Kingston-upon-Hull
Lancashire
Merseyside
Middlesbrough
North Lincolnshire
North-East Lincolnshire
North Yorkshire
Northumberland
Nottingham
Nottinghamshire
Redcar & Cleveland
South Yorkshire
Stockton-on-Tees
Tyne & Wear
Warrington
West Yorkshire
York

Wales and West Midlands

Cumberland House
200 Broad Street
Birmingham B15 1TD

Wales - Tel: **0121 609 6835**
West Midlands - Tel: **0121 609 6813**
Fax for both areas - **0121 608 1001**

Area covered: West Midlands
Herefordshire
Shropshire
Staffordshire
Stoke-on-Trent
Telford
Warwickshire
West Midlands
Worcestershire
Wrekin

Area covered: Wales
All of Wales

Eastern

Terrington House
13-15 Hills Road
Cambridge CB2 1NP

Tel: **01223 531 060**
Fax: **01223 532 089**

Area covered:
Bedfordshire
Buckinghamshire
Cambridgeshire
Essex
Hertfordshire
Leicester
Leicestershire
Lincolnshire
Luton
Milton Keynes
Norfolk
Northamptonshire
Peterborough
Rutland
Southend-on-Sea
Suffolk
Thurrock

Western

2 Rivergate
Temple Quay
Bristol BS1 6EH

Tel: **0117 900 8577**

Area covered:
Bath & North-East Somerset
Bournemouth
Bracknell Forest
Bristol
Cornwall

Devon
Dorset
Gloucestershire
Hampshire
Isle of Wight
North Somerset
Oxfordshire
Plymouth
Poole
Portsmouth
Reading
Slough
Somerset
Southampton
South Gloucestershire
Swindon
Torbay
West Berkshire
Wiltshire
Windsor & Maidenhead
Wokingham

South Eastern and Metropolitan London

Ivy House
3 Ivy Terrace
Eastbourne BN21 4QT

Tel: **01323 452 400**
Fax: **01323 726 679**

Area covered:
Brighton and Hove
East Sussex
Greater London
Kent
Medway Towns
Surrey
West Sussex

311

Other useful addresses

The Association of Lorry Loader Manufacturers and Importers of Great Britain (ALLMI)

14 Manor Close
Droitwich
Worcestershire
WR9 8HG

Tel: 07071 226 773
Fax: 01905 770 892

Scottish Qualifications authority

Optima Building
58 Robertson Street
Glasgow,
G2 8DQ

Tel: 0845 279 1000
fax: 0845 213 5000

Driver and Vehicle Licensing Agency (DVLA)

DVLA Customer Enquiry Unit – Licence Enquiries
Swansea
SA6 7JL

Tel: 0300 790 6801
Minicom: 0300 123 1278
Fax: 0300 123 0798

(Service available Monday to Friday between 8.15 am and 8.30 pm, and Saturdays between 8.30 am and 5.00 pm)

Driver and Vehicle Agency (Licensing) in Northern Ireland (DVA)

County Hall, Castlerock Road
Coleraine BT51 3TB

Tel: 02870 341 469
24 hour tel: 0345 111 222
Minicom: 02870 341 380

DVLA Drivers' Medical Group

Swansea
SA99 1TU

Tel: 0870 600 0301

Freight Transport Association Ltd

Hermes House
St John's Road
Tunbridge Wells
Kent TN4 9UZ

Tel: 01892 526171
Website: www.fta.co.uk

Historic Commercial Vehicle Society

Iden Grange
Cranbrook Road
Staplehurst
Kent TN12 0ET

Tel: 01580 892 929
Fax: 01580 893 227
Email: hcvs@btinternet.com
Website: www.hcvs.co.uk

HSE Infoline

HSE Information Services
Caerphilly Business Park
Caerphilly
CF83 3GG

Tel: 0870 154 5500
Fax: 02920 859 260
(See your telephone book for details of
your local HSE office.)

The Chartered Institute of Logistics and Transport (UK)

Earlstrees Court, Earlstrees Road
Corby, Northamptonshire
NN17 4AX

Tel: 01536 740 110
Fax: 01536 740 101
Email: enquiry@ciltuk.org.uk

Road Haulage Association Ltd

Roadway House
35 Monument Hill
Weybridge, Surrey
KT13 8RN

Tel: 01932 841 515
Fax: 01932 852 516

Skills for Logistics

12 Warren Yard
Warren Farm Office Village
Milton Keynes
MK12 5NW

Tel: 01908 313360
Fax: 01908 313006
Email: info@skillsforlogistics.org
Website: www.skillsforlogistics.org

The Road Operator's Safety Council

395 Cowley Road
Oxford
OX4 2DJ

Tel: 01865 775 552
Fax: 01865 711 745

Royal Society for the Prevention of Accidents (RoSPA)

Edgbaston Park
353 Bristol Road
Birmingham B5 7ST

Tel: 0121 248 2000
Fax: 0121 248 2001

Road Transport Industry Training Board (RTITB)

Access House
Halesfield 17
Telford TF7 4PW

Tel: 01952 520200
Fax: 01952 520201

Vehicle and Operator Services Agency (VOSA)

(formerly Transport Area Network and
the Vehicle Inspectorate)

The Enquiry Unit
Welcombe House
91-92 The Strand
Swansea SA1 2DA

Tel: 0870 606 0440
Fax: 01792 454 313

313

Categories of goods vehicle licences

Category	Description
C1	Medium-sized goods vehicle over 3.5 and up to 7.5 tonnes, with a trailer up to 750kg MAM
C1 + E	Medium-sized goods vehicle over 3.5 and up to 7.5 tonnes, with a trailer over 750kg MAM
C	Large goods vehicle over 7.5 tonnes, with a trailer up to 750kg MAM
C + E	Large goods vehicle over 7.5 tonnes with a trailer over 750kg MAM

Motor homes and recreational vehicles come under either category C or C1, depending on their MAM. If used on test, they must meet the MTV requirements for the relevant category.

For more information on licensing categories see DVLA leaflet INS57P which can be obtained via www.direct.gov.uk or directly from DVLA (see contact details on page 312).

Minimum Test Vehicles (MTV's) requirements

Any vehicle or vehicle/trailer combination presented for use at test must meet minimum test vehicle standards. These standards are part of European Community Legislation on Driver Licensing. Great Britain, as a member of the European Union, is obliged to comply with these requirements.

All vehicles used for Categories C1, C1 + E, C and C + E tests must have externally mounted nearside and offside mirrors for the examiner's use, seatbelts fitted to seats used by the examiner or any person supervising the test, a tachograph and an anti-lock braking system (ABS).

Trailers do not need to be fitted with ABS.

All vehicle combinations must operate the appropriate service brakes and utilise a heavy duty coupling arrangement suitable for the weight.

Vehicles fitted with electronic parking brakes are not allowed on test.

A tractor unit is not a suitable vehicle for category C or C1 test.

All the listed weights refer to the maximum authorised mass (MAM).

Vehicles and trailers used for tests must be unladen.

A vehicle displaying trade plates is not suitable for a driving test, as the conditions attached to trade licences do not allow for a vehicle to be used for this purpose.

All vehicles should have the relevant no smoking signs in the cab area to conform with the new regulations, recently introduced, concerning smoking in vehicles used for work purposes. (see page 144 for further information).

All test vehicles must also conform to all the requirements shown on page 316-317.

Medium-sized goods vehicles

Category	Description
C1	A medium-sized lorry with a maximum authorised mass (MAM) of at least 4 tonnes, at least 5 metres in length, capable of 80 km/h (50 mph) and with a closed box cargo compartment at least as wide and as high as the cab; Tachograph, ABS, seat belts and examiner mirrors.
C1 + E	There are two types of test vehicle in the C1 + E category: 1. A drawbar outfit made from a combination of a category C1 vehicle towing a trailer of at least 2 tonnes MAM with a combined length of at least 8 metres, capable of 80 km/h (50 mph) and with a closed box trailer at least as high and as wide as the towing vehicle. The trailer may be slightly less wide than the towing vehicle, but the view to the rear must be by use of external mirrors only. Tachograph, ABS, seat belts and examiner mirrors. 2. A medium-sized articulated lorry with a MAM of at least six tonnes with a combined length of at least 8 metres, capable of 80 km/h (50 mph) and with a closed box trailer at least as high and as wide as the towing vehicle. The trailer may be slightly less wide than the towing vehicle, but the view to the rear must be by use of external mirrors only. Tachograph, ABS, seat belts and examiner mirrors.

Large goods vehicles

Category	Description
C	A rigid goods vehicle with a MAM of at least 12 tonnes, at least 8 metres in length and at least 2.4 metres in width, capable of at least 80 km/h (50 mph). The vehicle should have at least eight forward ratios, a closed box cargo compartment at least as wide and as high as the cab, Tachograph, ABS, seat belts and examiner mirrors.
C + E	There are two types of test vehicle in the C + E category: 1. A drawbar outfit made from a combination of a category C vehicle and trailer with a MAM of 20 tonnes, a length of at least 7.5 metres from coupling eye to extreme rear and a combined length of at least 14 metres with a trailer at least 2.4 metres in width. The vehicle combination should be capable of 80 km/h (50mph), with at least 8 forward ratios and a closed box cargo compartment at least as wide and as high as the cab; Tachograph, ABS, seat belts and examiner mirrors. 2. An articulated lorry with a MAM of at least 20 tonnes, with a minimum length of 14 metres and a minimum width of at least 2.4 metres. The vehicle should be capable of 80 km/h (50mph) and have at least 8 forward ratios and a closed box cargo compartment at least as wide and as high as the cab; Tachograph, ABS, seat belts and examiner mirrors.

Cone positions

Ready reckoner: metric measurements

This list of metric measurements should prove useful if you want to practise the reversing exercise.

To calculate the reversing area's layout - identify the length of your vehicle in the left-hand columns and scan across to the right-hand columns for the relevant cone measurements. The cone positions are relative to the base line Z (see Diagram on page 259).

Metres	Feet	Cone A	Cone B
4.50	14.8	22.5	13.5
4.75	15.6	23.8	14.3
5.00	16.4	25.0	15.0
5.25	17.2	26.3	15.8
5.50	18.0	27.5	16.5
5.75	18.9	28.8	17.3
6.00	19.7	30.0	18.0
6.25	20.5	31.3	18.8
6.50	21.3	32.5	19.5
6.75	22.1	33.8	20.3
7.00	23.0	35.0	21.0
7.25	23.8	36.3	21.8
7.50	24.6	37.5	22.5
7.75	25.4	38.8	23.3
8.00	26.2	40.0	24.0
8.25	27.1	41.3	24.8
8.50	27.9	42.5	25.5
8.75	28.7	43.8	26.3
9.00	29.5	45.0	27.0
9.25	30.3	46.3	27.8
9.50	31.2	47.5	28.5
9.75	32.0	48.8	29.3
10.00	32.8	50.0	30.0
10.25	33.6	51.3	30.8
10.50	34.4	52.5	31.5
10.75	35.3	53.8	32.3
11.00	36.1	55.0	33.0
11.25	36.9	56.3	33.8
11.50	37.7	57.5	34.5
11.75	38.5	58.8	35.3
12.00	39.4	60.0	36.0
12.25	40.2	61.3	36.8
12.50	41.0	62.5	37.5
12.75	41.8	63.8	38.3
13.00	42.7	65.0	39.0
13.25	43.5	66.3	39.8
13.50	44.3	67.5	40.5
13.75	45.1	68.8	41.3
14.00	45.9	70.0	42.0
14.25	46.8	71.3	42.8
14.50	47.6	72.5	43.5
14.75	48.4	73.8	44.3
15.00	49.2	75.0	45.0
15.25	50.0	76.3	45.8
15.50	50.9	77.5	46.5
15.75	51.7	78.8	47.3
16.00	52.5	80.0	48.0
16.25	53.3	81.3	48.8
16.50	54.1	82.5	49.5
16.75	55.0	83.8	50.3
17.00	55.8	85.0	51.0
17.25	56.6	86.3	51.8
17.50	57.4	87.5	52.5
17.75	58.2	88.8	53.3
18.00	59.1	90.0	54.0
18.25	59.9	91.3	54.8

Glossary

ABS Anti-lock braking system (developed by Bosch) which uses electronic sensors to detect when a wheel is about to lock, releases the brakes sufficiently to allow the wheel to revolve, then repeats the process in a very short space of time – thus avoiding skidding.

Abnormal load A load which cannot reasonably or inexpensively be divided into two or more loads and therefore cannot be carried under the provisions of the Construction and Use Regulations.

ADR Abbreviation used for the European Agreement stating the Rules covering International Carriage of Dangerous Goods by Road.

AETR The European Agreement concerning the work of crews of vehicles engaged in International Road Transport.

Air suspension system This uses a compressible material (usually air), contained in chambers located between the axle and the vehicle body, to replace normal steel-leaf spring suspension. Gives an even load height (empty or laden) and added protection to fragile goods in transit.

Articulated Vehicle A tractor unit coupled up to a semi-trailer (commonly referred to as an 'artic').

Axle-lift device a device permanently fitted to the vehicle used to reduce or increase the load on the axles.

Axle weights Limits laid down for maximum permitted weights carried by each axle – depending on axle spacings and wheel/tyre arrangement. (Consult regulations, charts or publications that give the legal requirements).

Box trailer Normally a solid-sided semi-trailer that is loaded through rear doors.

BS EN ISO 9000 British Standards code relating to quality assurance adopted by vehicle body-builders, recovery firms, etc.

CMR The main document needed for transporting internationally by road, confirming the haulage company has received the goods and that a contract of carriage exists between the trader and the haulage company.

C&U (Regs) Construction and Use regulations that set out specifications which govern the design and use of goods vehicles.

CNG Compressed Natural Gas.

CAG Computer-aided gearshift system developed by Scania that employs an electronic control unit combined with electropneumatic actuators and a mechanical gearbox. The clutch is still required to achieve the gear change using an electrical gear lever switch.

City of London Security Regulations Anti-terrorist measures which mean that access to the City of London is restricted to only seven access points, involving closure of several other roads. Full details can be obtained from the Metropolitan Police.

COSHH Regulations 1988 The Control of Substances Hazardous to Health Regulations 1988 place a responsibility on employers to make a proper assessment of the effects of the storage or use of any substances that may represent a risk to their employees' health. (Details can be obtained from the Health and Safety Executive).

CPC in Road Traffic Management This Certificate of Professional Competence indicates that the holder has attained the standards of knowledge required in order to exercise proper control of a transport business (and is required before an operator's licence can be granted).

Cruise control A facility that allows a vehicle to travel at a set speed without use of the accelerator pedal. However, the driver can immediately return to normal control by pressing the accelerator or brake pedal.

Curtain-sider A popular semi-trailer and rigid load area design that has largely replaced 'flat-bed' load areas. It normally has a rigid roof and rear doors, with curtain sides that draw back on both sides of the loading area.

Diff-lock A device by which the driver can arrange for the power to be transmitted to both wheels on an axle (normally rotating at different speeds when the vehicle is cornering for example), which increases traction on surfaces such as mud, snow, etc.

Double-deck trailer These have two levels of load area and can improve business efficiency by increasing load volume, cutting unnecessary mileage and reducing fleet size.

Double de-clutching A driving technique that enables the driver to adjust the engine revs to the road speed when changing gear. The clutch pedal is released briefly while the gear lever is in the neutral position. When changing down, engine revs are increased to match the engine speed to the lower gear in order to minimise the work load being placed on the synchromesh mechanism.

Draw-bar combination The drawing vehicle is coupled to a trailer by a rigid towing device. Also referred to as a 'lorry and drag' or 'wagon and drag'.

Drive-by-wire Modern electronic control systems that replace direct mechanical linkages.

Driver CPC The Driver Certificate of Professional Competence indicates that the holder has attained the standards of knowledge required in order to exercise proper control of a Goods vehicle or Passenger-carrying vehicle.

Electronic engine management system This system monitors and controls both fuel supply to the engine and the contents of the exhaust gases produced. The system is an essential part of some speed retarder systems.

Electronic power shift A semi-automatic transmission system, developed by Mercedes, that requires the clutch to be fully depressed each time a gear change is made. This system then selects the appropriate gear.

Fifth Wheel Coupling A device that allows a tractor unit to be connected to a semi-trailer, using a 'pin' on the trailer and a plate (the fifth wheel) on the tractor unit.

Flatbed A basic flat floor on a semi-trailer or the flat load area of a rigid vehicle.

GCW Gross Combination Weight, applying to articulated vehicles.

Geartronic A fully automated transmission system developed by Volvo. There's no clutch pedal. Instead, there's an additional pedal operating the exhaust brake.

Groupage This means combining orders from several different sources or customers into efficient and cost-effective loads for onward movement.

GTW Gross train weight, applying to drawbar combinations.

GVW Gross Vehicle Weight, applying to solo rigid vehicles and tractor units. Also known as Maximum Authorised Mass (MAM).

HGV (Heavy goods Vehicle) - A commercial vehicle designed to carry goods. The combined weight of vehicle and goods exceeds 3.5 tonnes. HGV is still a term commonly used in the industry, although the correct term is now LGV (Large Goods Vehicle).

HSE The Health and Safety Executive. HSE produces literature that provides advice and information on health and safety issues at work.

Inter-modal operations Combined road and rail operations for the movement of goods where the 44 tonnes weight limit is authorised – subject to certain conditions.

ISO containers Also called intermodal containers, these are designed to transport freight by ship, truck or rail.

Jake brake A long-established system of speed retarding that alters the valve timing in the engine. In effect, the engine becomes a compressor and holds back the vehicle's speed.

Kerbside weight (KBW) The total weight of a vehicle plus fuel, excluding any load (or driver).

LGV (Large Goods Vehicle) The correct term now used to refer to a commercial vehicle designed to carry goods.

Laminated A process where plastic film is sandwiched between two layers of glass so that an object - upon striking a windscreen for example - will normally indent the screen without the detachment of large fragments of glass causing injury to the driver.

LEZ (Low Emission Zone) A specified area in Greater London within which the most polluting diesel-engined vehicles are required to meet specific emissions standards.

Lifting axle An axle that may be lowered or raised, depending on whether the load is required to be distributed to include the additional axle or if the vehicle is running unladen. Such axles may be driven, steered or free-running.

LNG Liquified (compressed) Natural Gas.

Load-sensing valve A valve in an air brake system that can be adjusted to reduce the possibility of wheels locking when the vehicle is unladen.

London lorry ban Nighttime and weekend ban on lorries over 16.5 tonnes MAM, applying to most roads in Greater London other than trunk roads and exempted roads. All vehicles other than special types or those concerned with safety or emergency operations must display a permit and exemption plate if they're to be used in the restricted areas. *Note* - Not all London boroughs operate the scheme.

Low Loader   A semi-trailer used for transporting heavy machinery.

Lorry-mounted crane   Lifting device mounted on vehicle chassis to enable one-man loading and unloading.

LPG   Liquified (compressed) Petroleum Gas.

MAM   Maximum Authorised Mass, also known as maximum permissible weight or gross vehicle weight, is the maximum weight of the vehicle that may be used on the road including the maximum load the vehicle may safely carry. This is normally shown on a plate fitted to the vehicle.

Mobile worker   A mobile worker is defined in legislation as 'any worker forming part of the travelling staff, ie drivers, crew, trainees and apprentices who are in the service of an undertaking which operates road transport services for passengers or goods by road for hire or reward or on its own account.'

MPW   Maximum Permissible Weight. Under the EC drivers' hours rules, the weight of the vehicle and that of any trailer (added together) or the towing vehicle's maximum permissible train weight - whichever is the less.

Muck-Away   An industry-recognised term for the bulk removal of surplus or waste materials by road from a construction site.

Multi-drop   A journey involving deliveries to several different places.

Operating Centre   Any commercial vehicle that is authorised on a Goods Vehicle Operating licence must be registered to an appropriate base - the operating centre.

Own-account   Goods Vehicle operators who are primarily moving goods produced by their own companies.

Owner-driver   a driver who is also the authorised operator of the vehicle, being self-employed rather than employed by a haulage company.

PG9   Prohibition notice issued by VOSA.

Plated weight   Department for Transport regulations for recording and displaying information relating to dimensions and weights of goods vehicles, indicating maximum gross weight, maximum axle weight and maximum train weight. In the case of trailers the plate indicates maximum gross weight and maximum axle weight for each axle. (This is in addition to any manufacturer's plate that's fixed to the vehicle or trailer).

PMW   Permissible Maximum Weight. This is the maximum weight permitted (also known as **MAM** or **GVW**).

POD   Proof of Delivery. This can be any of the usual delivery documents (delivery note, consignment note, waybill etc) or a special POD document. It normally shows the delivery address, date and time of delivery and what was delivered, as well as the recipient's name and signature.

PPE   Personal Protective Equipment. The basic set of PPE is recognised as a hi-visibility vest, hard hat, steel toe-cap footwear and gloves.

Range changer   Gearbox arrangement that permits the driver to select a series of either high or low ratio gears depending on the load, speed and any gradient being negotiated. Effectively doubles the number of gears available (frequently up to a total of 16 gears, including crawler gears).

Red Routes   Approximately 300 route miles in the London area have become subject to stringent regulations restricting stopping, unloading and loading. Also being introduced in other major towns and cities.

Re-grooving   A process permitted for use on tyres for vehicles over an unladen weight of 2,540 kg, allowing a new tread pattern to be cut into the existing tyre surface (subject to certain conditions).

Retarder   An additional braking system that may be either mechanical or electrical. Mechanical devices either alter the engine exhaust gas flow or amend the valve timing (creating a 'compressor' effect). Electrical devices comprise an electromagnetic field energised around the transmission drive shaft (more frequently used on passenger vehicles).

Retractable axle   this is the axle raised by an axle-lift device.

Road-friendly suspension   A suspension system where at least 75% of the spring effect is produced by air or other officially-recognised compressible fluid under pressure. See Annex II of Council Directive 96/53/EC(a) for defined equivalents within the European Community.

RPC   Reduced Pollution Certificate. Specific vehicle types, registered in the UK prior to October 2006, are able to obtain a Reduced Pollution Certificate. Vehicles with a valid RPC can be registered for a reduced level of vehicle excise duty (VED).

SAD   Single Administration Document - this is used to transport goods between EU member states. Such goods are now classed as having community status within the EU.

SAMT   Semi-Automatic Transmission system in which the clutch is only used when starting off or stopping.

Selective or block change   A sequence of gear-changing omitting intermediate gears, whilst correctly matching the speed of the vehicle. Sometimes known as selective gear-changing.

Self-steering axle   These are fitted on the rear of trailer bogies or multi-axle vehicles. They reduce tyre scrub, increase tyre life, aid manoeuvrability and marginally improve fuel consumption.

Skeletal trailers   Skeletal trailers have a bare chassis with twistlocks and are designed for carrying containers.

Splitter box   Another name for a gearbox with high and low ratios that effectively doubles the number of gears available.

Subcontractor   anyone who is subcontracted by another transport company to carry out deliveries on behalf of that company.

Supply chain   The chain of suppliers, warehouses, transport and delivery to the final customer. Some companies provide a complete supply chain logistics service for manufacturers or retailers.

'Suzie' Lines   These are the red air supply line (also known as the emergency line) and the yellow brake connector line between the vehicle and trailer.

Tachograph   A recorder indicating vehicle speeds, duration of journey, rest stops, etc. Required to be fitted to specified vehicles.

TARE weight   This is the weight of a container deducted from gross weight to obtain net weight or the weight of an empty container.

TBV   Initials of the French (Renault) semi-automatic transmission system that employs a selector lever plus visual display information.

TC   Traffic Commissioner, appointed by the Secretary of State to a Traffic Area so as to act as the licensing authority for Goods Vehicle and PSV operators in the area.

TIR   Referring to security system, specifically a cord, fitted by customs to secure a load from tampering.

TIR Carnet   Approved document showing full details of journey/load/packaging.

Thinking gearbox   The term used to describe a fully automated gearbox that selects the appropriate gear for the load, gradient and speed, etc by means of electronic sensors.

Toughened safety glass   The glass undergoes a heat treatment process during manufacture so that in the event of an impact (such as a stone) on the windscreen it breaks up into small blunt fragments, thus reducing the risk of injury.

An area on the windscreen in front of the driver is designed to give a zone of vision in the event of such an impact.

Tractor Unit   A vehicle that, on its own, cannot be loaded with goods but can be coupled to semi-trailers that can be loaded.

Trailer swing   This occurs when severe braking causes partial loss of control as the rear wheels of a semi-trailer lock up on an articulated vehicle.

Train weight   This is the combined MAM of the vehicle and the trailer it is pulling.

Tremcard   A transport emergency card that must be carried when transporting ADR loads. It gives detailed written instructions to the driver in the event of a crash involving a dangerous goods load.

Turbo-charged   The exhaust gas drives a turbine, which compresses incoming air and effectively delivers more air to the engine than is the case with a normal or non-turbocharged engine.

Turbo-cooled or intercooled   Refers to a system where the air from the turbo-charger is cooled before being delivered to the engine. The cooling increases the density of the compressed air to further improve engine power and torque.

Two-speed axle   A system whereby an electrical switch actuates a mechanism in the rear axle that doubles the number of ratios available to the driver.

Unladen weight   This is the weight of the vehicle before loading. It does not take into account the weight of the crew plus any extra equipment such as fridges, televisions etc.

Unloader valve   A device fitted to air brake systems, between the compressor and the storage reservoir, pre-set to operate as sufficient pressure is achieved and allowing the excess to be released. (Often heard at regular intervals when the engine is running).

VEL   Vehicle Excise Licence or road fund licence.

VRO   Vehicle Registration Office, dealing with matters relating to registration of goods vehicles, taxation and licensing.

Walk-round check   It is essential that every driver carries out a thorough walk-round check before using a vehicle on the public highway (see page 153-4).

WTD   Working Time Directive. This is a European Union directive limiting the number of hours people can work, and determining what breaks should be taken, minimum holiday entitlement etc. It applies to all kinds of employment, not just mobile workers, but currently excludes those who are self-employed.

Extra tips on fuel economy

Improving fuel economy

E very time you move off, do so smoothly - avoid harsh acceleration.

C hange down to the appropriate gear, but wait while speed decreases.

O n acceleration, try to skip gears where you can.

N ever leave it to chance - maintain your vehicle in good condition.

O bserve and keep within the rev counter green zone.

M inimise brake use - plan ahead and keep monitoring road conditions.

Y our top speed should remain constant - think "Gear high - rev low'.

Hazard labels

POISON

FLAMMABLE LIQUID

DANGEROUS WHEN WET

COMPRESSED AIR

OXIDIZER

5.1

RADIOACTIVE

7

Tying a dolly knot

Other Official DSA Publications

The Official Highway Code

Essential reading for all road-users – not just for learners. This current edition contains the most up-to-date rules of the road, many of which are legal requirements.

Book	ISBN 9780115528149	£2.50
CD-ROM	ISBN 9780115528460	£9.78

Available in British Sign Language
DVD and Book Pack ISBN 9780115529849 £9.82

Driver CPC – the Official DSA Guide for Professional Goods Vehicle Drivers

This official book is specifically designed to help LGV drivers prep for their initial Driver Certificate of Professional Competence (Driv CPC) by focusing on the syllabus of the two new modules: Case Studies and the Practical Demonstration Test. The new Driver CPC tests came into force from 10 September 2009.

Book	ISBN 9780115530012	£9.99
Downloadable PDF	ISBN 9780115530661	£9.99*

TSO
information & publishing solutions

The Official DSA Guide to Driving –
the essential skills
Book   ISBN 9780115528170 £12.99
Downloadable PDF   ISBN 9780115530609 £12.99*

The industry standard driving manual packed
with advice for learners, experienced motorists
and instructors. Includes guidance on essential
driving techniques, manoeuvring and
defensive driving.

Know Your Traffic Signs
Book   ISBN 9780115528552 £4.99

Essential guide to traffic signs. This handy
reference title illustrates and explains the vast
majority of traffic signs that a road user is likely
to encounter.

TSO (The Stationery Office) is proud to be DSA's official publishing partner.

6 Easy Ways To Order:

Online:	Visit www.tsoshop.co.uk/dsa
Email:	Email your order to customer.services@tso.co.uk
Telephone:	Please call 0870 243 0123. Please quote reference CQD when ordering
Fax:	Fax your order to 0870 243 0129
Post:	Marketing, TSO, Freepost, ANG 4748, Norwich NR3 1YX (No stamp required)
Shops:	Available from all good High Street book stores (including the TSO shop) or online bookstores. For interactive products please also visit selected computer software retailers.

Information & publishing solutions

*Provides immediate access at the press of a button. Available direct from TSO – visit www.tsoshop.co.uk/PDF

Prices correct at time of going to press but may be subject to change without notice.